MW00564056

Estate Grown:

Planting Roots
in Fiddletown

By Mara Feeney

All rights reserved. Printed in the United States
Gaby Press
P. O. Box 221
Fiddletown, California 95629
My Fiddletown/Mara Feeney. -- 1st ed.

ISBN 978-0-9819319-6-8

Cover Art: Mara Feeney and Marilyn Duffey
Photos: Mara Feeney unless otherwise noted
Cover and Interior Layout Design: Priceless Digital Media, LLC

Author's Note: Objects or events seen in a rearview mirror can appear distorted. Experience is subjective, and memory is sometimes fickle. This book's names, characters, places, and incidents are based on real people, places, and events. A few names have been changed to avoid duplication and/or to enhance privacy. This is a work of narrative non-fiction. No lies have been told intentionally, although some exaggerations may have occurred.

For Deborah
My Accomplice in All of This

"Be brave enough to live life creatively. The creative is the place where no one else has ever been. It is not the previously known. You have to leave the city of your comfort and go into the wilderness of your intuition. You can't get there by bus, only by hard work and risk and by not quite knowing what you're doing, but what you'll discover will be wonderful. What you'll discover will be yourself."

– *Alda, Alan*
Things I Overheard While Talking to Myself
Random House Publishing Group

TABLE OF CONTENTS

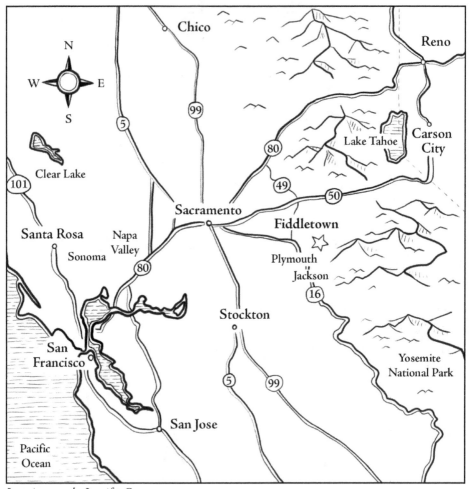

Location map by Jennifer Cameron

PROLOGUE

Yes, Fiddletown is a real place. It's in rural Amador County, about an hour's drive east of Sacramento, California's state capital. Like many other communities scattered along the foothills of the Sierra Nevada mountains in Northern California, Fiddletown owes its existence to the discovery of gold at Sutter's Mill in 1848 that sparked the famed Gold Rush. Before that time, the area was sparsely inhabited by Miwok Indians and Mexicans. Soon, swarms of migrants from around the world were setting up crude camps to pan for gold. Once the easy pickings were depleted, they moved on to seek their fortune elsewhere. Many Gold Rush-era campsites vanished with little trace, but Fiddletown evolved from a large tent camp into a small town. The availability of water and timber was vital to its success. The community attracted many Chinese immigrants who'd come seeking work. Others turned to agriculture, finding the soils and climate suitable for growing fruit, nuts, and wine grapes.

In 1853, a post office was established in Fiddletown. By 1854, the town's population had grown to around 2,000 permanent residents. There was a church, several hotels and stores, and a steam-operated sawmill. In 1855, the first school opened. Fraternal organizations and benevolent societies sprang up, along with saloons and dance halls. In the 1860s, a second school and a second church were built.

Those were the glory days. Fiddletown is a relatively quiet place now. While the Gold Rush was short-lived, people are still drawn to the Sierra foothills as if pulled by some magnetic force. Perhaps they are still seeking some kind of treasure in these golden hills.

When Deborah and I first discovered Fiddletown in 1991, there was a road sign indicating the official population was 100 persons. However, the local post office delivers mail to many more households in the 95629 zip code. The population now is predominantly white, but with a colorful mix of personalities, lifestyles, and political views.

"Downtown" Fiddletown sits in the bottom of a bowl surrounded by a ring of hills. The main road running east-west through town is called Main Street along the block or two where most of the historic buildings are clustered. Otherwise, that thoroughfare is known as Fiddletown Road. Hill dwellers cut through town on their way to jobs in Plymouth, Jackson, or Sacramento. San Francisco Bay Area residents and tourists whiz through on their way to camp, hike, or ski at resorts in the Lake Tahoe Basin. Most folks find little reason to stop in Fiddletown. We did stop, bought land, and settled in to a surprisingly rich experience, as these stories will reveal.

PART ONE

TERROIR

FIRST SIP

The Flying Saucer

Deborah and I moved to San Francisco in 1980 and settled in as if it had always been home, even though she was from Virginia and I from Canada. We'd met in college a decade earlier, when my roommate invited her to my twentieth birthday party. I thought she was the smartest, wittiest, most beautiful person I'd ever met. I loved her irreverence and no-nonsense approach to everything. I guess she thought I was pretty cool, too, because we became instant best friends, and later more than that, and we are still together more than half a century later. We eventually married once laws changed and it became legally possible to do so.

In 1980, Deborah had been accepted as a medical resident at the University of California, San Francisco. I found work with an engineering firm that had decided to branch out into environmental consulting, so they'd hear about major new infrastructure projects when they were still in the planning stages. I thought my job title, Staff Scientist, was hilarious, because I'd avoided science classes like the plague throughout my education. I was called a socioeconomist in Canada, but I suspect the men in charge thought that sounded too much like "communist."

We drove to 22nd and Guerrero one evening to see what the excitement was about. The area was transitioning at that time from a relatively affordable Latino neighborhood to a hip locale for tech workers. We found a parking spot a few blocks away and walked to the restaurant. The décor was inviting, the menu unusual, and the prices seemed reasonable. The place was busy, but we managed to snag two seats at the bar.

I don't remember what we ate that night, except that it was good enough to lure us back many times. I do recall what we drank. The bartender, Tony, recommended a bottle of Easton Zinfandel as the perfect accompaniment to our meal. He said he personally knew the winemaker, having worked with Bill at his Solano Cellars wine store in Berkeley.

Deborah thought the zinfandel we drank that evening just might be the best red wine she had ever tasted. She studied the label carefully and asked many questions. Tony told us Bill had recently bought land in the Sierra foothills to try his hand at grape growing and winemaking in the Shenandoah Valley.

"Wait just a minute," Deborah said. "I grew up in Virginia. That's where the Shenandoah Valley is. Who's ever heard of a Shenandoah Valley in California?"

"We have one in Northern California, too," Tony insisted. "It's in Amador County, in Gold Country. Wine grapes have been grown there since the mid-1800s. Some excellent wines are coming from the area now, so move over, Napa and Sonoma."

Neither of us had been to Amador County or any part of California's Gold Country. We decided we should explore the foothills the next time we found a free weekend. We had no inkling how that evening at the bar in the Flying Saucer would alter the trajectory of our lives.

The Shenandoah Valley

We headed for Amador County on a summer Saturday morning. We drove across the Bay Bridge and north on Interstate 80 toward Sacramento, where the air temperature was almost thirty degrees warmer than in the San Francisco fog. We took Highway 16 away from the capital and soon reached Plymouth. We coasted beneath a banner proclaiming the town to be "The Gateway to the Shenandoah Valley." We spotted a motel called the Shenandoah Inn and stopped to inquire about a room. The proprietor said there were none available.

"It's the weekend of the Amador County Fair, and the fairgrounds are right here in Plymouth. Our rooms have been booked this weekend for some time." His wife corrected him. "We still have the Bridal Suite available," she said. "But that's an extra fifty bucks a night."

We took it. We unloaded our scant luggage to stake our claim. A map of local wineries in the lobby helped us quickly orient ourselves for a tour of the Shenandoah Valley.

After stopping at the Pokerville Market for picnic supplies, we set out for a drive along E16, aka the Shenandoah Road. This valley was small, nothing like its Virginia namesake. It stretched only about five miles from one end to the other, with two loop roads creating a figure eight where most of the wineries were located.

The scenery was lovely, with vistas of rolling hills, waving vineyards, grazing sheep, and a mixture of pear, plum, and walnut orchards. Dark green patches of live oak forest contrasted with bright swaths of golden pastures dotted with lichen-spattered granite outcroppings. We stopped to taste at several small, family-owned wineries and found the wines to be surprisingly good. These wineries seemed more intimate and friendly than those we'd visited in the Napa and Sonoma Valleys. The tastings were free, and the person pouring often turned out to be the owner, winemaker, and/or vineyard manager. We asked about Easton wines and learned they had not yet opened a tasting room but were planning to do so soon.

We spent Saturday evening at the Amador County Fair, another unexpected delight. It was a classic, old-fashioned fair with pickle and quilt displays, cow and pig judging, baking contests, rodeo shows, bumper cars, cotton candy, and a Ferris wheel. That night, we tumbled into bed in the Bridal Suite, content with our day's adventures.

Fiddletown

On Sunday morning, we drove to Sutter Creek for breakfast. We were charmed by the old Gold Rush-era town, with its two-story stone buildings and wide wooden boardwalks. We strolled along Main Street, peering into art galleries, antique stores, restaurants, and an old-fashioned ice cream parlor. We perused the property listings posted on a real estate office window. Everything seemed cheap by San Francisco standards.

"Wow—look at this," Deborah said. "An eighty-acre ranch for $150,000, or this adorable Victorian home on a quarter-acre corner lot for $80,000. I wonder where that beauty is located."

"At that price, it must need a lot of work," I said. Just then, a petite, freckled woman with short blond hair stepped out the door and introduced herself as Sue. She offered to take us for a drive to show us some properties she thought might be in our price range. *What price range?* I wondered. We had not mentioned a price range, nor had we given any thought to buying rural property. But Sue was friendly and low-key. She insisted a drive around the hills couldn't hurt and wouldn't take long. Sue enjoyed introducing newcomers to the area and said she'd be happy to be our tour guide. Since we liked the Shenandoah Valley, she could easily show us a range of properties for sale in that area—just for fun. We looked at each other and shrugged. *Why not?*

Sue quickly learned we were professionals with busy careers. She assumed we'd want to get out of the city to relax on weekends. She showed us several properties, including a forty-acre wooded "executive retreat" in the hills above Sutter Creek, a twenty-acre undeveloped parcel on the Cosumnes River, and some five-acre lots in a new rural residential subdivision set in rolling, forested terrain. It was enjoyable riding around with Sue and learning about local history, but none of those properties appealed to us. Not that we were looking to buy anything, anyway.

"We don't like to put our feet up," I said. "We prefer to be active."

"Well, perhaps a small hobby farm would be more to your liking," Sue said. "I want to show you one more place since we're so close to Fiddletown." I chuckled at the quaint name. Sue didn't know exactly how the town got its name, but it was thought the immigrants who populated it in the 1800s brought their fiddles to make music in their spare time.

Sue told us the tiny rural community was tucked into a bowl just over the hill from the larger Shenandoah Valley. While it felt remote, it was only a ten-minute drive from Plymouth. "All on paved roads!" she added. That meant easy access to city services.

I peered out the window as we drove up Fiddletown Road. I thought I had never seen land so pretty. There were rolling pastures the bright yellow color of gold bars, dotted with dark blue-green oak trees and mossy rock outcroppings. The bright blue sky seemed oversized, like the sky over the prairies where I'd grown up. Straight ahead, I could see a massive single thunderhead cloud hovering over the horizon like a mountain of pristine cotton balls.

Sue said the property she was about to show us, an elderly couple's thirteen-acre hobby farm, had been on the market for quite a while with no offers. "Probably because it's neither fish nor fowl. It's too big for weekenders to manage, but it's too small for people who want to do serious farming. It might not be the kind of property you gals are looking for because it would be hard to manage from a distance. But I want to show it to you, anyway, so you can compare it with the executive retreat I showed you. Maybe you'll see that property in a new light. It's much larger but would require less upkeep than this one. And they're both about the same asking price."

I jumped out to open the gate. We eased up the steep driveway, past a hedge of lilacs and walnut trees loaded with nuts. A flock of quail led the way and then scurried into a thicket of pomegranate bushes. We arrived at a flat, graveled pad below a long mobile home on a brick foundation. There was a rock garden across the front of the place, where white and yellow roses and bright pink and purple verbena tumbled over rust-red rocks. A fine water mist was spraying the rock garden, cooling everything down.

A short, elderly woman wearing a housedress and apron came down the steps to greet us. She introduced herself as Norma and offered us iced tea, which we gratefully accepted. Norma said no matter how hot the temperature got, there was always a cooling breeze blowing up the hill from downtown Fiddletown. She led us to a picnic table in the shade of a massive oak tree. We looked over a large vineyard flanked by walnut and pear orchards directly across the road. "This is our western view," Norma said. "We come here to watch the sun set over those hills. You wouldn't believe how pretty it can be." *I can believe it,* I thought.

Deborah had done research on winegrowing in the area and learned that the Shenandoah Valley is a designated American Viticultural Area, or AVA. AVA designations are granted by the federal government to geographically distinct areas with unique attributes. Of the several hundred AVAs in the United States, approximately half are located in California. A wine carrying an AVA designation on its label is generally considered more prestigious than one with a more general appellation of origin, such as "Amador County" or "California."

"Is that vineyard part of the Shenandoah Valley AVA?" Deborah asked. Norma didn't know, but Sue had done her homework. "No," she said. "The Shenandoah AVA ends just over the hills north of here, but this area has its own designation. It's the Fiddletown AVA, with only a handful of growers in it. The vineyard we're looking at is quite old, probably planted during the Gold Rush, and it's known for producing excellent old vine zinfandel."

"Is this property also part of the Fiddletown AVA?" I asked. Sue confirmed it was. I thought I saw a curious, dreamy look pass over Deborah's face, but I might have confused it with something I was feeling myself.

As we chatted, an old Ford tractor pulled up to the two-story barn beyond the mobile home. A portly man in denim overalls got off the tractor and removed his sweat-stained hat to beat some dust off of it. As he approached, I noticed his stubble. It indicated he didn't believe in shaving daily.

"Howdy," he said, extending a hand twice the size of mine. "I'm James. You folks want a tour? I'm not going to show you everything because there's a lot of oak forest, but I'll show you around the cultivated parts if you like." Deborah and I accepted. Sue preferred to stay in the shade with Norma.

We strolled around with our sweating tumblers of tea as James pointed out the locations of the pecan grove, the vineyard, the stone fruit orchard, the seasonal vegetable garden, and the perennial garden. He said the latter had three twenty-foot rows of asparagus, half a dozen artichoke plants, and a bed of raspberries. There were thirty pecan trees, five walnut trees, ten peach trees, three apricots, four cherries, three pears, and around 250 grapevines—mostly wine grapes, but also some Thompson Seedless and Red Flame table grapes. There were some unusual and exotic things, too, like carob trees, a trellis full of slip-skin grapes like Concord and scuppernong, and several exotic jujube trees which draped like willows and produced oblong fruits that resembled dates but were crisp like apples.

James said he and Norma had nine kids and numerous grandchildren to keep out of trouble, so they'd had plenty of help developing their farm. It was a family labor of love. But now he and Norma were getting old. It was time to retire. They wanted to move back to Texas, where they'd grown up and where the cost of living was much lower than in California. None of their kids were in a position to take over their place.

Well, I want to! I was surprised to find myself thinking. The property seemed like a wacky wonderland, a gardener's paradise, a miniature Garden of Eden.

"We could live off the land here," I whispered to Deborah.

"Yeah, but how would that work when we have our city jobs?" she said. "No renter would take care of a place like this."

I wasn't thinking of renting the place out; I was dreaming of spending my weekends, holidays, and retirement here. I typically don't converse with inanimate objects, but I had the distinct sense this farm was talking to me. "Come settle here," it whispered. "Look how gorgeous I am. You will never tire of me. You can fondle my foliage, pluck my fruit...."

Hold it right there, Buster. I am in a committed relationship! But the land didn't care. "Bring your partner, bring your friends—the more, the merrier! I'll nurture and sustain you all. I can't promise you happiness—that's up to you. But I promise you fulfilling, meaningful experiences and a lifetime of honest labor."

I snapped out of my trance. Deborah is a scientist. I didn't dare mention the land was speaking to me. But I knew she enjoyed learning new skills and appreciated good wine.

"Can you imagine the thrill of popping the cork out of a bottle of your own estate-grown zinfandel?" I asked.

"It'd be way cheaper and easier to pick up a few cases from those wineries we visited yesterday," she replied. She seemed skeptical but not entirely negative. Perhaps there was a small opening...

"It would take years to bring a raw piece of land up to speed," I said. "This place is a turnkey operation. The well and irrigation and septic systems are all in place. There are electrical outlets everywhere you look. The sheds and outbuildings are already built."

"Yeah. And it looks like they all need a good scraping and painting, maybe new roofs—or perhaps demolition."

The buildings did look a tad run-down, but they seemed serviceable enough to me. Norma had made the trailer cozy. The garden was exploding with vegetables ready to harvest. The trees were heavy with fruits and nuts. There were even chickens laying eggs in a coop. And a woodshed full of split wood and dry kindling. Such bounty!

Admittedly, we had no farming experience. But we were relatively young and energetic, and we were quick learners. *Life is an adventure; we enjoy new challenges!*

Deborah told Sue we had to get going. It was a two-and-a-half-hour drive back to the city, and we both had to work the next day. Sue returned us to Sutter Creek, gave us her card, and said she'd be happy to show us more properties any time.

Deborah drove home, taking the curves as fast as I would. I turned down the radio, stopping Bonnie Raitt from belting out "Nick of Time" quite so loudly, and asked: "So what did you think of those properties we looked at?"

"Hmmm. I'm not sure. The Fiddletown place made me remember how much fun I had gardening with my dad as a kid. He always planted a huge summer garden in the backyard— tomatoes, green beans, lima beans, sweet corn, okra, you name it. It was my job to help Dad plant, weed, and harvest. He always said if the economy went to hell or the world went to war, we'd survive eating kale and shooting squirrels," she said. "I don't know if any of those places would be right for us or if buying property way out in the hills makes any sense. We should be clear about what we're looking for before we leap into buying country land. Maybe some other investment would make more sense in the long run."

Of course, there probably were smarter investments, but that wasn't my point. I was talking about something else—an adventure, taking a leap, responding to a new opportunity, heeding an unexpected call...

Deborah asked what I'd thought about the places we'd seen. "I thought the executive retreat had lovely views, but the interior was way too Laura Ashley for me," I said. "And there'd be nothing to do there except watch the deer eat anything you might try to grow. The other places seemed too ordinary, nothing special. I liked the Fiddletown property a lot, though. Don't ask me why. Maybe it's my farming roots." I had Canadian wheat farmers on my mom's side and Australian sheep ranchers on my dad's. But there was something more. I felt smitten by the land, its colors and smells, those rolling hills with vineyard views. These feelings were sensual and difficult to explain, so I went for the practical.

"We could have a pantry full of nuts, dried fruits, and wine to survive marauding hordes, nuclear devastation, environmental collapse, or financial ruin. Is that crazy?"

"Yeah, it's crazy," she replied. "I never would have guessed, when I met you twenty-some years ago, you'd ever want to be a farmer. An artist, a poet, or a teacher, maybe. But a farmer—who'd have thought? You're full of surprises." She squeezed my hand and pressed down on the accelerator.

We rode the rest of the way home in silence. I knew Deborah well enough to know she was probably mentally reviewing the patients she'd see in the morning. I was dreaming about James and Norma's hobby farm. I couldn't get the images out of my mind. I felt stirred up. It reminded me of falling in love—the way you can't stop thinking about a person, how you still feel connected even when apart. I had never had such feelings about an object like a piece of property. *Why is this happening?* I wondered.

We stopped to buy corn, peaches, tomatoes, and basil at a Lockeford farm stand. Then we drove through the Altamont pass, between the tall, eerie windmills and the "Jesus Saves" messages carved into the hilly landscape. We cruised past the twinkling lights of Pleasanton, Dublin, and Oakland, into the cool fingers of fog reaching through the Golden Gate toward the Bay Bridge.

THE OFFER

It was a busy work week. I had to focus on consulting reports due to clients, leaving no time for reveries of country living. Until Sue, the real estate agent from Sutter Creek, rang.

"Hi. I don't mean to bother you," she began, "but I have some news I thought you might be interested in. I had a call today from the owners of the Fiddletown hobby farm. Norma thought she might have detected a small spark of interest in you two—something she has not seen in other folks I've taken there in the past year or two. She wants me to tell you they're willing to consider a reduced offer."

"How much reduced?" I asked.

"It's up to the buyer to decide how much to offer," Sue said. "But it's not every day I get a call from sellers inviting a below-asking price offer. I know they're anxious to move to Texas. Norma also told me James decided to replace the wooden steps at the back of the house but didn't mention it to her. She stepped out the back door to hang some laundry, fell, and broke her ankle. That was the last straw. She told him it was Time to Retire!"

"Ouch—I bet James is in the doghouse," I said. "I appreciate the call. Let me talk it over with Deborah."

"Okay, no pressure. To be honest, I was surprised you considered that place. Most clients rule it out right away, saying it looks like a huge amount of work. You must have lots of energy."

"We are kind of hyperactive," I confessed. "We work hard at our jobs, but we like to play hard, too. We like to learn and do new things, rather than sit home watching television."

"Well, good for you. Just let me know if you want to proceed," Sue said.

Deborah and I did talk it over. We'd enjoyed our weekend getaway, but now that we were back in the city, we felt ambivalent about buying country land. It seemed so far away, a long drive with a lot of chores waiting at the other end. On the other hand, we were invited to put in an offer, perhaps well below the asking price. If we could buy the thirteen-acre hobby farm at a bargain rate, maybe it would be a good long-term investment, and we could have some fun with it in the meantime. We'd both just turned forty. We'd finally paid off our student loans and were beginning to save some money. We 'd bought our first home in the Rockridge neighborhood of Oakland and put a lot of work into remodeling it. That house had more than doubled in value in less than three years. Selling it had allowed us to buy a Victorian building in San Francisco, including rental units to help us pay the mortgage. Our unexpected success made us think we were real estate geniuses, and we should invest our savings in more California real estate. We decided to make an offer about a third below the asking price for the hobby farm. If we didn't get it, so be it. If we did...well, there would be considerable challenges ahead.

I called Sue, half expecting her to guffaw at our proposal. She did not. Instead, she filled out an offer form and faxed it over for us to sign. Then we waited. I felt nervous, excited, and scared at the same time. I half hoped the sellers would reject our offer. Life would go on nicely if we did not own this farm or ranch or whatever it was. If they accepted it, there would be no more weekends biking in Monterey, hiking in Yosemite, or skiing at Lake Tahoe for the foreseeable future. We'd be tied down with vines to prune, tomatoes to can, eggs to gather, barns to paint. Yikes.

I strolled to Church Street for lunch and, afterward, browsed the shelves in Aardvark's Odd Ark, a barn-sized used bookstore with a comforting, musty smell. There was no Agriculture section, but there was one labeled "Gardening."

Eureka! I spotted one Sunset book on how to grow just about everything I'd seen thriving in Fiddletown. It was a magazine-sized paperback titled *How to Grow Fruits, Nuts, and Berries.* Each crop had a double-page spread crammed with information on planting, pruning, pests, irrigating, fertilizing, harvesting, etc. It covered all of James's orchard plantings—pecans, peaches, cherries, walnuts, pomegranates, grapes, raspberries, and even jujubes. Then I spotted a similar book entitled *Growing Vegetables*. The slim volume addressed everything from artichokes to zucchinis. *These two books contain everything I need to know,* I thought smugly as I peeled off four one-dollar bills to pay for my purchases.

Sue called back mid-week. "Guess what? They accepted your offer!" she said. "James grumbled about the price, but Norma was delighted to finally receive an offer."

"Oh, wow...I guess that's good news," I said. I asked about next steps. Sue said we'd have thirty days to inspect the property and decide if we wanted to go through with the purchase or modify our offer. She said she had a recent well test and septic inspection report that seemed exceptionally good. "I sell lots of properties around here with wells in the ten- to twenty-gallon-per-minute range, and this one is rated one-hundred-plus GPM, enough to supply a commercial ag operation or a winery."

Because the house was a mobile home, she advised us against paying for a termite report. She said it would make more sense to spend the money on a whole-house warranty covering the appliances, from the well pump to the dishwasher. If any of those were to fail in the first two years of ownership, the policy would pay the full cost to replace them.

"Tell you what," she said, "I'll throw that policy in for you out of my own commission. What do you think?" I thought that sounded good.

We received the reports in the mail within a few days. The well report indicated the well was indeed rated 100+ GPM and noted it had been artesian at one point. I had nostalgic notions about artesian wells like those in *Jean de Florette* and *Manon of the Spring,* terrific French movies about peasant water wars starring Gerard Depardieu. I called Sue to ask why the well was no longer artesian. She said someone had "stolen" it.

"Initially, James had trouble finding a good water source on the property. They tried drilling in three different locations, to no avail," Sue said. They kept hitting aquifers yielding only 8–10 GPM. "That's enough to keep a modest home in water, but not enough to grow crops. So they tried again and again." After consulting a water witcher, James asked a local well company to drill near the property's southwest corner. He'd pay to go as deep as 500 feet if they had to.

The crew began drilling. And drilling. They reached all the way to 500 feet, finding nothing more than a trickle. James told them to stop. He couldn't afford to waste more money. But the crew felt bad for him and decided to drill just a little further, at no additional charge. At 520 feet, they found water. Lots of water. An artesian well, with sufficient pressure from deep inside the earth to send the water spurting out of the ground like a Texas oil gusher. Of course, James and Norma were thrilled.

The artesian well was a source of pride for the family until their downhill neighbor drilled another well close by and slightly lower in elevation. The groundwater stopped shooting out of the ground on James and Norma's land. Instead, it was gushing on the adjacent property. The neighbor created a large pond to contain the overflowing water, right on the property line. James felt ripped off every time he saw ducks splashing in water that ought to be his.

"The well still produces a hundred-plus GPM, but James was upset about losing the artesian," Sue said. "I think that's the main reason they decided to go home to Texas."

Some neighbor, I thought, not fully grasping how the nasty neighbor could soon be mine. We set a date to return to Fiddletown. Sue offered to be present for the inspection. I told her we didn't think that was necessary, but she insisted. This sale had been a long time coming; she didn't want anything to scuttle the deal at the last minute.

BLISSFUL IGNORANCE

It was a glorious late summer day when we returned to Fiddletown, considerably cooler than on our previous visit. It was delightful to drive out of thick Bay Area fog into sunshine. We shed our windbreakers and fleece jackets along the way and gleefully donned our sunglasses.

When we arrived in Fiddletown, we saw Sue sitting on the front patio with Norma, who had her right leg propped up on a chair. "I'd offer you some tea, but I just can't today," Norma said, pointing to the cast on her ankle. She invited us to go inside and inspect her home. It would have to be a self-guided tour. As we climbed the front, she urged us to pay attention to the kitchen cabinets because she and James had paid extra to upgrade to solid wood.

On our drive to the foothills, Deborah and I had joked about becoming "trailer trash"—because the house was a standard 15-by-72-foot trailer on a permanent foundation. It looked simple from the front, long and narrow. Once we stepped inside, we discovered a spacious family room had been added to the north side, with a classic black wood stove on a raised brick pad. The home had two bedrooms and two bathrooms, all on the small side but tidy and clean. The kitchen felt inviting, with two windows to let in natural light from north and south. The larger window near the stove framed the western sunset view. The trailer seemed cozy because of Norma's special touches—gingham curtains, handcrafted knickknacks on shelves and walls, and the scent of cakes baked in her kitchen with the solid wood cabinets. The place surpassed our expectations for weekend getaway housing.

I was anxious to tour the property again with James. I'd brought a pad of paper and a pen this time, planning to take copious notes. I didn't know how to distinguish table grapes from wine grapes, let alone care for all the things growing on this land. I needed a crash course in farming. James agreed to show me around again while Deborah took part in a work-related conference call. Norma kindly let her use the house phone, as no one we knew had mobile phones back then, and cellular service was not available in Fiddletown, anyway.

I trotted along behind James, trying to match his big strides and take notes simultaneously. He waved his arms, talking constantly as we raced through the vineyard. I scribbled away, hoping I might remember what my notes meant later, but I had trouble keeping up with him. He would say things like: "The cuttings over there came from an historic California mission near Paso; those over there came from a different mission further south. The grapes in this block are all native to North America; the rest are European varieties. This block here is all table grapes; those over there are a mix of red and white wine grapes, but there are also some table grapes, including some champagne grapes."

"Is that because you make champagne out of them?" I asked.

"No," he replied. "I think it's because they're so tiny they look like champagne bubbles." He said the main block of grapes was zinfandel, grown from cuttings taken from the century-old vineyard across the road. He pointed to the west, and I stopped scribbling notes long enough to appreciate the western view again. I noticed a section of the old vineyard had been recently planted with small trees and asked about it.

"Well," he said, "the owner is a businessman from the Bay Area. He thinks California's going to have a glut of grapes and a shortage of walnuts because so many walnut orchards are being torn out to make way for new homes. So, he decided to take out some old vines and plant walnuts instead. I guess he'll find out if he's right or wrong in a decade or two."

James strode toward the fruit orchard situated between the vineyard and the perennial garden. I resumed taking notes. There were three cherry trees—two Bings and a Queen Anne. There were three apricot trees, all Blenheims. The ten peach trees were all "volunteers" sprouted from peach pits tossed into the old chicken coop, so he couldn't tell me what kind they were. There were half a dozen walnut trees, all Carmelos, which produce large, delicious nuts too big for commercial processing facilities to handle. The walnuts were scattered around the barn and trailer, but thirty mature pecan trees were clustered on an acre of land along the eastern edge of the vineyard. James was reeling off the names of the pecan varietals as we dashed through the shade of the thirty-foot-tall trees.

"I'll never get all these names down," I protested.

"Don't worry about that. I made a map of the pecans. I'll give you a copy," James said. I asked about the hoses encircling some of the trees. He said those were soaker hoses he moved to different trees every day so by the end of the week, each tree would have had about twelve hours of slow soaking. Deborah and I would have to devise a different method, given our schedules.

We looped around the vineyard and returned to the perennial garden. James pointed out a thicket of wild plums, a hedge of pomegranates, three twenty-foot rows of asparagus, a raspberry patch, and a bed of artichokes. As we admired the bounty, one of the artichoke plants began to vibrate, then wave erratically. Suddenly, it was pulled belowground, disappearing entirely.

"Damn gophers!" James exclaimed. "If you rebuild these beds, be sure to attach some sturdy chicken wire or hardware cloth to the bottom, or these critters will drive you nuts!" I noticed several white cats circling the garden and asked if they helped catch gophers. He said they helped a bit, but it was almost impossible to eliminate the varmints.

I gave up trying to jot down what everything was called. Instead, I concentrated on recording the crucial farming tips James was rattling off:

- Prune wine grapes in March; harvest around September-October.
- When the walnut casings crack in fall, smack them with the twenty-foot-long pole (in top of the barn), and the nuts will fall to the ground.
- Prune the olive trees when they bloom.
- Fight mildew in the vineyard with sulfur; apply when the weather is cool or warm and wet (but not after it gets too hot).
- Peaches need to be pruned very heavily every year.
- Use grapevine cuttings to fill in the open areas of the vineyard—put two to three buds underground, leaving one or two aboveground, and a new vine will grow.
- Deer prefer white grapes. Tie strips of Bounce (fabric softener) on vines as a repellent. Deer hate the smell of it.

- After the first rain in fall, broadcast a cover crop mix, such as purple vetch and oats, in the vineyard. Plow under the following spring.
- Wrap all the aboveground pipes in winter, or they will freeze!
- The barn attic needs venting.

As we returned to the trailer, I felt overwhelmed. I had so many questions I didn't know where to begin. I was puzzling over something James had said earlier about the water. "You mentioned iron from the well can wreak havoc on appliances, so we'll need to keep on top of it. Which appliances did you mean, and how do we 'keep on top of it'?" I asked. Norma's freckled face turned the color of a garnet yam. She glowered at James, perhaps thinking he was trying to sabotage the sale.

"I meant toilets and sinks...and the dishwasher. There are good products available now, though. Norma can tell you about them," James said as he beat a hasty retreat to the barn.

Norma insisted it was no problem. Some minerals in the well water could leave reddish stains. But these were easy to remove with the right product and a little elbow grease. She named the cleaners she preferred to use and insisted we go inspect her toilet bowls to see there were no visible stains. "A little scrubbing with a pumice stone works best." She said, shaking her head over her husband's silly warning. "The well water is perfectly safe to drink."

Deborah suggested we ask James to show us what was in the barn and outbuildings. The barn was a substantial two-story building, with a pulley for lifting heavy objects like hay bales to the upper floor. There were lots of hoses and empty rabbit cages he said he'd leave behind if we could use them. I said "Yes!" at the same time Deborah said "No!" Often, where she sees clutter, I see potential.

"Okay, I guess," she said. I could tell she thought we'd haul that stuff to the dump someday, but it wasn't worth a fight.

James showed us the chicken coop, which was freshly painted, relatively clean, spacious inside, and had a fenced yard around it. There was another small building that had been a sheep shed once but now was used for storage. James proudly showed how it had both electricity and water—crazy luxuries for a small outbuilding. On a nearby hilltop sat a rambling metal shed with a haunted feel. This was where James had once raised pigs, but the stalls were empty now. It was staggering to think of all the projects in these buildings—and the work they entailed.

An hour of inspection was all we could take. We thanked James and Norma for their time and all the information. Sue escorted us to the car.

"Well?" she asked. "Are you satisfied with what you saw?" Deborah and I shot each other a glance.

"I guess so," I said. "I'm not sure what we're getting into, but the price seems reasonable for a lifetime of hobbies."

"We should have asked for the tractor as part of the deal," Deborah said. "We don't even own a lawn mower!"

"Well, I happen to know James already promised that tractor to his son," Sue said. "Don't worry. You won't need equipment until spring." She suggested we keep an eye out for garage and estate sales, good places to find useful tools.

On the drive home, Deborah said the two slim volumes on gardening I'd bought at our used bookstore in the city were not going to cut it. She suggested we go by UC Davis, home of Northern California's best Agriculture and Viticulture programs. That would be the place to buy some serious how-to-farm books.

Fortunately, the UCD bookstore was still open when we arrived, and it did indeed have a huge Agriculture section. There were tomes on optimizing your apricot or pear crop and a large book entitled *The Chickpea in the 90s*.

"Look at this!" I grinned as I showed it to Deborah. "Who'd have thought a whole book could be devoted to the humble garbanzo bean...let alone its trends over a single decade, as if it were a nation-state or the Women's Movement?" She had a stack of books she wanted to buy on viticulture, cover crops, and stone fruit production. Her favorite was a thick volume titled *Weeds of the West*. She handed a charge card to the cashier and invested over $200 on farming advice.

As we drove back toward the freeway, we noticed a barn at the side of the road with a large Garage Sale sign. We pulled over to investigate. I approached a thin woman wearing a lace-trimmed apron over her jeans and asked if she might be selling any useful farm equipment.

"Oh, you should have come along earlier," she replied. "Most of the good stuff has been picked over by now. We had lots of garden implements and workshop tools, but most of those were snapped up before noon." *Too bad,* I thought.

Deborah picked up a long, skinny weed whacker. "Does this thing work?" she asked the woman.

"Oh sure," she replied, "but it's electric, so you can only go as far as your extension cord will reach. It's handy for trimming up around the house, and it's a lot quieter than those gas models. We're about to close up here, so I'll let you have that for five bucks." We felt smug returning to the city with our stack of how-to-farm books and our first piece of landscape taming equipment.

That evening, as we opened a bottle of Amador County zinfandel to toast our land acquisition, little did we imagine that within a few years, we'd be the owners of three weed whackers, two gas push mowers, a riding mower, two chain saws, a wood splitter, a chipper-shredder, and two diesel Kubota tractors with half a dozen attachments for discing, raking, rototilling, mulching, leveling, and mowing. And we had absolutely no idea we'd need every bit of that equipment.

Photo by Kay Ellyard

MOVING IN

Once the property was in escrow, we experienced a mixture of excitement and trepidation. Something about this adventure felt right, somehow meant to be. At the same time, it seemed utterly insane. We were city girls! We lived in a Victorian flat in the middle of San Francisco. We had professional jobs. We knew nothing about agriculture or viticulture, and we lacked proper tools. Yet here we were, planning to take over a thirteen-acre hobby farm and manage it on weekends. *What were we thinking?*

Our friend Anne lived in Calaveras County, adjacent to Amador County. We'd met Anne at a deck-building party in Santa Barbara, where we'd helped mutual friends improve their yard. We'd taken an instant liking to each other as we sawed and hammered redwood planks. Anne had invited us to visit the 160-acre ranch she managed in Calaveras County, and we'd done so several times. We decided to pay Anne another visit once our property was in escrow, so we could practice skills like wood splitting and egg gathering that might be useful when we had a country home of our own. I recall sitting for hours studying the chickens while Deborah became enamored of the latest addition to Anne's menagerie, a black puppy named Scooter.

Anne's brother and his wife had visited the previous weekend. As they were driving through Angels Camp, they'd seen a boy sitting by the side of the road sobbing. They'd stopped to ask him what the matter was, and he'd shown them a cardboard box containing a single black puppy. The boy said his dad was going to drown the pups if he couldn't get rid of them. He'd given them all away except for this one...a female with big brown eyes and long black eyelashes—the runt of the litter. They felt sorry for the boy and relieved him of his last puppy, assuming it would fit right in at Anne's ranch with all the other dogs, cats, cows, horses, sheep, chickens, and parading peacocks.

In a way, Scooter did fit in. She shared a bed with a kitten that had coloring similar to her own—black with a splash of white on the chest. One of Anne's older dogs would play tug-of-war with Scooter, letting her grab one end of a knotted sock. He'd then swing her in circles, all four paws flailing as she flew through the air. Anne thought Scooter was sweet, but she didn't need another animal to care for. She decided Deborah and I could provide the perfect home for Scooter. Now that we had country property, she insisted, we'd need a dog. We returned to the city with an adorable pooch—as unexpected an acquisition as our land in the hills.

Escrow closed at the end of August. We rented a U-Haul truck on Labor Day weekend, crossed the Bay Bridge, and headed north on Interstate 80. Our first stop was at a furniture outlet advertising a mattress sale. We bought a couple of beds and mattresses and a bookcase for good measure. Our next stop was Sacramento, where my colleague and friend Janice had been living for a year, working on a temporary consulting assignment in the state capital. She'd rented a studio apartment and outfitted it with the basics. Janice happened to be finishing her consulting gig and moving back to San Francisco that weekend.

"I won't need any of this stuff anymore, so you are welcome to take whatever you want," she told us. "Anything left over is going to the thrift shop." The furniture was not top quality, but it was clean and serviceable—and free. We took a Naugahyde sofa, love seat, coffee table, dining table, chairs, floor lamp, end table, pots and pans, towels, table settings, bowls, and measuring spoons. We loaded everything and drove our van full of loot eastward into the hills.

As we approached Fiddletown, I noticed something different about the green sign at the roadside. Someone had used chalk to cross out the official population of 100, replacing it with "98."

"That had to be Norma and James," I said. I asked Deborah to pull over. I erased the chalk marks, restoring the population to 100. Even though we would not be full-timers, we felt committed to becoming part of this community in some significant way.

We found the keys where Sue had left them. We took a long walk around the property, admiring this land we now possessed with amazement and humility. We'd never owned acreage before, and we both felt a strong urge to protect and nurture it.

We spent most of the afternoon unloading boxes and putting things in their place while Scooter sniffed around inside and out. Janice's furniture fit perfectly into the living room. The kitchen was too small to accommodate her dining table and chairs, so we put those in the family room beneath the window that looked onto a rock garden bright blue with Ceanothus blossoms.

Several people dropped by to welcome us that weekend. The first was Pam, who lived in the big white rammed-earth house on the hilltop across the road. She said she and her husband, George, would be hosting a wine and cheese soirée in a few weeks. She invited us to come and meet some of our new neighbors. We thanked her and said we'd be there.

Later, Dodd and Mary walked across their pony pasture to introduce themselves. They were our closest neighbors, with their house situated in a patch of oak trees across the creek to the northeast of us. We learned Dodd was a lawyer, a pilot, and a former rodeo cowboy, although he'd spent most of his career working as a principal in various foothills schools. Mary did consulting work, helping schools comply with the ever-changing laws governing employee working conditions and civil rights issues.

"We were so excited to learn about you two moving here," Mary said. "I hope we're not being presumptuous...but we thought two women from San Francisco were likely to be liberal."

"Yes," Dodd added. "And we're hoping now there might be *four* Democrats in Amador County, counting us!" We all laughed. I thought Dodd was joking but would learn soon enough the Democratic Party booth at the Amador County Fair is a lonely place indeed.

In the late afternoon, we strolled around to assess priorities for farm work. I reviewed the list of farming tips I'd received from James. It seemed a hodgepodge of unrelated concepts, most of which were not pertinent to this time of year. There were tips about spring pruning, late fall harvesting, and winter freeze protection. *What about late summer or early fall?* I wondered.

We tied fabric softener strips along the periphery of the vineyard, as James had suggested, to deter deer. We harvested some grapes that tasted ripe and hand-watered a few plants, but we couldn't think of any other pressing farm chores that needed doing. We decided to harvest the bounty of tomatoes, peppers, onions, and eggplants from the garden. The chickens had gone to new homes, but Norma had left a dozen fresh eggs in the refrigerator, so I made a scrumptious frittata for dinner. We experimented with several different pasta sauce recipes, so we could freeze some of the bounty for later use. Our favorite discovery was this simple tomato sauce recipe from Marcella Hazan:

Core and peel tomatoes, squeezing out most of the seeds. Fill a medium-sized pot with the fruit, add a stick of butter, and a peeled onion cut in half. Simmer for a long time. Serve over your favorite pasta. Enjoy with salad, crusty bread, and red wine.

The result was a buttery, oniony, essence-of-tomato concoction that tasted like heaven.

This farming life is not so difficult, I thought, as we enjoyed our simple meal with a glass of wine on the front porch. The temperature seemed perfect as the setting sun filled the sky with yellow, orange, and pink streaks. Eventually, the sky darkened and exploded with constellations we had never ever seen in the city. Even the Milky Way was plainly visible, gleaming like a welcome mat stretching toward the future.

Photo by Bob Kleinbrahm

THE MIDDLE AGE SPREAD

Anne came over to see how Scooter was faring and to tour our new property. She brought her new friend, Marianne, a redheaded nurse practitioner who worked in a clinic in Jackson. We strolled around the 13.25 acres together, marveling at everything. Anne's home in Calaveras County was about 1,000 feet higher in elevation than Fiddletown. The land there is covered in pine trees, manzanita, coyote brush, and a shrub called mountain misery. I smugly thought "our" part of the foothills was prettier. It's more open, with oak-studded rolling hills, pastures, orchards, and vineyards. It reminded me of Tuscany.

Our cultivated vineyard, orchard, and gardens occupied about two acres. Another eight acres were taken up by oak forest. The remaining land was open meadows. We were thrilled to discover a small seasonal creek and a natural spring on the property. We saw a flock of wild turkeys, a red fox, and a covey of quail as we ambled. The trees were teeming with chirping birds and chattering squirrels, and we could hear the acorn woodpeckers jackhammering at trees and telephone poles, making holes to store nuts for winter.

We found a few interesting artifacts along the back road including a hand-forged square metal spike and a chipped stone pestle of the kind the Miwok Indians used to grind acorns to provide sustenance through the winter months. It was worn to a smooth polish. There was a sense of history here.

Our property felt like a living thing, an entity of sufficient substance that warranted an official name. We tossed around many possibilities, but by the time we reached the trailer, a clear winner had emerged: The Middle Age Spread. Deborah and I had just entered our forties, and it was clear this land would dominate our time, attention, and energy in the coming years, so the name seemed to fit. Thirty years later, the name would no longer seem so perfect, but it would always remind us how we'd invested our prime.

NEW NEIGHBORS

We finished work, packed the car, and headed for Fiddletown on Friday evening. We sat in rush hour traffic that would only worsen in subsequent years but arrived in time to see a spectacular sunset painted over the vineyards in streaks of deep rose, orange, and yolk yellow.

We spent Saturday catching up on farm work, and then we spruced up to attend Pam and George's wine and cheese party. Their house sits on a hilltop and is visible from almost anywhere in the valley. Its whitewashed walls, Saltillo floors, and tiled fountain had a distinctly Mediterranean feel. George gave us a tour of the home, with the kitchen and dining room at one end of the house and bedrooms off a long corridor leading to a study.

"They're going to have to carry me out of here," George said when we reached the library, which had a spectacular view of hills and valleys stretching toward the Bay Area. We could see Mount Diablo in the distance. Pam told us George enjoyed spending his free time here writing papers on the history of neurology.

She introduced us to other neighbors, including a winemaker named Bill and his wife, Jane, who was a caterer and food writer. Bill mentioned he'd owned a wine store in the East Bay before moving to Fiddletown and establishing a winery in the Shenandoah Valley.

"Are you Bill Easton?" I asked. "Yes," he replied.

Deborah told him about our experience at the Flying Saucer, meeting his former employee and discovering his fine wine. Bill told us about the Rhone wine program he was developing in Amador County. He believed Fiddletown had the ideal "terroir" (the combination of soil, climate, and *je ne sais quoi*) for Rhone varietals.

"If you decide to plant Syrah," he said, "I might be interested in buying your grapes. Call me if you want to discuss it."

Wow, I thought, *we've barely moved in, and we're getting offers for grapes we haven't even planted yet!* I glanced at Deborah and could tell she was thinking similar thoughts. Perhaps we'd made a brilliant investment decision after all.

We met the couple who lived in a home just north of us, on the other side of the Moose Lodge. Jim was a Cherokee Indian interested in making wine, though he was a teetotaler. They didn't grow any grapes on their own property, but Jim would visit local vineyards after harvest and glean any grapes that might have been overlooked, as well as the small secondary clusters that ripen later than the primary crop. His wife, Jenny, was a home health care worker. We'd seen llamas grazing on their five-acre property and learned they also bred Sharpei puppies. I asked them about the Moose Lodge that sat between our two homes.

"Oh, we just try to ignore the Lodge and everything about it," Jim replied. "Your downhill neighbor, Zack, runs the Lodge. I think he has some fancy title like 'Governor' now."

"When we first moved here," Pam said, "Zack came over with his chain saw, cut down a couple of oak trees that were growing along our driveway, and hauled them away. I think he was trying to make a point that this valley is his, and he wanted to be sure we knew it."

That raised my hackles. I told Pam I would have called the police or the district attorney to have the guy arrested immediately. "George doesn't like to make waves," Pam said. "We took it as our introduction to country living. It's not like we needed those two trees." *Still,* I thought, *the nerve of that man!*

Bob and Marjun, who were raising ducks and geese and kids, lived just across the rise to the southwest. Bob was a high school teacher, musician, and home winemaker. Marjun, who spoke with a faint Danish accent, was short, funny, and gregarious, with a warm smile illuminating her freckled face.

"Who's the guy I've seen driving around here who looks like the cartoon character Mr. Magoo?" I asked. "He's quite old and wrinkled, wears a floppy white cotton sun hat, and slumps down so far he can barely see over the steering wheel."

"That's Ziggy," Pam said. "When you see him coming, you want to head for the other side of the road. I think he may be legally blind. He really shouldn't be driving. It's too dangerous."

"Ziggy's a character," Marjun added. "He has a pig named Bacon who lives in his house. The pig takes showers with Ziggy—and sits on his sofa to watch TV with him!"

A friend of Pam's who was visiting from Berkeley sought us out to say she loved housesitting for people in Fiddletown. "It's like an Italian vacation without the airfare," she said. "The smell of the air and the tone of light at this altitude remind me of Italy. And of course, the rolling hills and vineyards add to the effect." She gave us her phone number in case we might need someone to look after our home and pets in the future.

Everyone we met that evening seemed polite and solicitous, interested in knowing what Deborah and I did for a living and curious to know how we'd come to purchase James and Norma's place. They made us feel comfortable and welcomed to the neighborhood.

Jim and Jenny were the first to leave the party. They had a new litter of puppies to tend to. As soon as they got home, they called Pam to let her know they'd almost hit an emu wandering in the road. This news caused a stir. After a few glasses of wine, the remaining guests felt we must save the emu! We swarmed down the driveway and onto the main road. Sure enough, a solo emu stopped to stare at us with its dark, moist eyes. We joined hands and formed a big circle around the tall bird. Then, we stepped in unison, calmly herding the emu toward a pen near Pam's gate. Our emu wrangling succeeded. Pam and George posted notices, but no one ever claimed the bird, so they kept it and named it Big Bird. They assumed it was a male until the day she laid a big green egg.

After the soirée, we returned to our trailer, where Scooter greeted us with a frenzy of wags and kisses. We went to bed feeling smug about our property purchase and looked forward to getting to know our new neighbors better.

Even Zack. I intended to show that man he was not going to mess with me.

FENCING

One of the first property improvement projects we tackled was completing the fencing around our land. We had no intention of pasturing animals; nonetheless, fencing seemed important. Most properties around us had it. The flyer Sue had used to promote our place touted ranch fencing "almost all the way around" the perimeter. This made us think of the fencing as an unfinished project, a work in progress. We would get it done.

We studied our neighbors' fences. The sturdiest, newest fences enclosed vineyards to deter deer. These typically were made of eight-foot-tall welded wire mesh attached to sturdy metal poles, with corner posts secured in concrete. Ranches had a patchwork of fencing styles, including many tumbledown remnants of historic fences made from hand-hewn wooden posts and barbed wire. These were likely strong and secure at one time, but now the wire was rusted and sagging, and the posts were rotted, leaning, and stuffed with acorns by Sierra woodpeckers. While these fences had a certain charm, they'd no longer contain livestock. When neighbors installed new fencing with metal T-posts, they often left the older wood posts in place. Perhaps for nostalgic value—or simply because it was easier than removing them.

One week, when we'd decided to take a Friday off, we went to the Fiddletown post office to rent a mailbox. Our postmaster, Alice, asked us to fill out an application. As I did so, she said if we needed any help around our place, her son Tracy was strong and hard working. "He's real handy," she said, passing me a slip of paper with his phone number on it. I asked if he could install fencing. "Fencing's my boy's strong suit," she replied.

We called Tracy to enlist his help. What his mom said proved to be true. He was a very hard worker. Tracy was only twenty years old but amazingly strong. He had a barrel chest, thick neck, no waist, and bulging shoulders and thighs. I wondered if he lifted weights, but I was too shy to ask. Maybe there was no need for gym time with the kind of work he did. Tracy could install fencing by himself, assisted only by a winch and his pickup truck.

I felt a great sense of satisfaction once the perimeter fence was complete. Deborah's response was a bit different. It made her view the cross-fencing on our property more critically. James had used it to contain sheep in one area while the grass in other pastures continued to grow. Since we had no intention of keeping livestock, she questioned why we needed any cross-fencing. She thought it preferable to gaze across our estate with her view uninterrupted by useless runs of wire. The cross-fencing didn't bother me; I thought it might be useful someday. But once a thing started bugging Deborah, she had a hard time letting it go.

We tried to hire Tracy to remove some of it, but he didn't return our phone calls. I asked Alice about her son, and she outlined a sad story involving an affair gone wrong, alcohol, and an almost fatal automobile accident. Tracy had been medevaced to a hospital in Sacramento. He needed multiple surgeries and would not be available for work for some time.

Our neighbor Pam referred us to Joe, a handyman who lived a mile away, near downtown Fiddletown. We invited Joe to look at the job. When Deborah explained what she wanted done, he said: "Jeez, nobody ever takes out perfectly good fencing! I guarantee you, you'll be paying me or somebody to reinstall it someday." Even after Deborah insisted she was serious, Joe defied her instructions to haul the old fencing to the dump. Instead, he stockpiled the posts and wire on his property, where they'd be handy when she came to her senses.

FALL BOUNTY

It remained relatively hot through September and October, so Deborah and I applied ourselves to maintaining a weekly watering regimen for the fruit and nut trees, the perennial garden, the vegetable beds, our tiny patch of lawn, and the flower gardens around the trailer. We experimented with several types of battery-operated irrigation timers. None of them seemed completely reliable, so we continued to water everything manually. Between the two of us, we would put in the equivalent of a forty-hour workweek each weekend, moving sprinklers and hoses, managing our crops, and tending our gardens. This made me very happy to see my desk on Monday mornings. I'd relish sitting in a chair in front of a computer screen most of the day.

The bounty from our newly acquired land continued to surprise us. The tomato plants kept on flowering and producing sun-ripened fruit. There were summer and winter squashes, melons, artichokes, and a new crop of fall raspberries. We enjoyed the late variety peaches, then an abundant harvest of pears, walnuts, pecans, and pomegranates. We tried to preserve this cornucopia by drying, canning, and freezing.

It felt strange to be reaping the fruits of someone else's labor. In a fit of guilt and gratitude, I mailed a small package to James and Norma, who must have thought I'd lost my mind...shipping pecans to Texas! They probably laughed about the "Citiots" (a special contraction of "city" and "idiots" reserved for people like us who move to the foothills from urban areas) who'd bought their old place. We never heard from them, although we thought of them often. Whenever some marvelous new flower would bloom as the seasons changed, I would silently thank Norma. There were signs of James's welding talent everywhere. For example, he'd turned old wheel hubs into garden hose hangers. These were sturdily mounted on metal posts held firm by buried coffee cans full of concrete that had hardened in place.

We had no idea what to do with the jujubes, those exotic oblong fruits with the consistency of a date but the taste of an apple that grew on three willowy trees planted between the perennial garden and the vineyard. Since they were supposedly of Asian origin, we showed them to our Chinese dry cleaners in San Francisco and the Persian brothers who ran a popular coffee shop in our neighborhood. They looked puzzled but tasted the jujubes to be polite.

I then took some to the Korean woman who ran a sandwich shop around the corner from our city home. She went crazy when she saw my carton full of shiny, brown fruits. She clapped her hands and stomped her feet, doing a little dance behind the sandwich counter. Once she calmed down, she explained that in Korea, jujubes are thought to be very lucky—bringing good health, long life, vitality, harmony, great sex, wealth, love, and good fortune to all who consumed them. She explained they could be eaten raw, or they could be chopped up on rice, used in stir-fries, or simmered for broth or tea. She offered to take all the jujubes I had, saying her extended family would be very grateful. In exchange, she offered us free sandwiches and all the meat scraps Scooter could eat. Thus, the Korean sandwich shop became one of the regular stops Scooter would make on our city walks. Our pup quickly learned which stores along her urban "trap line" had dog biscuits or jerky treats and which ones gave cold-cut ends to smart dogs in exchange for a trick.

Deborah and I became adept at scouting garage sales and estate sales on our commutes to and from the hills. We found all sorts of treasures: an old wheelbarrow, a bench grinder, a heavy-duty vise. We stashed these treasures in our barn, alongside the empty rabbit cages, nut drying racks, and miles of hoses that had come with the property.

My mother came from Canada to visit, curious to see our country estate. Her grandparents had been real farmers, settlers on the Manitoba prairies. She'd spent most of her life in Winnipeg but frequently visited her cousins who lived on farms in MacGregor, a short journey west by car or train. In Manitoba, the Red River delta soil is rich and black. Her first pronouncement upon seeing the red dirt on our land was: "What crappy-looking soil!" Our dirt, often mistaken for clay, consists mainly of decomposed granite. It looks red due to its high iron content. Mom soon acknowledged our soil did seem exceptionally productive, capable of growing just about anything. She was particularly impressed with the Mission grapevines, gnarly giants with thick trunks, yielding forty or fifty pounds of grapes per vine.

We enjoyed fresh-pressed, estate-grown grape juice daily. Most consumers have no idea how fabulous and shockingly sweet and delicious the juice of wine grapes can taste. We learned the wines that end up around twelve percent alcohol start with a sugar content roughly twice as high—24 to 25 percent— which explains why the juice is so intensely delicious before it ferments into an alcoholic beverage.

"Why is the commercial market dominated by boring Concord grape juice and bland Concord grape jelly when we could be drinking zinfandel juice and slapping zin jelly on our toast?" Deborah asked. "This is California, so why do we have only generic, artificially flavored grape Popsicles when we could have cabernet, chardonnay, or pinot noir?"

Mom and I preserved exotic grape jams: zinfandel, mission, scuppernong, and sauvignon blanc. We foot-stomped buckets of hand-picked grapes just for fun. My mother giggled like a schoolgirl in response to the tickling sensation of grapes bursting and squishing between her toes.

Since we had an abundance of wine grapes, Deborah and I began researching how to make wine. It seemed relatively straightforward: pick, crush, press, ferment, and—voila! It's a process humans have been using for millennia to transform fruit juice into alcohol. Of course, one can get fancy, killing the bacteria and natural yeasts found on grape skins and introducing specific yeasts to influence the style of wine. One can press the juice off the skins sooner rather than later for lighter wines. Or select different woods for barrel-aging the wine to impart desired flavors to the end product.

We decided we should give it a try. We had no sophisticated equipment to monitor grape chemistry, but we regularly tasted our ripening crop. When the wine grapes seemed delicious (and hungry birds arrived to feast on them), we used bussing trays as picking bins, returning to the trailer with about fifty pounds of luscious purple clusters. We dumped our harvest into a clean metal washtub, and I did my best Lucille Ball imitation, crushing the fruit with my clean bare feet. The foot-stomping technique was remarkably effective. We soon had a tub full of bright pink liquid, with skins, stems, and seeds floating to the top. We removed some of the stems to prevent them from imparting bitterness to the must. We carried the washtub into the trailer and placed it in a cool corner of the family room. We gave it a good stir before we left for our city jobs and hoped for the best.

When we returned the following weekend, we immediately rushed to see how our brew was coming along. The surface was topped with a scummy gray foam, and the room smelled vaguely like vinegar. Deborah dipped a small ladle into the tub and pulled out a sample of the dark liquid. She took a wee sip, screwed up her face, and raced out the back door to spit into the shrubs.

"Oof, that is some nasty stuff," she said. "I wouldn't even want to cook with it." I asked if we could make vinegar out of it.

"No. I've read you have to start with good wine to make good vinegar. Good wine is not what we have here," Deborah said, casting a disparaging glance at our tub of glop. Although we felt discouraged, we let our brew bubble for another week, on the off chance it might improve. It did not. We tossed the foamy mess onto the compost heap we'd started near the chicken coop. We should have dumped it further away, somewhere down in the oak forest, to avoid the pungent aroma of failure that would linger in the garden for months.

CUSTOM FARMING

James had given us the names and phone numbers of several local men he thought might be able to help us with serious farm tasks (like discing, mowing, tilling): Delbert, Dennis, and Dick. Delbert was the County Agricultural Extension agent who could provide sound advice and also happened to live just down the road. Dennis and Dick were local guys who owned lots of useful equipment and had logged many hours using it. Sometimes, if they weren't too busy, they would do contract tractor work for others. I decided to call them all.

I called Delbert first and asked if he might be available to give us some advice on how to farm properly. "That's my job," he said. We learned the University of California collaborates with County Departments of Agriculture all over the state to provide advice about best practices to local farmers. We marveled at this free service, apparently paid for by our tax dollars. It probably was in the state's interest to help know-nothing newcomers avoid making mistakes that might threaten to ruin California's agricultural economy. We arranged a time for him to come by and talk with us the following weekend.

When Dennis answered the phone, he asked what exactly we wanted done. I said frankly I didn't know since we were brand new to farming, but James had told us he was sharp and handy and owned a tractor.

"You mean James took off with his old Ford tractor?" he asked.

"Not exactly," I said. "He gave it to his son, with all the implements." Dennis produced a low whistle through his teeth.

"Well, Lord, you ladies are going to need a *lot* of help in that case," he said. He agreed to drop over for a chat. I said I looked forward to picking his brain and hearing whatever advice he might have to offer.

I left a message for Dick. He returned my call later the same day, saying he was too busy to take on any new customers. Nonetheless, he invited us to drop by his ranch, only a few miles away. He said he liked to meet new people moving into the area. More importantly, he'd been keeping handwritten notes of his observations on farming and viticulture in the Shenandoah Valley for years. He said he'd be happy to give us a copy of his notes if I thought they might be useful. I jumped at the chance and arranged to come by the following Sunday to pick them up.

Del showed up shortly before noon on Saturday morning. Without even looking at the gardens or vineyard, he began criticizing the way James had farmed. "That man was constantly plowing," he complained. "Sometimes I think he just wanted to get out of the house, so he'd get on his tractor and go disc, and disc, and disc. Some of that's fine—if applied sparingly and at the right time and place. But too much of it destroys the soil structure and turns dirt into useless dust that won't grow anything."

He suggested we amend our soil by adding compost and planting a cover crop. "Let it grow all winter, then till it under in spring—but don't overdo the tilling! After a few years, the soil might have a chance to heal," he said. I asked what he meant by cover crops, and he explained these were plants like clover, vetch, legumes, and mustard that can fix nitrogen in soil, loosen hard-packed soil, prevent erosion, and encourage beneficial microbes.

"Some plants use nitrogen as they grow; others build it up," he explained. "If you don't have a good vegetation cover, your topsoil can wash away. If we get a big storm, small channels can become big ones mighty fast. Then your topsoil slides off, muddying up our creeks and silting up the Sacramento Delta and San Francisco Bay."

Yikes, I thought. I wanted to ask Delbert when those rains would come, as we had not seen a single drop since we'd bought our property. So far, our main challenges had been trying to keep living things alive through drip irrigation and hand-watering. I realized I'd never paid a lot of attention to the weather in the city. If it was rainy, I'd simply wear a raincoat or take an umbrella. Now, as a landowner, I had to worry about rain washing our topsoil down the hill and wrecking San Francisco Bay.

"If this were my place, you know what my top priority would be?" Del asked. Of course I wanted to know. "Two words: erosion control," he said. "You know those rivulets cutting down the front slope of your property over there next to the road?" I hadn't noticed them. "If you don't get right on top of those, they'll quickly grow big enough to swallow a Volkswagen. I see it happen time and again around here. First, a bit of runoff, then a gully, then the topsoil washes away. All you're left with is dead subsoil that won't grow anything and a bunch of giant, ugly cracks in the earth."

"What should we do?" I asked, feeling a certain level of panic.

"Well, there are a lot of expensive things you could do, but just spreading some straw over any bare, sloping areas can be effective, as well as inexpensive. The point is to discourage the runoff from following the same channel all the time. Straw helps hold the water in place, and encourages it to disperse over a wider area, rather than continue to carve deeper and deeper ruts in the same spot." He advised us to keep an eye on the weather forecast over the coming months and to have some bales of straw ready to put down before the first heavy rain. We thanked him for taking the time to come over on a Saturday, and he wished us good luck.

Del's advice seemed simple enough, except we didn't have a truck to haul around bales of hay and fifty-pound bags of cover crop seed. Our little Honda hatchback was not going to cut it. *Farm girls need a farm truck,* I thought, as Deborah browsed her how-to-farm manuals to learn more about cover crops, erosion control, and soil building.

Dennis showed up a few hours later, driving a massive pickup truck pulling a flatbed trailer. Attached to the trailer with chains was a small orange tractor. *It's adorable,* I thought. He parked near the trailer and got out to shake hands. He said he happened to be familiar with our place because he used to come over and help James and his sons with major welding projects.

"Your barn's got all the right electrical hookups; it's a great setup for welding," he said. I had no idea. I made a mental note to take up welding someday, should I need another hobby.

Dennis was kind enough to walk around and talk about the seasonal farming tasks that should be done on a place like this—seed drilling, mowing, tilling, raking. "Believe me, you're gonna wish you had your own tractor instead of waiting on somebody like me to do the work for you. Everybody gets busy at the same time around here, so it's hard to get the help you want when you need it. When the weather and soil conditions are just right for tractor work, everyone gets at it on their own place first, of course. When they find a minute to help someone else, it's often too late—pouring rain or whatever. I brought my old Yanmar tractor over here to show you gals because it's a spare one I don't use much anymore. She's still got a lot of life left in her. I could let you have her for five thousand dollars, a real bargain. I can even throw in a discer for the same price, but I'd have to charge you two hundred fifty extra for my old rototiller, which needs some modification to make it attach properly to the three-point hitch." *What's a three-point hitch,* I wondered, *and how in hell would one modify an implement to attach better?*

Deborah and I glanced at each other. Of course, we'd love to have the tractor, but we already felt overwhelmed with new things to learn and buy. We'd spent a lot of our savings on the twenty percent down payment, and now we had two monthly mortgage payments. We thanked Dennis for his offer but said we'd prefer to hire him to work for us. He agreed but felt sure we were making a big mistake.

"When you change your minds," he said, "I'll teach you how to drive 'er." He asked if it would be okay to leave the tractor at our place, so it would be handy when he came over to use it. We had no objection, so he pulled out the ramp, unlocked the chains, rolled the little orange tractor down the ramp, and parked it under the overhang on the open side of our barn. *She looks right at home there,* I thought.

On Sunday morning, we drove to the Shenandoah Valley to the address Dick had provided. He was outside feeding his chickens when we arrived. He invited us for a stroll around his ranch to see for ourselves how well he maintained his walnut trees and vineyard. He also showed us the yard full of agricultural implements he had available to rent.

"It's tough to make a living at farming," he said. "You have to get creative and diversify if you want to succeed economically." I asked if he also rented tractors.

"No! Every serious farmer has their own tractor. It's just the accessories I rent out—tillers, sprayers, and the like." We told him Dennis had agreed to do tractor work for us. I also mentioned Delbert had advised us to focus on erosion control and planting cover crop seed. Dick scoffed at the idea of paying money for expensive seed mix.

"Just throw some of the cheapest fertilizer you can find on any bare spots you have," he suggested. "The soil around here holds about a million seeds per cubic inch. Just give it some nourishment, and those seeds will sprout."

"But won't we just end up growing weeds?" Deborah asked.

"I don't have any problem with weeds," Dick said. "After all, what's a weed? It's just a plant growing where you don't want it to. Weeds can be just as useful as anything else to prevent erosion, contribute organic matter, and even add nitrogen to the soil. Why throw your money away on seed when there's already so much seed, just needing a nudge to start growing?"

Dick invited us into his house, where he handed me a stack of his Xeroxed notes, stapled into sections by topic. We thanked him for his advice and his willingness to share what he'd learned from decades of farming with folks like us who were new to it all. He said it was his pleasure, and we could call him anytime if we had questions about what he'd written or if we wanted to rent equipment— or anything else. Or just come over for lunch. He didn't get out much and was curious about what other people did for a living.

That evening after supper, I flipped through the stack of Dick's handwritten notes. The section titles were enticing:

- Drainage Issues
- Cultivation Methods
- Dry Farming
- Thoughts about Planting a New Vineyard
- Strip Spraying
- Vine Spacing
- A Word about Tillage
- Why Grass Is Your Friend
- Trellising 101
- On the Matter of Fencing
- What I Think about When I Fertilize

Well, I thought, I guess I have my winter reading cut out for me.

LUCK AND A TRUCK

On Sunday evening, we drove back to the city, arriving well after dark and feeling spent from weekend farming adventures. I poured a glass of wine, got into my pajamas, and sorted the mail. There was a letter from my mom, saying how much she'd enjoyed her recent visit. She thought buying the farm was a good thing, not foolhardy. She was excited we'd get to enjoy such a beautiful spot on the planet for many years to come. She enclosed a check to support the endeavor—my own frugal mom.

Her check led me to call Dennis the next day to say we'd buy his Yanmar tractor after all. We set a date for tractor handling lessons. I also called Mom to thank her and tell her we were now the proud owners of a used tractor named Bernice in her honor. She was delighted we'd put the money toward something so practical.

On Monday morning, I walked Scooter to the Korean sandwich shop to deliver more jujubes to the delighted proprietor. She handed me a bag containing about five pounds of dog treats, ends from all the hams and roasts and cheese loaves she'd used in her shop and saved for Scooter.

It was a pleasant fall day, so I walked home the long way along Market Street, where I spotted it: a cherry red Ford pickup truck with a For Sale sign in the window. *If only,* I thought. I kept walking, trying to ignore the fluttering sensation in my heart.

I thought about Delbert's and Dick's advice. We would have to spread lots of straw and fertilizer and cover crop seeds to rebuild our soil and avoid silting the Sacramento Delta and San Francisco Bay. I thought about all the harvest bounty we were hauling from our garden back to the city to distribute to grateful friends and colleagues who could not grow decent melons or tomatoes in the fog. And we were going to need bigger tools, like lawnmowers, that wouldn't fit in our hatchback. And perhaps the day might come when we'd have to deliver our grapes to a winery...

I circled the block and walked back to the truck. It had a few minor paint scrapes but was clean inside and out. The seats had been lovingly covered with fabric stamped in a Southwest Indian pattern. I copied down the phone number on the sign, displaying enticing words like Low Mileage, Original Owner, Immaculate.

When I got home, I called the number. A pleasant young man answered. I asked him why he wanted to get rid of such a beautiful truck. He told me he'd just moved to San Francisco from Albuquerque. He loved his truck but found it hard to park on our crowded streets. He got expensive parking tickets and realized the truck was not as useful in the city as on a ranch in New Mexico. He wanted to trade it in for a compact car or try taking public transit for a while to see if he could do without a car altogether.

When Deborah came home from work, I informed her we had an appointment to test-drive a vehicle in fifteen minutes. She looked surprised and perhaps a bit annoyed with me, tired from her day of seeing patients in the Veterans' clinic. But I saw her perk up when Ted pulled into our driveway in the cherry red Ford Ranger pickup. As soon as she saw it had a stick shift, she was sold.

"As long as this thing works, it looks like exactly what we need," she said.

"Farm girls need a farm truck!" I said.

We drove it around a few blocks, with Scooter on my lap and Ted folded onto the bench seat in back. The engine, brakes, and transmission all performed as they should. Ted was impressed with Deborah's mastery of stick-shift driving, admitting it was a hard sell to most San Franciscans who had to cope with hill driving.

We negotiated a reasonable price and asked Ted to give us twenty-four hours to obtain a cashier's check. When he returned the next day, we gave him the check, and he handed us the title and keys.

"Hey...nice truck!" one of our neighbors shouted when he saw what was parked in our driveway. "I've always wanted to own a fire engine red pickup truck!"

"It's cherry red!" I said. I couldn't wait to put our new truck to work in Fiddletown.

THE LODGE

The following weekend, I drove our new pickup to the hardware store in Plymouth. I asked the young men who worked there to stack as many bales of straw as would fit in the bed, plus as many bags of 10-10-10 fertilizer as would fit inside the cab. Our friends Anne and Marianne were coming for a visit. We planned to entertain them sprinkling all-purpose fertilizer on bald spots in the vineyard and spreading straw on the eroding front slope Del had warned us about.

"Gee, we could be having this sort of fun at home," Anne teased.

"I know!" I said. "But isn't it better to spend quality time with your friends?"

Deborah turned to Anne and said: "We used to see you regularly, coming to the foothills for our quarterly fix of country labor. I have a feeling we won't be driving to Calaveras as often anymore. It looks like we have a lifetime of projects right here."

"I understand," Anne said. "But we're only an hour away. We all need to take a break occasionally!"

After we finished our tasks, Marianne suggested we check out the Moose Lodge next door. "I've seen these fraternal organizations around, but I've never been inside one," she said. "I'm curious to see what goes on in there. I know some of my patients are members."

After working hard, we looked a mess. Our hair and clothes were riddled with spikes of straw—all the bits too large to go up our noses. Anne suggested we clean up before going over to the Lodge.

"Aw, hell, let them think we're a bunch of hayseeds," Deborah said. "Maybe it'll earn us some respect."

"Or a reputation," I added.

We did a bit of "dry cleaning." We blew our noses, washed our faces, combed our hair, and brushed the straw off our work clothes as best we could. Then we walked up the main road to the Lodge. The place was not fancy—basically a large, barnlike building with a metal roof and siding. "Perhaps the inside has more charm," Deborah said.

It didn't. There was a large open room with a partially tiled concrete floor that had seen better days. Long folding tables were surrounded by dented metal chairs, giving it the feel of an elementary school cafeteria. A bar stretched almost the entire length of the south wall. It had a polished wooden top and a black foot rail. The front was covered in padded red vinyl with thoughtfully placed purse hooks for ladies—although only men occupied the bar stools. There were two small windows, one at either end of the bar, looking directly onto our property.

"I guess you'll give these guys hours of free entertainment," Anne whispered. Marianne giggled and said: "I can hear them now: 'Hey, fellas, let's watch these city gals try to run a farm without men. That'll be better than anything on the TV.'"

We approached the bar, where half a dozen men, ranging from middle-aged to elderly, sat nursing their drinks. "Hello, gentlemen," I said. "We just bought the property next door, so I thought we should come over and find out something about our next door neighbor. Can you tell us about the Lodge—what you do and what it takes to become a member?"

They looked at us and glanced at each other. "Wait'll Zack hears about this," I heard one of the men mumble. Finally, the bartender spoke up. The Moose Lodge, he said, was a philanthropic organization supporting an orphanage and an old folks' home in the Midwest. Dues were $40 per year for men. There was a separate support group called the Women of the Moose, whose dues were only $10 a year.

"Why such a difference in dues?" I asked.

"Well, it's the guys who do more of the work around here," he said, just as several women came out of the kitchen and began setting tables, putting out pots of flowers, silverware, plates of butter, and baskets of rolls. The aroma of chili or stew wafted from the kitchen.

"No offense, but it looks to me like the women are doing more work at the moment," I observed.

"The ladies are setting up for a special dinner," he said. "They do most of the kitchen work. But it's the guys who maintain the building and grounds and run the place. Our most popular event is the monthly Burn Yer Own Steak night, and men do all the grilling then." We asked how to become members and were told the only way for us to join would be through a husband, brother, or father who was a Moose.

"We can't just join by ourselves?" I asked.

"No," the bartender said, "but if you want to stay and have a drink, one of us could sign you in as guests."

"No need to bother," Deborah said. "We'll go home and have happy hour next door, where no membership's required."

"Who wants to be a Moose-ette, anyway?" I said as we walked back down the road.

DOGS AND CATS

Our parents used to accuse my brother and sister and me of "fighting like cats and dogs." The metaphor seemed appropriate at the time, but our dog, Scooter, did not fit that mold.

As a young pup, Scooter had a knack for selecting inappropriate love objects. Her first obsession was with a caged hamster owned by friends we stopped to visit on our way to the foothills. Scooter would sniff under the bathroom door where the hamster resided, whining and whimpering pathetically until someone would take pity on her and open the door. She would rush in to lie beside the cage of her beloved, panting, moaning, and producing a steady stream of little love yelps. We'd have to put her in the truck for fear she'd hyperventilate.

Shortly after we bought our property, we took a walk along our country road with our visitors, Kay and Linda, with Scooter prancing along beside us. We walked past the Moose Lodge, through a stretch of oak forest, and then down into a valley with golden pastures where some cows and horses were grazing. We turned around when we reached the far side, where the road reaches up a steep hill and then curves to descend into the Shenandoah Valley vineyards. As we turned toward home, a young kitten with tortoiseshell coloring jumped out of the brush and onto the warm asphalt. She planted herself in the middle of the road in front of us and began to yowl. She arched her back and stood her ground as Scooter rushed over to sniff her. For this, Kay named her Moxie.

Kay picked the kitten up and tucked it inside her zippered fleece jacket. As we resumed our walk, we heard more mewing coming from the roadside bushes. Soon another tiny kitten emerged. He was black from nose to tail, with a patch of white fur on his chest and beautiful bright green eyes. Deborah named him Tuxedo. Tux was more timid than his sister, but he didn't want to be left behind. Kay scooped him up and zipped him inside her jacket, too.

As we walked, we discussed what to do with the kittens. Kay and Linda couldn't take them home because Linda was allergic to cat dander. I thought they might be useful as mousers on the farm, but how could Deborah and I manage them when we were only there on weekends? We couldn't drive them to and from San Francisco, where they'd be in a strange place with a nosy dog pestering them.

Our neighbor Pam had seven cats at that time. We called for advice, and she offered to help. We made a home for the kitties in a protected spot in the top of the barn. We would care for them on weekends, and Pam would come over and feed them on weekdays until they were old enough to fend for themselves.

Moxie treated Scooter with scorn, ignoring her whenever she tried to dominate or intimidate her. Tux, on the other hand, was easily spooked. Whenever Scooter approached him, he would do his best imitation of a Halloween cat—with his back arched and claws extended, along with a comical stream of hisses. The tiny kitten tried his best to appear as threatening as a fire-breathing dragon. Scooter didn't buy it for a minute. She continued her campaign to approach and sniff the black cat, unsure whether to chase or lick him. Tux's resistance lasted only a few weeks. After that, he decided to give up and make friends. He and Scooter became best pals. Tux maintained his wariness of humans, but he became devoted to Scooter. The two would cuddle on the front porch like an old married couple, content to spend hours in each other's company. Sometimes Tux would groom Scooter, licking her all over, or he would lie contentedly with his head draped across Scooter's back. Occasionally, the two of them would get amorous, but Scooter would soon tire of trying to hump the small, supple black cat.

WINTER

After months of dry heat, Rainy Season thundered in. The sudden deluge created new erosion channels in the vineyard, as the wind tore leaves and nuts off the walnut trees. Rain pounded on the metal roof of our trailer, sending Scooter into fits of shivering. When the electricity went out, we found flashlights and built our first fire in the woodstove. It took some practice to get the draft just right. Once we did, we were delighted to learn how thoroughly the small stove could heat the whole place.

We enjoyed a candlelight dinner of split pea soup and grilled cheese sandwiches made on the woodstove. For dessert, we had estate-grown pears poached in zinfandel. I hoped the power would not be restored for a while.

Pears Poached in Spiced Zinfandel – from *Zinfandel Cookbook: Food to Go with California's Heritage Wine,* by Jan Nix and Margaret Smith, Toyon Hill Press, 1995

- 2 c. zinfandel
- ½ c sugar
- 6 black peppercorns
- 6 whole allspice
- 2 whole cloves
- 1 cinnamon stick
- 1 bay leaf
- 4 medium-firm ripe pears

Combine wine, sugar, and spices in a non-reactive pan. Bring to a simmer. Peel the pears with a small knife or vegetable peeler, keeping stems intact. Leave whole or cut and core, as desired. Place pears in the liquid. Simmer uncovered for 10-15 minutes (longer for firmer pears). Turn pears occasionally to cook evenly. When the pears are soft, lift them out with a slotted spoon and place them in a wide bowl.

Increase heat and simmer syrup until reduced by one-half. Pour syrup over pears and let cool. Refrigerate, covered, for 24 hours if desired. To serve, place pears in dessert bowls. Strain syrup over the fruit. (I like to serve warm with a dollop of whipped cream.) Makes 4 servings.

When the storm clouds retreated the following day, we drove to the hardware store to buy rubber boots and more bales of straw we could spread to prevent further erosion. We also decided to tackle the winterizing projects James had mentioned. We rolled up hoses and gathered sprinklers and stored them in the top of the barn. We wrapped the well pump, water lines, and aboveground faucets with insulation to prevent them from freezing in case of a cold snap. We called a number we'd seen posted at the hardware store and ordered a cord of seasoned oak firewood for delivery.

After a few weeks of on-and-off precipitation, the hills suddenly turned green, as if someone had flipped a switch. It seemed miraculous. We had enjoyed our autumn walks through golden hills, but now we enjoyed them even more. The countryside resembled Ireland in spring.

Our first Fiddletown Christmas was delightful. We gathered pine, toyon, and cedar branches and lots of mistletoe to make holiday swags and wreaths. We hung twinkling white lights around the trailer and decorated a live potted pine tree. Scooter enjoyed ripping open gifts under the tree, whether they were meant for her or not. Santa brought me a tool belt and a pitchfork for Christmas. Deborah got a chain saw, so we spent some of the holiday cutting downed wood and stacking it to dry for future use, burning brush as we worked.

We drove to Calaveras County to have Christmas dinner with Anne and Marianne. There is often snow in the pine and manzanita belt by late December, but that year the temperature was unusually warm. We ate our holiday meal in T-shirts on the sunny deck. When my Canadian relatives called to wish me a merry Christmas, I spared them a weather report; it would have been too cruel. I felt euphoric, with so much to be thankful for—good friends, sound health, interesting work, a loving partner, the best dog in the world, a home in an amazing city—and a second home in the beautiful Sierra foothills.

Before returning to San Francisco for a New Year's Eve party, we planted our living Christmas tree along the property boundary we shared with the Moose

Lodge. We decided to plant a tree every year, to enhance our privacy and deter the Moose from peering out those bar windows to see what we were up to.

I used to wonder what farmers did all winter, but we soon discovered there was no shortage of things to do in January and February. We moved the walnuts and pecans from their drying racks into sturdy plastic bins for long-term storage. We thinned the iris and daffodil bulbs, sharpened our saws and axes, and burned brush piles. We fertilized and mulched the orchard. We cut the spent asparagus ferns down to the ground, so new green shoots would emerge in the spring. We trimmed the raspberry canes. We studied our how-to-farm books and chatted with neighbors and hardware store guys as we planned our spring projects. Deborah attended a couple of pruning workshops, then got to work pruning the walnuts, pears, pecans, apricots, peaches, and cherry trees—relegating the roses, wisteria, and decorative shrubs to my care. Our friend Susan, who was recovering from a broken heart, visited frequently once she discovered there was no better therapy for getting over the loss of a good man than pruning grapevines.

Occasionally, work or social obligations would keep us in the city on a weekend. The Middle Age Spread seemed such a treasure, we preferred to have someone enjoy it, even (or especially) when we could not. One weekend we turned it over to our city handyman, a mellow British man, who invited some friends up for a Buddhist retreat. Another time, my Black tennis instructor took his blonde Swedish girlfriend there for a few days. These were not the sort of people typically seen around Amador County. I'm sure the neighbors and the Moose Lodge crowd noticed and wondered even more about us.

As the winter rains brought vibrant green landscapes and dry creeks gurgled to life, Deborah declared winter to be her favorite season. She loved the cool temperatures, the abundance of downed wood to cut with her new chain saw, the short days, and the cozy evenings by the woodstove. Me, too.

FIRST SPRING

The late winter landscape was glorious—green pastures, bucolic grazing cows, puffy white clouds. But spring turned out to be even more amazing. We marveled at the steady parade of voluptuous buds and perfumed blossoms. Each weekend brought a different bright palette of colors. In early March, there was an eruption of daffodils and crocuses. Once the daffodils began to fade, the freesias, sparaxis, California poppies, and irises took over the floral fireworks show. Soon after, the plum trees and apricots were white with blossoms. By late March, the peaches, pears, and quince were all in bloom, and then the lilacs erupted, filling the air with their perfume. How could spring not be my favorite season? It was intoxicating. I was constantly, silently thanking Norma for laying the groundwork for this dazzling show.

In April, the rains diminished, and the heat came on suddenly. I thought green grass on remote hillsides was lovely, but I was not so fond of it popping up in lusty clumps in our raised garden beds and gravel driveway. I began pulling it out by hand, at first blade by blade, then by the fistful. It became apparent I would never keep up. I called Anne for advice.

"You need Roundup!" she blurted, as if this should have been obvious.

"What's Roundup?" I asked. Anne put her hand over the receiver. I could hear her tell Marianne I wanted to know what Roundup was, followed by peals of laughter.

"Jeez, if you don't know what Roundup is, you'd better find out quick," she said. "Ask any of your neighbors, or just go to the hardware store and get some. Buy the concentrate and some kind of sprayer to apply it. That's what your driveway needs. You'll never pull the grass up by hand," she said. "Besides, you'll have plenty of other stuff to keep you busy." We hired Joe, who had a four-wheeler with a pull-behind spray rig, to blast our driveway with Roundup.

When we returned the following weekend, the grass had turned yellow and was shriveling up.

"Wow! Roundup is amazing—and frightening," Deborah said. In the 1990s, it seemed everyone was spraying poisons to control weeds, especially on roadways and along fence lines and vineyard rows. (A few years later, once we understood the effects on the planet and available alternatives, we'd switch to using only organic growing methods.)

There was more pruning and lots more weeding to be done in the subsequent weeks. The grasses and mustards and dandelions in the vineyard and orchard grew quite tall, but it was still too wet to mow or weed-whack. We started hoeing the weeds out of the vineyard by hand, which was not easy. We'd launch into this work feeling feisty, but after several hours, our backs ached and our palms were blistered. We were exhausted—and discouraged to see how little of the vineyard we'd tamed. We were even more discouraged the following week to see the areas we'd already hoed had sprouted weeds all over again. Dick was right about the millions of seeds in each cubic inch of soil, just waiting for the right conditions to spring to life.

Deborah devised a new approach. She borrowed our neighbor Dodd's rototiller and began to steer it through the vineyard. My job was to follow behind and hand-hoe the areas she missed as she maneuvered the tiller around each vine. This went a bit faster, but it still would take forever to get the vineyard weeds under control.

"Aerobic weeding!" Deborah cheered.

"Yeah, yeah, who needs a gym?" I said, glancing wistfully at some chunky customers ambling out of the Moose Lodge after a leisurely Sunday brunch and a few Bloody Marys.

As the weeks ticked by, the temperature rose, further stimulating the growth of weeds and other living things. My diary filled with brief, panicky entries:

- Weeds run amok!
- Weed and weed-whack and mow; till and hoe.
- More whacking and mowing!!!
- Weed and mulch!!
- Spent all day Saturday pruning the upper vineyard.

- Rain all day Sunday. No mowing possible!
- Asparagus, irises, tulips up. Weed and mow and whack.
- Growth overwhelming!!!!

By the end of April, we felt desperate. We realized how inadequate our hand tools and electric weed whacker and push lawn mower were. We placed an urgent call for assistance to Anne and Marianne. They kindly came over the next day with an array of gas mowers and weed whackers and blowers. They had plenty of work to do at their own place but felt sorry for two city career girls faced with their first spring in the Sierra foothills, lacking the equipment, knowledge, and experience to cope. The hills echoed with the sound of small engines all day. By the time they left, at least the areas around the house and garden had been tamed a bit.

"Maybe we should've purchased a quarter-acre lot in town instead of thirteen acres," I said.

"Yeah, well, that's water over the dam," Deborah said.

The next weekend, we could see the lawn and garden needed work again. We ignored it and tackled the orchard instead, trying to liberate the fruit trees from the jungle of vetch strangling them. Deborah found an area thick with weeds resembling giant dandelions, some as tall as she was. These had to be dug up with a potato fork. I'd never seen anything like it.

That weekend, a K-Mart flyer arrived in our post office box, advertising riding lawn mowers for just under a thousand bucks, with zero percent financing. I sped to Jackson in the pickup truck to fetch one before they were all gone.

A photo in our Fiddletown album shows me taking the first ride on the mower. The grass and weeds were about five feet high, completely obscuring the vineyard. As I blazed a trail through this head-high jungle on the new riding mower, Scooter followed behind, now able to walk into the vineyard along the green alley I mowed rather than having to leap over the growth like a gazelle.

Our three twenty-foot rows of asparagus started producing in March. First there was a trickle, then a stream, then a torrent. I was surprised to learn it is actually possible to get sick of asparagus. We became very popular during asparagus season, returning to the city with sixty pounds of the luscious green spears to distribute to friends and neighbors on Monday mornings.

Deborah and I were on our knees one day, harvesting more asparagus than we knew what to do with, when we heard Scooter barking. And barking. And barking. This did not sound like one of her "Mighty Dog Is Here" broadcasts. It was high-pitched and insistent. I went to find her and saw what had her in such a tizzy—a nest of tiny kittens tucked into an overturned stump. I picked one up by the scruff of its neck, and it turned into a mini-monster, hissing and spitting at me with tiny claws extended. In the following weeks, Scooter would make regular patrols to locate the feral kitties, so we got to check on their progress as their mother moved them around to save them from our mowing and whacking madness. Once, to get them out of harm's way, she moved them into the huge metal burn box James had welded—a rusty contraption we dubbed the Crematorium. It didn't look very clean or comfortable, and soon the white kittens were covered in patches of soot. Still, it did provide solid protection from predators and rain—and wild women with weed whackers.

Along with the litter of kittens, we found nests of baby birds, pockets of grass filled with families of mice, baby voles, and gophers. The air seemed chock-full of pheromones, prodding all vegetable and animal life into fertility. I suggested we could make our fortune renting out the Middle Age Spread to infertile couples at this time of year since the Life Force was so palpable.

TEN REASONS

We took a week off in May to stay in Fiddletown. We'd planned to do a lot during our mini-vacation—go biking or hiking every day, catch up on work in the vineyard and orchard, invite neighbors over for dinner or a glass of wine. But somehow, the week raced by at twice the speed of a normal workweek.

The light and temperature seemed perfect. There was not a cloud in the sky, and gangs of birds were chirping a loud morning chorus. I didn't want to leave.

"I want to live here all the time," I declared.

"Well, so do I—but we have commitments in the city. Not to mention incomes to earn," Deborah said.

"Can't we plan to spend the entire month of May here every year?"

"That doesn't seem unreasonable," Deborah said. "Other people manage to plan month-long vacations. Maybe we should, too."

We actually *could* have stayed longer because we'd taken three whole weeks off work. But we had longstanding plans and had already purchased airplane tickets to visit a friend spending a sabbatical year in France. Now, we didn't want to be anywhere but Fiddletown, but it seemed crazy to cancel our trip to Europe. At least the idea of spending next May on our land cheered us. To reinforce our resolve, we each made a list of ten reasons why we should spend the entire month of May in Fiddletown in the future.

Deborah's List:

1. The days are long, so you can accomplish loads of outdoor work.
2. The chain saws and weed whackers and mowers all need cleaning and tuning.
3. The vines need suckering and tying.
4. The fruit trees are loaded with tiny fruits that need to be thinned.
5. The irrigation systems need to be checked and adjusted.

6. You can get together with friends to taste zinfandels, as it's not too hot to enjoy red wine in the late afternoon.

7. Last chance to burn brush before the summer burn ban descends.

8. It's time to pull out the winter garden and plant the summer one.

9. The water lines in the vineyard should be blown out, to remove the dirt and acorns the woodpeckers stuffed into them over the winter.

10. It's a good time to dig out nasty weeds and thistles before the ground dries and hardens like concrete.

Mara's List:

1. The weather is divine.

2. The morning light is magical.

3. The sky oozes racy colors at dawn and at dusk.

4. The temperature is perfect for sleeveless outdoor work.

5. It's warm and dry enough to hang a hammock and put out the garden bench.

6. The sugar snap and shelling peas are just coming in.

7. The asparagus needs to be harvested daily.

8. The barn swallows are constructing fabulous mud homes on the barn.

9. The barn cats are shedding their winter fur and love to be combed.

10. The roses are blooming (and the irises, columbines, lupines, etc.).

I could have kept my list going for a long time.

SUMMER HEAT

We made our two-week trip to France. It was lovely there, but we found ourselves missing Fiddletown. Why were we sitting in cafés among strangers when we could be home dining with friends on the front porch? The food was great, but we were excellent cooks ourselves. Were there unique sights to see? Of course, but we missed our own vineyard views. At least it was an opportunity to polish old language skills—French for me, German for Deborah.

Deborah had been studying her favorite tome, *Weeds of the West*. She started identifying weeds in the French countryside. "Look—we have these same weeds in Fiddletown," she'd say. "This one's a mullen, and that one is dock."

When we stayed with our friend Beth in her rented *mas* (an old French farmhouse that once sheltered both people and livestock), we'd study the grape trellising methods in the Gigondas region, debating their pros and cons. We ate our fill of ripe, sweet cherries and hiked to a nearby Roman-era quarry, where we were the only visitors. Still, most days, we wished we'd stayed home to watch spring unfolding in Fiddletown.

When we returned to the foothills in early June, we were astounded to see all the things we'd spent the past months mowing, whacking, and hacking back appeared to be dead. The hills, which were a vibrant, verdant green when we departed, had turned gold in our absence. The sweet peas blooming profusely when we left were now burnt brown. We learned all the energy we'd applied to beating back growth in spring must be applied to keeping things alive in summer—which apparently can arrive abruptly, without warning. We experienced a new type of panic as we hauled the hoses, irrigation lines, and sprinklers down from the top of the barn and worked feverishly to get them in place and operating again. At least the grapevines and nut trees withstood a few arid weeks without shriveling, as most of the vegetables and flowers had done.

As the days grew hotter, our stamina for outdoor work was tested. We could work in the vineyard for only a few hours before wilting ourselves. We had to retreat indoors frequently to rest and cool off. We decided some sort of pool might be necessary. An in-ground pool seemed expensive and extravagant, so we purchased a simple above-ground pool. Once it was installed, we could work in the vineyard for an hour or two and then jump into the pool fully clothed. We'd be good for another vineyard shift, staying cool as the water evaporated. Our friend Don came for a visit and helped us build a pool deck big enough to hold a picnic table and a few lounge chairs for summer entertaining.

We occasionally hired Joe to help us with certain tasks. Joe was talented and sharp. He quickly realized how little we knew about country living and farming. Our ignorance showed when he dropped by one day to warn us the rattlesnakes had come out of hibernation.

"Rattlesnakes! There are rattlesnakes here?" I asked.

"Of course there are. They have a wide range in Northern California, from down in the Bay Area all the way up to Lake Tahoe," he said.

"I've never seen or heard of a rattlesnake sighting in San Francisco," I said.

"San Francisco's too cold for them, with fog blowing in off the ocean. But they do get into people's garages in the warmer suburbs, like Danville or San Jose," he said. "Up here, you just have to watch where you're stepping in the summertime. And don't stick your hands into rock piles or anywhere you can't see clearly."

It seemed like generally good advice to watch where you put your hands and feet.

"The good news is they prefer not to mess with people," Joe said. "They're reclusive, like the black widow spiders."

"We have black widow spiders, too?" I said.

"Well, of course we do! You didn't know that? There's probably dozens of them living under your trailer." To prove his point, Joe walked over and opened the door of the water heater closet on the south side of the trailer. There were plenty of daddy longlegs, but we didn't see any black widows.

Joe insisted they were in there, and he showed me how to tell. Regular spider webs are weak and wispy, easily broken with a brush of a hand or a broom. Black widow spider webs are much stronger, almost as tough as guitar strings. He said these spiders are round as peas, shiny black, and the females have a telltale red hourglass on their underside. I assured him I would not be flipping such spiders to check their markings.

I asked if there was anything we should be careful about besides rattlesnakes and black widows. "Nah, that's about it," he said. "Except for the mountain lions. People see them once in a while, but there haven't been any 'incidents' reported around here. Oh—and if you happen to react to poison oak, there's plenty of it growing in the woods, and it's hard to see sometimes." I asked him to show me what it looked like, too, so I could avoid it. We walked around the lower road, and he pointed out shrubs and plants with shiny oak-shaped leaves in clusters of three. He failed to show me another type, the ropy vine climbing into trees. The next time we were clearing brush, one of those vines touched my wrist in the tiny gap between my work glove and work shirt. Soon I was covered with itchy red welts.

We became accustomed to co-existing with the spiders, snakes, mountain lions, and poison oak. We kept a respectful distance and stayed out of each other's way for the most part. The beauty and bounty of the place seemed well worth it. We could share.

Though the summer heat felt brutal during the day, we appreciated it once the tomatoes ripened. Tomatoes grown in a hot, sunny place are nothing like the tomatoes bred for long shelf life—or even the ones we tried to grow in our cool city backyard. In Fiddletown, we felt rich in amazing tomatoes, so flavorful. I canned them by the bushel for winter use. We had tomatoes on toast for breakfast, with a hint of garlic and a drizzle of olive oil. For lunch, we had BLTs or plain tomato sandwiches with extra mayo. We had *insalata caprese* (sliced tomatoes with fresh mozzarella or goat cheese, ribbons of basil, and a generous drizzle of excellent olive oil) with dinner—or pasta with a simple sauce of tomatoes with a touch of garlic and lots of basil. Perfection.

When we learned fig trees also thrive in the heat and produce bounteous crops of bodacious fruit, we found one more reason to adore summertime in the foothills. I loved to eat them raw, in salads or for dessert. Especially the plump, sweet brown turkeys. We discovered one could split them, tuck some goat cheese into a half, wrap the fig with a strip of prosciutto, and grill them for appetizers. The fig would caramelize, the cheese would melt, and the prosciutto would become crispy. Ambrosia.

ZACK

One summer evening, I sat out on the pool deck, admiring Don's carpentry and the particular light that occurs when afternoon transitions into evening. Suddenly, I heard and felt something—a rustling—just outside my right ear. Although I had never been shot at in my life, my first thought was that a bullet had just whizzed past my ear. I instinctively jumped out of the lawn chair and slid onto a low step beside the pool.

Had I imagined it? I didn't think so. There was still a faint ringing in my left ear, and the hair around my ear seemed to be standing on end. Given where I'd been sitting, the bullet—if that's what it was—would have had to come from the south, where Zack and his wife lived, along with a few helpers who lived in old trailers near his entrance gate. *Why would they want to harm me when they don't know me?* I wondered. *Unless...*I shivered to recall stories I'd heard about gay couples moving to the rural south only to find dead cats stuffed in their mailboxes.

I returned to the trailer, still wondering. When Deborah came in for supper, I told her about my experience.

"No way," she said. "You must have imagined it. People don't go around shooting at each other in this part of the world. It's not the Wild West anymore." Since I wasn't entirely sure what had occurred, I decided to let it go. I also thought it might be a good idea to go meet this Zack fellow one day soon. The opportunity arose sooner than expected.

Shortly after my ear-tingling experience, Zack decided to shut off his artesian well—the one he'd allegedly "stolen" from James and Norma—to do some maintenance on his pond. He didn't warn us. As soon as he turned a lever to stop the flow of water, the "artesian" property returned to our well. Instead of discharging into Zack's pond, the water rushed through pipes that hadn't been used in years, shooting out of an old dolphin fountain, part of a Japanese footbath James and Norma's son had built. Once the footbath filled, water rushed through old drainage pipes and emptied into the ditch along the main road. We could hear whooshing water from the trailer. I ran down the hill to see Zack standing beside the pump house next to his pond. I waved. He walked over. I introduced myself. He said howdy, said he'd heard something about two women from San Francisco buying the property next door. He asked if I was the doctor or the lawyer.

"Deborah's the doctor," I replied. Though I'm not a lawyer, I didn't think it could hurt to have him think I was one. I told him whatever he'd done had sent water shooting through pipes at our wellhead. He said he was just taking care of some planned maintenance. He walked away, suggesting I might want to call a well company to fix my problem.

I looked inside the shed that held the electrical equipment for our well pump. I found the name of the company that had drilled the well and installed the equipment. I walked back up the hill to the trailer to call them. Fortunately, someone answered the phone and said they could send a repairman out within an hour. He installed a special seal at our wellhead to block the flow, so Zack's actions could no longer affect our system.

Soon afterward, we had a pipe burst at the wellhead. We noticed a sudden drop in water pressure up the hill and wondered what had caused it. Meanwhile, water was blasting from the broken pipe. It rushed downhill and eroded several deep ruts across Zack's driveway. Soon someone came onto our property uninvited and shut off our well pump. We were planning to irrigate the vineyard that day. Having no water got our attention. I went to investigate and discovered the problem. I called the well company, and once again they sent someone out promptly to fix it—since being without water in summertime is considered the highest priority emergency in foothills communities.

I happened to see Zack in the grocery store the next day. I walked right up to him and said: "Hey, Zack, I want to thank you for shutting off our well pump when our pipe burst. I hate paying for electricity to pump water that's being wasted. If it happens again, you can call me—my number's listed in the phone book—so I can go and turn it off myself." He blushed and looked flustered. "Uhhhhh..." was all he managed to say before I wheeled my shopping cart around him and vanished into the next aisle.

Zack's number was in the phone book, too, I discovered a few years later when something came up I wanted to discuss with him. He'd started a new practice of leaving a radio blasting from a small shack near his entrance gate. It would blare night and day, disturbing us, especially at night. I called and had words with Zack's wife about it, complaining the music rose up the hill and straight into my bedroom window, disrupting my beauty sleep. I explained I desperately need my beauty sleep and can get quite cranky when I'm tired.

"Well, it's our security system," she said. "We've had some things stolen from our barn and workshop. We hope the radio'll make people think there's someone down there all the time." I get out of sorts when my sleep is interrupted. For that and other reasons (I love regular meals and exercise and being outdoors, for example), I would make a lousy prisoner of war.

"Well, could you at least turn your security system down, so it doesn't keep us awake at night?" I asked. I thought it was a reasonable request, but apparently, she did not. One summer night, after being awakened by a blast of mariachi music, I sat straight up in bed, wide awake and royally pissed off. Sometimes I think I inherited my father's hot temper and short fuse. Most of the time, I can control it; other times, especially after several nights of sleep deprivation... not so much.

I got out of bed and dressed. I drove the cherry red pickup down the hill in the dark, with the lights off. I entered Zack's gate and coasted up to the little shack with music emanating from it. I left the truck idling while I walked into the shack and pulled the plug, shutting an announcer up mid-sentence. When I returned to the truck, I noticed my pruning shears sitting right there in the cup holder, so handy. I strolled back into the shack and cut the radio cord for good measure. It felt like an act of punctuation.

Beauty sleep was restored, at least for a time. I'm sure Zack knew full well who did the deed. But it was done in the days before security cameras became affordable and ubiquitous, so there was no evidence.

MOOSE WAR AND PEACE

Among the flyers and bills in our post office box was a notice from the Planning Department informing us of a development proposal in our vicinity. I read the notice and studied the figure several times. It seemed the Moose Lodge was intending to develop an RV park—right along our property line. I told Deborah what the notice said, and she let me know what she thought of it: "They're out of their fricking minds! Who in the world would drive an RV to the middle of nowhere to drink cheap beer at that place?"

A date had been set for a public hearing, so I got busy researching the Moose Lodge's history. Apparently, the Oro Madre chapter started in one of the old buildings in downtown Fiddletown, but there were conflicts with residential neighbors over traffic and noise. One of the Moose members owned a chunk of land about a mile away and got permission from the county to subdivide it into rural residential lots, each five to fifteen acres in size. He donated one of the smaller parcels to the Moose, so they could construct a brand new Lodge away from the town center.

Since most of the newly subdivided lots were zoned R1A—for residential and agricultural use—the Moose had to apply to the county for a conditional use permit to operate a club with a bar and commercial kitchen. Meeting notes indicate the Moose promised to keep all activities indoors to not disturb the neighbors in their proposed rural setting. The county made them go so far as to double insulate the wall facing the closest residence and advised them to keep the doors closed whenever they had events. Since then, more homes had been built on the parcels surrounding the Lodge, including ours.

When the laws changed to prohibit smoking in bars and restaurants, the Moose built a shed-like annex off the east side of the Lodge and dubbed it the Old Puffers Club. It had a wood stove and a metal roof to keep the smokers warm and dry, with gaps between the siding and roof for ventilation. Next, they built an outdoor kiddie playground and later added horseshoe pits. So much for the prohibition on outdoor activities. If we saw kids wandering in the woods close to our property line, we'd shout a warning to be careful of the poison oak and rattlesnakes. That typically sent them scurrying back to the Lodge to find their parents. Still, there were times when people who'd had a few too many drinks would carry on loud conversations outdoors for hours.

We'd seen the odd RV parked at the Lodge. Sometimes there would be a single one parked there for months. The rumor was it belonged to some pal of Zack's, a fellow Moose who was down on his luck or trying to recover from one addiction or another. I was very involved in Habitat for Humanity San Francisco at the time, so I understood the concept of providing a hand up. The squatters were generally quiet and didn't bother us, but there were exceptions. On rare occasions, we'd call the sheriff to complain. We learned the meaning of "HBD" in a police report—Had Been Drinking.

We installed a gate with a coded entry to prevent angry men from driving onto our property, honking their horns to indicate what they thought of us for interfering with their free camping gig. (This sometimes happened after they HBD.)

We had no problem with the Moose helping people in need occasionally, especially quiet senior couples needing a place to park their RV for a while. But creating an official RV park to invite strangers to camp anytime was a different kettle of fish.

I organized the neighbors. We wrote letters to the Planning Commission expressing our concerns. We launched a series of Letters to the Editor in the local newspaper. (In response to one letter I sent, the editor called me to say my letter was some of the best writing he'd seen in a long time, but it exceeded the word limit for Letters to the Editor. He encouraged me to split the content into two letters, so he could publish them both.)

Neighbors showed up in force at the Planning Commission hearing. The commissioners were surprised the proposed project got such a strong response from nearby residents. The Moose Lodge was relatively remote, and they hadn't heard any complaints about it until then. We told them about how the Moose were not adhering to the conditions of their existing permit, so we encouraged them not to approve RV camping. The commission voted 5-0 to deny the Moose permission and even warned them they better comply with their existing permit or risk having it revoked altogether.

We left the meeting feeling encouraged that people potentially affected by a local government decision could voice their concerns and be heard and understood—and the officials could then make an objective decision based on reasonable information. That's how little we understood county politics.

The Moose Lodge appealed the Planning Commission decision to the Board of Supervisors, the ultimate arbiter in our local jurisdiction. At the hearing, a great deal of emotion and plentiful lies were expressed by the busload of Moose members who showed up to fill the room. They came as much to defend the reputation of the fraternal organization as to fight for RV camping rights at one particular Lodge. They presented fists full of letters from Moose members, passionate about how the Lodge was the center of the county's cultural universe and how RV camping was necessary to save the Lodge financially. Some of the testimony was utterly fabricated. They claimed neighbors had denigrated Moose members before the Planning Commission, practically accusing them of being misfits and criminals. Some of their letters referred to some neighbors as the type of people who would not offer shelter to a tired traveler and his pregnant wife— an apparent biblical reference to Joseph and Mary. In other words, they assumed we were not "good Christians"; therefore, whatever we had to say could and should be disregarded.

There are five county supervisors, each elected to represent a district. The supervisor for our area at the time was a member of the Moose Lodge. Rather than disqualify herself from this discussion, she commandeered it. After hearing the testimony pro and con, the other supervisors looked at her and said: "This is a tough one, Stephanie. We'll go along with whatever you think is right for your district." Stephanie thought an RV park was right.

Fortunately, the county staff defined limits for the use permit. A Moose representative said they wished to host up to eight RVs, perhaps twice a year. The planning director encouraged the Moose to request twice as much to allow some "wiggle room." They were given a permit to host as many as fifteen RVs, no more than four weekends per year. In addition, the RVs would have to be parked at least twenty feet from the property line in consideration of neighbors.

The neighbors were spared a major, year-round RV park. Still, the Moose had succeeded in expanding their non-conforming land use. The place was a club, more like a pub, in an agricultural and rural residential area. They now had permission to attract visitors to enhance their booze and meal sales to help keep the Lodge afloat financially. At least the patrons would retire to their RVs instead of driving our rural roads after they HBD.

Shortly after the fight over RV camping subsided, efforts were made on both sides to bury the hatchet and improve relations. Fighting with neighbors never feels good. Some Moose Lodge members wanted the club to be viewed as a charitable organization rather than a cheap bar. They wanted to be better neighbors.

The next time Deborah and I were working in the vineyard, a couple of women walked over from the Lodge, bearing glasses of ice water and exclaiming how hot we looked working in the sun. I thanked them but pointed out that we had our own canteens. I thought it was sweet of them to think of us. When they left, however, Deborah vowed to redouble efforts to establish a visual barrier between our vineyard and the Lodge by planting more trees along the property line and drenching them with Miracle Grow.

AGENT "00" MOOSE

During the public hearings about RVs, I'd mentioned the Lodge next door to my home was a club I couldn't join because I was not the wife, mother, daughter, or sister of a Moose. Not long afterward, Moose International changed its policy, as many men-only clubs were doing at the time. They established a new chapter for "unattached" ladies, so you no longer had to be related to a male Moose to enjoy Lodge privileges.

Deborah and I were out weed-whacking one day when a stranger walked up the driveway. I flipped up my face shield and pulled off my ear protectors to hear what the man had come to say. He seemed nervous, as if he'd been sent to launch peace talks with aliens from another planet. The man said Zack had stepped down, and he was the new governor of the local Moose Lodge. He'd been sent to invite Deborah and me to become members. He explained about the new chapter for unattached ladies. It was called Home Chapter #00. He handed me an application form and encouraged me to consider joining.

The day was a hot one, and I'd been working hard. The first question that flew to my lips was not "What's the role of women at the Lodge?" or "What sort of charitable works do the Moose support?" It was: "What kind of beer do you have on tap over there?" The governor blushed and stared at his shoes, wrestling a grin. I bet he couldn't wait to get back to tell the boys that alien females like beer! He composed himself and said, unfortunately, the Lodge no longer had draft beer. It just hadn't sold well enough. But they carried a range of the standard canned beers that all taste like water to me. I told him I'd think over the invitation.

Deborah was annoyed with the Moose over the RV camping issue, as well as their lies, unkind words, and mean behavior at the public meeting. She felt they'd as much as labeled us "trailer trash," in addition to displaying their anti-gay prejudice by referring to us as "those women from San Francisco" and to our neighbors, Russ and Al, as "those men with shrill voices." She refused to have anything more to do with them. But the anthropologist in me was too curious about Lodge rituals to miss an opportunity to observe for myself. Just getting on their mailing list to receive information about upcoming events would be worth it. I filled out the application and dropped it off at the Lodge with my check for ten dollars—a small price to pay to become Agent Double-0 Moose.

Despite the formation of the new chapter for unattached ladies, it turned out one still had to have a local sponsor to become a Moose Lodge member. Someone had volunteered to be mine. Was it Stella? Or Thelma? The latter had sent me a note inviting me to attend an initiation ceremony on a particular Tuesday evening, which would mean taking time off from work. I drove up from the city on Tuesday morning and spent the afternoon mowing, weeding, and mulching. The time flew. When I glanced at my watch, I realized I would be late for the ceremony, even though it was right next door. I quickly changed into clean jeans and a blouse and drove to the Lodge.

In the middle of the cavernous main room, a dozen folding chairs had been set up in short rows, as if for a church service, with several chairs in front turned to face the small congregation. Women were milling about, dressed in what appeared to be their Sunday best. Some even had corsages pinned to their gauzy cream or lilac-colored dresses. Upon the arrival of the Late One, who was also the only woman in the room wearing pants of any sort, they took their places, and the ceremony began.

The rituals made me feel grateful I'd been raised Catholic, because there was a lot of standing up, sitting down, bowing this direction and that involved. The ceremony was replete with symbolism, much of which had to do with the life cycle of a rose: how in winter it might look like just a thorny stick (glances cast in my direction), but how in spring it might bud and leaf out, and how in summer it might actually fulfill its wondrous potential and produce numerous blossoms of great beauty. The gist of the message seemed to be, no matter how hopeless things might look (such as thorny bare branches or a "different" sort of Moose Woman), one should not give up hope. With care and nurturing, even the thorniest of gnarled twigs might surprise you and blossom into a thing of wonder...eventually.

When the ceremony was over, the sponsors treated new members to a beverage at the bar. I welcomed the invitation and pondered whether to order my Jack Daniel's straight up or on the rocks. I joined the others who were placing their orders. Every one of the women ordered a caffeine-free Diet Coke. Having shown up a) late and b) inappropriately attired, I didn't think I should muddy the waters further by ordering something so scandalous as an alcoholic beverage. Instead, I demonstrated I could be a team player by ordering a Diet Coke, but with the caffeine, please.

Our sponsors wasted no time getting down to brass tacks. Now that we new initiates had become Women of the Moose, we'd be expected to volunteer time serving the Lodge. Did we feel called to cleaning, organizing children's programs, waiting tables, or cooking meals? I explained that, because of my career obligations and farm duties, my free time was very limited. I couldn't sign up for a regular shift, but I might consider pitching in as a relief bartender once in a while. After a short silence, one of the women said she'd pass the information along to the fellow who managed the bar. He never called me.

A few weeks later, I was out pounding stakes to support our new plantings along the property line. Deborah had insisted on buying well-established plants in bigger pots, so they'd create a privacy screen between our vineyard and the lodge sooner. Because the new plants were taller, the stakes had to be substantial. I was standing on the hood of our riding lawn mower, trying to pound a metal fence post in with a short-handled maul. It was all I could do to raise the heavy hammer above shoulder level. Two men strolled out of the Lodge toward their truck, which was parked close to where I was working. I took a swing with the maul, missed the post altogether, and smashed it into my left kneecap. I bit my tongue to avoid cursing. I didn't want those guys to know I was in pain.

One of them called over to suggest I invest in a steel post driver, specially designed to make the job I was trying to do much easier. I thanked him for the suggestion, which reminded me we had one of those very implements hanging in the barn—a gift from Anne and Marianne, who knew it was an indispensable piece of equipment for country living. I'd forgotten all about it. As I rode off to fetch it, hoping to preserve my other kneecap, I heard one man say to the other: "What she needs, Herb, is a man!"

SHARDS

One positive outcome of the Moose wars was that we got to know our Fiddletown neighbors better. Through organizing for the hearings, we'd met Al and Russ, who owned a sixty-acre parcel across the road from us, below Pam and George's property. They also owned a condo about six blocks from our flat in San Francisco. When we met, they gave us permission to take long walks on their property for recreation and exploration. Their land had a big pond, lots of deer trails, seasonal creeks, and evidence of Gold Rush–era activity. There were stone cabin foundations, tailings piles, and strange contours created by placer mining, which involved blasting water to remove dirt and expose ore.

Al and Russ had owned their land in Fiddletown for decades. After meeting us, they decided they should improve it. Russ said they'd bought their land as a long-term real estate investment. They thought owning country land was as good as money in the bank or in the stock market—it would only go up in value, especially anywhere in California. They'd had success creating businesses, so sometimes they thought about developing a rural resort, a getaway for city folks who wanted to enjoy a weekend of rustic living off the grid and out of phone range. After seeing the Middle Age Spread, they decided to build a home for their own enjoyment.

"You ladies and your friends always look like you're having a damn good time and your place always looks so lovely, we thought 'Well, why don't we go ahead and build a house and workshop here and enjoy our land like Mara and Deborah do.'"

"Keeping up with the Joneses," I teased.

"Exactly!" Al and Russ said simultaneously.

They debated about what type of home to build. In the end, they decided on rustic A-frame log cabin. My first thought was that a log cabin might seem out of place in Gold Country. Perhaps that style belonged upcountry, among the pines and snow-capped mountains, but I hadn't seen any log cabins in Fiddletown or the Shenandoah Valley. However, there were experiments in geodesic domes and straw bale houses happening, so why not? Al said they'd located a cabin builder in Auburn, and they'd paid ninety percent of the construction and installation cost up front. They seemed very excited about it.

Deborah said what I was thinking: "Ninety percent up front doesn't sound right, Al. I've never heard of such a thing."

"Well, they have material and labor costs at the start of a project," Al said. Even though we'd never built a home from scratch, we were familiar with the concept of progress payments for construction projects. We hoped our neighbors weren't getting ripped off.

Al and Russ got their building permit and hired a contractor to pour the concrete slab foundation for their new home. Several weeks later, we walked over to check on the site. Al and Russ were absent, but there was a stack of plywood and some shrink-wrapped pre-hung windows on site. The next time we walked over, we saw the same heap of materials, except by then, many of the windows had fallen over and broken, perhaps due to a windstorm. There were shards of glass everywhere but no signs of construction progress. I called Al's phone number and left a message.

"Hey, guys, we haven't seen you in a while and wanted to check in. We were at your place today, and it appears many of the windows that were delivered are broken. We thought you'd want to know." Al called back a short while later.

"Aaargh!" he said. "I don't know where to begin. I'm afraid the supplier simply absconded with our funds, and all we have to show for it is that pile of plywood and broken glass. It's nothing short of a full-blown disaster."

"Oh no! So sorry. What'll you do now?"

"I'm too disgusted with the whole mess to be sensible right now. I'm letting Russell handle it because I get so worked up I'm likely to have a heart attack, and it's simply not worth it. We have to go the legal route to try to recoup anything we can, but frankly, it's not looking promising at the moment. But enough of that. Let's talk about something more pleasant."

"Why don't you guys come for dinner next time you're in the hills?" I said.

I felt they deserved a special treat, so I offered to buy a fat rabbit from the Rabbit Lady we'd discovered over on Laurence Road. "She raises them right here in Fiddletown to supply to Sacramento restaurants and local farmers' markets. Deborah can grill it with a honey-Dijon glaze. What do you say?"

"That sounds fabulous!" Al said, so we set a date.

We served grilled rabbit as promised, along with Russian red kale from the garden sautéed with olive oil, shallots, balsamic vinegar, and a splash of wine. We also oven-roasted red potatoes tossed with olive oil, garlic, and rosemary. The meal cheered all of us up.

Grilled Rabbit with Lemon and Honey Mustard

Adapted from a recipe by Arthur Mangie, Wooden Angel Restaurant – Published in *Cook's magazine,* July/August 1986 edition

Ingredients:

two 2 ½ lb. rabbits
Salt and pepper

Marinade:

2 T minced parsley
4 shallots
2 cloves garlic
2 bay leaves
1 c. white wine
¼ c olive oil
1 ½ T fresh thyme leaves

Lemon and Honey Mustard:

¼ lemon
½ jalapeño pepper
2 T honey
¼ c. Dijon mustard

Clean the rabbits and cut each into about 8 pieces. Sprinkle with salt and pepper and set aside. For the marinade, mince parsley, shallots and garlic. Break bay leaves into pieces. Combine all in a shallow dish and add the rabbit. Refrigerate about 8 hours, turning the pieces occasionally.

For the Lemon and Honey Mustard, grate 1/8 tsp lemon zest. Seed and mince jalapeño pepper. In a small bowl, whisk together the zest, 2 tsp of lemon juice, honey, Dijon, and pepper.

When ready to cook, pre-heat grill. Transfer rabbit pieces from the marinade to the grill. Cook about 10 minutes on each side. Brush on the Lemon and Honey Mustard and continue cooking until the meat tests done (about another 10 minutes).

Arrange the rabbit on warm plates, topping with any remaining mustard mixture. Enjoy!

A LOG CABIN

When Al and Russ came over a month later, they gave us an update on the house.

"This has been the most frustrating experience ever," Russ said, "but there's a tiny silver lining in the cloud—we'll get to write off our losses on our income tax returns. It's not much, but it's better than nothing. If we're lucky, we might get more panels or logs or *something* out of this fiasco, rather than just pennies back on the dollars we spent."

The men had developed a Plan B: they'd design a simple log home themselves, hire a draftsman to prepare the drawings, and then build it over time, using whatever materials they could salvage from the builder and doing much of the work themselves. They did receive a few more windows as partial settlement and were able to incorporate those into their design. Once they had their building permits, however, Russ announced construction mess was not his thing. He said he wouldn't return to Fiddletown until the garbage disposal was installed in the finished kitchen.

We felt sorry for Al, having to oversee the project by himself. We offered him free use of the small guest cottage on our property, so he could be close to the construction site and spend his money on building supplies rather than hotel rooms. He was most appreciative and provided the barn cats with weekday companionship for many months until the cabin framing was completed and the weather improved. After that, he camped on his own property.

One evening, as we were putting away our tools for the night, Russ paid us a surprise visit.

"Don't tell me! Is the garbage disposal installed and running?" I asked.

"You know it is, honey, or I wouldn't be up here!" Russ said. "I've come to invite you for supper tomorrow. You've been so good to us, we want to treat you.

You simply cannot say no!"

"What can we bring?" I asked.

"Just yourselves!" Russ said.

We showered and drove over the following evening. The winter rains had filled their pond to the brim. We followed the road that crosses over the dam to reach their home among the oaks. The finished log home was charming. There was not much in the way of furniture, but they'd made a makeshift table from two sawhorses and a panel of plywood.

"We're feeling so rustic over here, I've cooked up a sort of a cowboy stew," Russ said. "It's full of beef and potatoes and carrots in a gravy that took hours to perfect. So, please take a seat, and let's dig in!" We'd brought over a bottle of local zinfandel. Al opened it and filled our paper cups for a toast. We had a hunch there'd be many wonderful moments shared under that steeply pitched roof.

POOR DEER

Pam and George were the first on our road to install real deer fencing—eight-foot-tall fencing with sturdy metal poles and cross-bracing. The welded wire had a tighter weave toward the bottom to prevent even small creatures like rabbits or voles from invading. Pam and George were determined to protect their newly planted vines.

The fencing worked. It changed foraging patterns in the valley. We'd seen a smattering of deer on our land previously, but soon we had a deer freeway across our property. Our vineyard came under heavy attack. A vine would barely put out a new green shoot before a ravenous deer would be munching it. It was clear we were going to have to install deer fencing ourselves if we wanted our vineyard to amount to anything. As a bonus, we'd also be putting a more serious barrier between our land and the Moose Lodge, discouraging social drinkers or kids from the temptation to hop the low ranch fence to explore our property.

Our new deer fencing did the trick. It kept deer out of our vineyard, orchard, and garden as if we'd posted a big sign saying: "Oasis Closed. Your Kind No Longer Welcome Here." It would have been ideal to enclose the entire property, but even fencing three of our thirteen acres cost a small fortune. It was worth it! The deer disappeared. At least for a while.

It wasn't long before our neighbor Zack began installing deer fencing around his property, which suggested the deer freeway had moved again. Unlike Pam's fencing, which was built with quality materials by workers with benefits, Zack's fence went in his way—at the lowest possible cost with maximum use of materials from his on-site landfill. Why remove old fencing when you can drive in lengths of rusty pipe next to it and add strings of recycled barbed wire to reach the desired height?

Once his project was done, the deer would wander up the road and leap over our remaining ranch fencing. They soon discovered the fruit and flowers growing around our trailer. It made Deborah crazy to find our table grapes and gladiolas munched off by hungry ungulates. She tried home remedies she'd read about: scattering shavings of Irish Spring soap, sprinkling urine around the flower beds, and hanging bars of Ivory soap around the vines. Nothing worked.

We tried more inventive schemes. We installed a floodlight with a motion detector, but to little effect. Joe suggested adding a radio to the mix so when the deer came around to nibble our table grapes, they'd be blasted by music and bright lights. This approach seemed promising, until the canes grew long enough to set off the system by waving in the breeze, waking us up in the night. One evening, when Deborah went out at dusk to turn off a sprinkler, she was suddenly bombarded with floodlights and a loud voice proclaiming, "And the Son of God was made flesh!" It scared the hell out of her. Time for more fencing.

Perhaps in reaction to Zack's approach, we were extra sensitive about aesthetics. We made sure our new run of deer fence was set well back from the roadway, so it would not make drivers feel claustrophobic. Deborah found the rolls of new welded wire we'd ordered too jarring to her sensibilities. Too bright and shiny. She didn't want to wait years for the wire to dull, so she asked Joe to figure something out. Joe loved this sort of challenge. He thought long and hard about how to remove the sheen and make the fence look as if it had been already in place for years. He finally fixed on a vinegar solution, which he poured into an old sheep trough. He bathed the rolls of new fencing in the trough, turning them every twelve hours, until the finish was sufficiently dulled to meet Deborah's standards (and earn her admiration). Next, we had Joe remove the perfectly good ranch fencing Tracy had installed along the main road just a few years earlier— being the Citiots we were.

ROOTSTOCK

P am and George had protected their vineyard with sturdy deer fencing, but then they let the vineyard get overgrown. They didn't own a tractor and soon learned—as Dennis had warned us—you can't rely on others to do custom farming for you when you want it done. Everyone is busy when pruning, cane thinning, or mowing needs to happen. Pam's husband, George, was a physician with little interest in manual labor. The vineyard was Pam's project, in his view.

Once the grass and weeds grew waist-high, Pam was afraid to set foot in the vineyard because she might step on a snake. As a result, the vines lay untended, sprawling across her hillside, instead of being staked and grafted to syrah as originally planned. The vines languished as an abandoned experiment, an unfulfilled dream.

Phylloxera began to devastate California's vineyards in the 1990s. Vineyards all over the state were being ripped out and replanted, causing a sudden shortage of the phylloxera-resistant rootstock recommended by the UC Davis viticulture program. Nurseries were scrambling to replant, but there's no hurrying Mother Nature. It would take years to catch up on their backlog of orders.

I went for a walk with Pam one day and told her we'd inquired about ordering new vines, only to be told there was a two-year waitlist due to the shortage of rootstock. Our light bulbs went on at the same instant. We stopped and looked at each other, smiling as we realized she was sitting on eight acres of gold. She contacted a nursery, and they were delighted to come and harvest her 110R rootstock, paying her seventy-five cents for each pencil-length stick the thickness of a pinky. Pam transformed from failed vineyard manager to brilliant businesswoman overnight. She collected a sum in the six figures for those cuttings. She invested her unexpected windfall in a new well and planted another five acres of grapes. She bought a tractor and hired Joe to help her manage the new vineyard.

Now that both our place and Zack's were deer-fenced, Pam's new plantings were hit hard. The deer would file through the Moose Lodge property to the north of us, cross the road, and enter Pam's newly planted vineyard. So Pam spent more money to enclose that area in deer fencing, too. Now the main road had an almost-continuous run of deer fencing, from the edge of town to the Moose Lodge, a stretch of over a mile—except for the historic vineyard right across the road from us, with its century-old zinfandel vines.

Around this time, we heard a rumor that the historic vineyard had gone into a sudden decline. Those gnarled vines that had produced zinfandel right through Prohibition suddenly seemed to lose their vitality. People speculated the vines finally had reached the end of their useful life. My hunch was the deer in our small valley were concentrated there now.

When the property sold soon afterward, the new owner, Gino, began to make major changes. He ripped out walnut trees, cut limbs, and burned stumps in mighty smoldering fires that burned all winter long. After months of grading and preparation, he installed deer fencing. It was brash and glaring—obviously not soaked with care in any vinegar bath.

We felt sorry for the deer. To cross the road now, they had to navigate from the wooded hollow on Dodd and Mary's property, across the Moose Lodge property, walk a short distance along the main road, and then down the narrow easement road between Pam's property and Gino's. They had to walk a half-mile down that narrow path to reach Al and Russ's sixty-acre property, which was festooned with NO HUNTING signs. There, the deer were free to roam, welcome to munch on grass and sip from the pond at their leisure.

THE FIDDLETOWN
OPERA HOUSE

Once their log home was completed, Al and Russ came to Fiddletown more often. They'd frequently drop by to ask our advice on rural matters. We assured them we were no experts, but we were surprised how often we knew the answers to their questions. Apparently, we'd learned a lot in a few short years.

The first time they saw a rattlesnake on their property, the men called in a panic, asking for help. Deborah and I loaded the shotgun, rakes, and shovels into our cherry red pickup truck and headed out. It felt like a scene from *Ghostbusters*, only we were Snake Busters.

When we arrived at Russ and Al's, they and several guests were standing in a semicircle near the shed, pointing at a pile of lumber stacked against the building. I pushed boards aside with my rake to expose the snake, and Deborah blasted it with her first shot. The onlookers gasped. I struck the dead snake with the shovel, severing its head for good measure. The men burst into applause.

"Hooray for Warrior Princesses!" someone yelled. "Thank god for women with tools and guns!" another added. They offered to pour mimosas from a Thermos for us, but we had too much farm work to do to risk getting light-headed so early in the day. Since we had so impressed the men with our grit, can-do, and know-how, Al consulted with us about another country problem they were experiencing.

"Can you tell us what to do about the grass taking over our driveway and those nasty thistles springing up along the ditch?"

"You need Roundup!" Deborah and I said simultaneously, sounding quite authoritative. Al and Russ and their friends shook their heads, marveling at all we knew. (We were simply passing on what we'd learned from folks who'd lived in the foothills longer than we had before we embraced organic methods.)

A few weeks later, Russ came roaring up our driveway in a car we hadn't seen before. It was a lowriding, flashy, finned automobile with lots of chrome and a red plush interior. He loved buying cars he thought were irresistible bargains. He'd drive them for a while and resell them.

"Girls! Girls! Girls!" he shouted. "You simply must come over this evening for dessert and coffee. We have a real treat in store for you. You can't say no!"

"What is it, Russ?" Deborah wanted to know.

"Oh, you'll find out," he said. "Eight o'clock! Sharp!" He spun off, spraying gravel in his wake. We returned to our chores, wondering what surprise might lie in store for us.

Russ was waiting at the door when we arrived. "Welcome, ladies, welcome!" he said. "Come right in, now." He led us into the living room, where Al was seated at an upright grand piano.

"Are you guys musical?" I asked.

"Well, of course we are!" Al said. "Didn't you know Russell and I met at the Opera House in Los Angeles some twenty-five years ago? We both adore music."

"Play something for them, Al!" Russ said as he went into the kitchen to pour the coffee.

"Well, let's see now...all right, but don't expect perfection," Al said. He adjusted the piano bench and began playing a complex classical piece, looking quite serious. We were very impressed.

"Sounds like concert hall quality to me," I whispered to Deborah.

Russ reappeared, carrying a tray. He handed each of us a cup of coffee laced with Bailey's Irish Cream and a slice of a multilayered, store-bought cake with green and pink icing. He tapped Al on the shoulder. "My turn!" he said, as he scooted Al off the bench with a hip bump. Russ then ripped into the keyboard, pounding out Broadway tunes and singing the lyrics, as well. He was not a bad one-man vaudeville show.

"Russ, I had no idea you were so talented!" I said when he took a break to take a bow.

"Honey, you don't know the half of it!" he replied. "I can dance, too. Wanna see my gams?"

"No, Russ, we'll take a rain check on that," Deborah replied hastily.

We learned Russ actually had performed for a living in Los Angeles at some time in the past. He and a woman friend created shows and played on the nightclub circuit. He'd even had a bit part in an obscure movie.

"Well, now we should have a talent show," I said. "I can play a few tunes on my trumpet, and Deborah can play the first three notes of 'We All Live in a Yellow Submarine' on her saxophone."

"Yeah—because they're all B's," Deborah said. "I didn't get too far with my lessons." She reminded us we had other talented friends. Marilyn used to play the drums in a band, Marianne played the sax for real, and our friends Anne and Janice and Vicky all loved to sing. Kay would be great with a tambourine, and Linda would play the harmonica or kazoo...

"All we need is someone who plays violin, and we could enter the annual Fiddlers' Jam," I said, "but then I should give up the trumpet and play the jugs, instead. It probably takes the same amount of wind—or hot air."

"Oh my god, could we really do that?" Russ asked. We were all thinking about what fun it might be...if only we didn't have demanding careers, a five-hour commute round trip between San Francisco and Fiddletown, tons of urban duties, and acres of rural chores. Where would we find the time for practice and jam sessions?

"Encore, encore!" I cried, clapping. Deborah joined in, whistling and stomping.

"Al, play us some more of your serious music," Russ said. Al played several more familiar-sounding snippets, from *Carmen*, perhaps, earning more of our sincere applause.

"If you guys are such music buffs, don't you miss spending your weekends in the City, going to the opera or the symphony?"

"No," Al replied. "We've seen so many operas already—in San Francisco, L.A., New York, Paris, and Vienna. Now we're content to go to the Fiddletown Opera House, where we can watch world-class performances in comfort."

"What do you mean?" I asked.

"You don't mean to tell me we haven't shown you the Fiddletown Opera House yet?" Al exclaimed. We looked puzzled.

"Follow me!" Russ said.

He led us up a circular staircase into an open loft, where four oversized La-Z-Boy chairs were lined up in front of a giant TV screen. Next to the TV was a bookcase full of videotapes.

"Here we can watch the most fabulous operas, performed by the world's best talents. We avoid the traffic and parking problems and don't even have to worry about what to wear," Al said.

"I'd love to see *La Bohéme* sometime," I said, looking at a video jacket showing Pavarotti when he was thinner and had more hair.

"Al—she's discovered our little secret! We watch these videos over and over and feel assured that if the performers are not aging—well, then neither are we."

We set several dates to return to the Fiddletown Opera House for performances. I looked forward to settling into one of those comfortable recliners to soak up more world-class culture, served coffee or wine and cake. Who knew we'd find such access to the arts in a tiny, rural community?

WATER SKIRMISHES

Anne Dillard once penned wise words about how irrigation requires cooperation and civilization. That may have been true historically, from the dawn of agriculture until the twentieth century. I'm sure there are outposts of the planet where irrigation is still practiced as a civilized, cooperative endeavor. But sometimes in California, it feels like it's every man for himself.

In the Sierra foothills, it generally doesn't rain at all from May to October or November. Water is critical for growing anything in summer, as well as for fighting fires in the fall. So, people skirmish to ensure they have an adequate supply to meet their needs without considering that groundwater is a finite commodity. By capturing and using more water themselves, they may be taking it from others—like Zack did when he "stole" the artesian well from his neighbors.

Even before the twenty-first century, fire danger was palpable in the Sierras, where the hot, dry summers turn pine trees and manzanita into perfect kindling. With wind, a fire can wipe out an entire valley in hours or even minutes. It's a real concern and a common enough occurrence that most people think about when it will happen, instead of whether it will happen to them. After years of drought and climate change, California wildfires became more frequent, more fierce, and deadlier. It doesn't help that folks who move to California are often unfamiliar with living in drought-prone areas. For too long, developers have built homes on "cheaper" land, further into wildland areas where water is crucial.

Whenever anyone sinks a new well in the foothills, neighbors get nervous, wondering what the effect will be on the unseen and poorly understood network of underground aquifers. Our neighbors Dodd and Mary began having problems with their well soon after Pam sank another well on her property for her new vineyard.

Dodd came over one day in full panic mode. He and Mary were about to host a wedding party for a niece, with fifty guests expected—and their well had run dry. We were able to help by allowing them to run hoses from two faucets on our property, so the important event was salvaged. Subsequently, they hired a water witcher and dug a new well because property in the foothills without sufficient water is not much use and loses its value.

One of the features our agent, Sue, had touted about our property was the impressive, one-hundred-gallon-per-minute well. That's a lot of water—enough for almost any commercial agricultural endeavor or even a winery, which requires lots of additional water for processing and for keeping equipment clean. Nonetheless, during our first summer in Fiddletown, we ran out of water three times. We'd drive up from the Bay Area on Friday night, arriving late and tired. We'd turn on the kitchen faucet to fill Scooter's water bowl only to find nothing issuing from it. Someone would have to tromp down the hill with a flashlight to hit the restart button on the well pump. We had no way of knowing exactly when the pump had shut off (because it was sucking air), but usually, by the time we arrived, the well casing had had sufficient time to refill. It was disconcerting not to know how long our land had been without water, how much our automated irrigation program might have been disrupted, and when it might happen again. We called Sue to discuss the matter.

"Well, yes, you guys are tapped into a hundred-gallon-a-minute aquifer, but of course, your actual water supply is limited by the diameter of your well casing and the size of your pump," she said. This was news to us. We called in some well experts to see what could be done about it.

The experts were as varied in appearance as they were in opinions. One arrived in a large commercial truck with an extended cab. It was a four-door "dually" with four tires in back to support extra weight. It had a huge hoist and the company logo painted on the side doors. Another arrived in a beat-up pickup truck with two golden retrievers riding shotgun. He was wearing a frayed cap and oil-stained coveralls, and his hair and shirt were adorned with bits of grass. Another drove up in a sedan, wearing a suit and tie, pulling out a briefcase full of color brochures.

One expert advised us to simply lower our pump, setting it deeper inside the existing well casing. (It was already 250 feet below ground, but the well casing extended to 520 feet below the surface.) Another suggested we buy a bigger pump with more horsepower. Another said we should "drill out" our well and install a bigger casing, so it would store more water, ready to use whenever we needed it. None of the suggested improvements would be cheap, and some could easily cost $10,000 or more. Yet none of the experts could guarantee the results we wanted, and each of them disparaged the advice of the others.

"If you drop your pump lower, you might just suck up more particulate and burn your pump out faster," one said.

"Put in a bigger pump and you'll be taking water out of the well casing more efficiently, so you'll run out of water faster and more frequently," said another.

"You can throw away money to drill a bigger well casing, but where's the sense in that if you can't keep the smaller one you got now filled?" mocked another.

We consulted with our local handyman, Joe. "Hell, if it was my money, I'd put up with the situation until it reached a real crisis point and then act. Why spend money making changes when there's no guarantee it'll improve anything?" We decided to go with Joe's approach for the time being.

Eventually, after a few more dry-well events, we grew frustrated and spent some money lowering the pump we already had. That improved the situation until our downhill neighbor Zack tore out his pear trees, planted thousands of new vines, and started irrigating them.

After a stretch of ten or twelve days in August that stayed around 100 degrees, our vineyard was beginning to wilt visibly. We decided to water the vines overnight, but when we went to turn the drip system on, nothing happened. I called my favorite neighbor, Zack, and asked how much water he'd been pumping lately.

"I planted all those baby vines on the hill this summer, you know, and they didn't deliver the vines until the end of July, so with this heat, I've been running water to them every day."

"Well, our vines are shriveling up over here, and our well seems to be dry," I said. I figured his reply would be something like "Ha-ha, go to hell," or "That's not my problem." Instead, he said: "Oh, jeez! I'll go turn mine off right away! You go ahead and give yours a good watering overnight." Perhaps he responded the way he did because of his mistaken notion I'm a lawyer. Or maybe he was simply trying to be a good neighbor or show consideration for a fellow farmer. Whatever his reason, I appreciated it very much.

Within a few hours, we were able to pump water from our well again, but we were fed up with uncertainty. We couldn't stand the idea of jeopardizing our vineyard, orchard, and garden, nor of being dependent on Zack's goodwill to keep water flowing from our faucets. So, we invested more money installing a pump with twice the horsepower (the biggest that would fit inside our existing well casing) and lowered it further down. Mercifully, these investments had the desired effect. We'd have other dry well episodes to address with new pumps and storage tanks in the future, but for the time being, we had enough water.

Relations with our neighbor Zack improved a bit. His equipment graveyards and clutter continued to annoy us, just as I'm sure our "lifestyle" bothered him. But we began a custom of waving as we passed each other on the roadway. I think we realized that, despite personal differences, we were joined at the aquifer, so a certain amount of cooperation would be prudent.

THE S & M SWAP SHOP

For years, Deborah and I would titter each time we drove past a sign in Fiddletown pointing the way to the "S & M Swap Shop." That's something you'd expect to see in the Castro neighborhood of San Francisco, but not in a tiny, remote community in the Sierra foothills. One day, we decided to investigate what the sign meant. We followed the arrows, which led us east out of Fiddletown to a spot where colored plastic flags fluttered above the roadway. On the left side of the road, there was a large yard filled with cafeteria tables covered with stuff. From the car, it looked like a giant garage sale with an odd assortment of rusty chains, stacked plates, chipped ceramic jugs, teacups, and hardware.

We parked and got out to take a closer look, which only added to our puzzlement. There was an entire table full of rusted padlocks, all missing their keys. Some looked as if they'd been cut off with bolt cutters.

"What would anyone do with these?" I asked.

"I have no idea," Deborah said, "but what about these?" She held up a couple of old traps missing their spring mechanisms.

"Everything out here's ten percent off—today only," a voice behind us announced. An elderly gentleman had emerged from the weathered wooden barn with a classic cigar store Indian guarding its front door. The proprietor introduced himself as Steve. He appeared to be in his eighties, somewhat thin and fragile, with wisps of white hair curling out from under a denim cap with flannel-lined ear flaps. "If you need an antique ashtray, you've come to the right place."

"We don't smoke," Deborah said.

"Yeah, but you eat, don't you? Look at this set of three butter-yellow bread plates. You don't find those every day. And this pitcher with the matching glasses—only one of 'em cracked." Steve was on a roll. "Do you gals have horses or cows? I have all kinds of hard-to-find items—this horse collar, for example."

He held up a rigid leather item that looked as if it weighed a hundred pounds and had seen better days. It might have been used in the 1930s.

"Nope—no livestock, either," Deborah said.

"I thought you must be city folk," Steve said.

"Why do you say that?" I asked.

"Simple—no truck," he replied.

"Ah, but we *do* own a truck," I said. "We just happen not to have it with us today. And you're half right—we're city folk most weekdays, but we spend our weekends and holidays and any other time we can right here in Fiddletown."

"Weekends don't hardly count," Steve said. "But perhaps you ladies would be more interested in the fine cut glass I have inside instead of my bargain 'pick piles' out here. Come along, and I'll give you a tour."

"So...are you the 'S' of the 'S & M Swap Shop'?" I asked, gesturing toward the sign at hanging the entrance.

"Yes, indeed, that's me. The 'M' is for my wife, Mary," he replied, "but I'll have to change the name of the business because she recently passed." His voice caught, as if he were still trying to get used to being an S without his M.

"Sorry to hear that," Deborah said.

"Aw, hell, I'm kinda glad about it. She was in so much pain these last few years. It's a blessing she finally found relief. She had arthritis something awful. Nothing seemed to help. At last, she's free of all that," he said. "I'm gonna have to change my sign, too. I'm replacing it all the time, anyhow. You wouldn't believe it, but the sign's been stolen ten or twelve times these past two years. I just can't understand it. When I was a boy, we used to find some sport in shooting at signs, but we wouldn't steal 'em. Why, I caught some fraternity boys from Chico red-handed just last week, trying to take the darn thing down. Where's the thrill in sign theft?"

I was tempted to tell Steve why the sign was such a hot commodity, but there seemed no point with the enterprise's name about to change. Steve led us into the Swap Shop to show us the treasures therein. The shop was dank and dusty, with wooden floors that might have been level and sound at one time. The main room was chock-full of more junk—empty biscuit tins, dolls missing heads or limbs, chunks of mineral rock, coat hangers with crocheted covers, wooden nickels, old political campaign buttons. Stuff was displayed on shelves along each wall and on a table in the center of the room, with just enough room to squeeze around it. There were rooms off to the left and right that appeared to have been added at different stages. The room to the right contained mostly tools, organized by type. There were bins of metal files, loads of old wood planes, and used saw blades of every size and shape.

"If you can't find it here, you don't need it," Steve assured us. "But I saved the best for last. You gals follow me." The small room off the entrance seemed extra fancy. It had been Sheetrocked and painted, and it held glass display cases.

"Do you ladies know your glassware?" he asked.

"Not really," I said.

"Well, it's a shame because I have some exceptional pieces here." He walked behind one of the cases and slid the back panel open to remove several medium-sized bowls in blue, green, and red cut glass.

"These here are a rare type of glass. I've forgotten its name, but some treasure hunters are thrilled to discover the collection I have right here. I've had customers from as far away as Sacramento drive out here to see what I've got—heard about it from a friend or whatnot. Apparently, this is rare stuff. I even have a couple of purple ones that start out a deep plum and fade to pale lilac over time. Mary knew more about glassware than I do. But look at these gold-rimmed teacups. These are hard to find, and here I have six of them, in just about perfect condition. I'm asking eighty bucks for the lot. Couldn't you gals use these?"

"I'm not much of a tea drinker, Steve," Deborah said, "but I do like to sip wine. Do you have any wine glasses?"

"Over there in the corner is where you'll find the stemware," he replied.

"Where do you get all this stuff?" I asked.

"Oh, here and there. I go to estate sales. I read the want ads. I do a little bartering and haggling. But I can't let you know all my secrets," he said with a wink.

"Well, I guess this is a case of pearls before swine," I said. "We're just not into collecting things. To be honest, your tool room interests me the most."

"That's a shame because these are rare and unique pieces," Steve said.

Deborah spotted a set of eight champagne flutes on a corner shelf and negotiated to buy them for a dollar apiece. I made an offer on a batch of rusty tools (heavy on wrenches) I thought I might be able to use for my railing project. Steve held surprisingly firm on the prices chalked on each rusty piece. Apparently, there were no volume discounts. I put some back and paid for the rest.

"Say, are you the kind of gals who like to cook?" Steve asked as we headed for the car.

"Depends what kind of cooking you mean," Deborah said.

"Well, I've got ripe plums on the tree over there. My wife used to make jam out of 'em. They're ready now, and they're real good, but I can only eat so many. I'd be pleased if you'd take away as many as you want. Otherwise, they're just gonna fall on the ground, rot and make a mess, and go to waste. If you can use 'em to make jam or bake desserts, I'll even give you the sugar, too. There's a ten-pound bag in the house I'll never use." When I expressed interest, Steve led us into the house, through a small coat room, and into the kitchen. He opened another door and walked into a closet-sized pantry lined with shelves. "Here you go," he said, handing over an unopened sack of sugar.

"Let me get a couple of grocery bags, and we'll fill them with plums," he said.

Deborah was giving me a look. I know—we had enough projects going on already—but picking plums seemed like some type of pleasant community service. Guy loses wife, has plums, needs help. We hadn't bought any fancy cut glass, but we could make some plum jam for this nice man, perhaps help him not miss his Mary so much. I accepted the plums and sugar and told Steve I'd come back one day soon with some jam for him.

We returned to the Swap Shop a few weeks later and took Steve two pints of plum jam. I also gave him a fresh pear tart I'd made to sweeten his day (we were overrun with ripe pears that week). We brought along a mini garden tiller we'd bought recently and found inadequate to our needs. It was so light it would bounce across the surface of the soil rather than dig into it. Deborah had been about to take it to the dump when I suggested we take it to the Swap Shop and let Steve sell it instead.

The man's eyes lit up when he saw the tiller. "Does it work?" he asked. We assured him it did and explained why we were frustrated with it. Deborah showed him how to start it and how to work the gears.

"This isn't going into the shop—I'm keeping it for myself," Steve said. He carried it behind his house, where he had some raised garden beds. "This'll come in handy here," he said. He showed us around his garden, pointing out all the peppers and tomatoes he was growing. "The season's pretty much over now, but I'm going to send you home with some of my homemade salsa," he said.

We expressed admiration for the tidy garden beds, as well as for Steve's domestic skills. Because of the plums, we'd assumed Mary was in charge of the kitchen. Steve explained he and Mary had had a division of labor that worked well. She oversaw glassware and fine china sales at the shop, while he was responsible for sales or trades involving tools, equipment, and minerals. On the domestic front, she handled most of the housekeeping, and he'd done most of the outdoor work, but they both liked to preserve things. To not step on each other's toes in the kitchen, they divided the labor. Mary handled fruit preserves while Steve oversaw the production of savory things. So, while making plum jam would be her bailiwick, pickling was his. He went into the pantry and emerged with two pint jars of homemade salsa, one mild and one hot. "You better have a beer handy when you try this one," he said. "I grow the hottest jalapeños this side of Jalisco."

As we walked away from the house, Steve asked how much we wanted for the tiller. Deborah replied it was junk to her, so she'd be happy if he could put it to good use, no payment necessary.

"No way—we have to swap for an item of such caliber," Steve insisted.

"But you've already given us two pints of your salsa," I said.

"That doesn't count," he said. Apparently, it violated Swap Shop policy. Steve returned to the barn and emerged with a handful of treasures from the tool room, including some of the pieces I'd put back in the bins on our last visit.

"Here, you must take these—and this," he said, handing me a flat piece of serpentine rock with a fuzzy item glued on top of it. The fuzzy thing had two white plastic eyeballs with black pupils swirling around.

"What is this?" Deborah asked.

"It's one of my very own creations," Steve said. "I make lots of those in the slow hours around the shop. A certain percent of the population is interested in rocks, and there's a certain percent interested in crafts. This here marries the two fields and seems to make the rock and the creature all the more valuable to all comers. I sell a lot of those!"

"Well, okay, thanks," I said. "And thanks very much for the tools. I'll put them to good use."

"No, wait. We're not square on this deal yet," Steve said. He ducked back into the shop. He emerged holding a glass cylinder, some kind of votive candle with the image of a saint painted on it.

"It's still not enough, but now we're getting closer," he said.

"You've given us enough already," Deborah said. "We didn't expect any compensation at all." Steve insisted. He reached through the truck window and placed the candle on my lap. On the ride home, I inspected it and discovered a couple of bugs entombed in the melted wax inside.

"Who on earth is buying Steve's stuff?" Deborah asked. I didn't have an answer, but I felt enriched for having discovered Steve and his treasures. He eventually did replace the sign with one simply saying "Steve's Swap Shop." No one tampered with it again.

FREE CHICKENS

Growing up in cities and suburbs, I was accustomed to buying eggs twelve to a package, all the same size, clean and white. But our property had come with a chicken coop, and I thought a chicken coop should have chickens in it. I mentioned this to Deborah and recall her saying something like, "Good idea, honey, but we'd have to live here full time to take care of any animals."

I can be patient. Deborah generally goes along with my ideas eventually—or pretends to. Resistance makes me dig in deeper. "Good idea, honey" does not. Many ideas simply fade away after mild encouragement. Others do not.

Our coop measured about nine by eleven feet, and it was a generous nine feet tall inside. It had several roosting bars and a row of nesting boxes. It was solidly built but needed maintenance like most of the buildings on the Middle Age Spread. The roof leaked. The paint was peeling. I convinced Deborah we should fix the building, if for no other reason than it was an eyesore the way it was. So, we spent a weekend scraping, sanding, patching, painting, and reroofing the coop. It looked so good we dubbed it the Chicken Hilton.

Still, it had no occupants. I'd see signs at the local hardware store announcing, "Free Chickens!" with a phone number. Our friends in Calaveras County had chickens, so I called my local chicken experts.

"Hey, Anne. I see signs now and again advertising free chickens. Why would anyone give away perfectly good chickens?"

"It could be because they have too many roosters, or their layers are too old to be productive anymore," she said.

"So, they're looking for someone to provide them a retirement home?" I asked.

"Sure—but I bet people who call those numbers want to eat the chickens. My guess is most of them end up in a stew pot," she said.

The next time I saw a sign, I jotted down the number. When I called, a woman answered on the second ring.

"Yeah, I had a bunch of chickens to dispose of because we're moving out of state. But I've had so many calls, all I have left is three roosters."

"I'll take them!" I said. The woman offered to deliver them since she had errands to do out our way. *Free roosters delivered to your door,* I marveled. A few hours later, the woman dropped off a cage containing three roosters, two large and one small. The biggest one was a classic rust-red rooster, with a bright red comb flopping over his forehead. Next was a white rooster with black spots all over, resembling a Dalmatian. I thought of names for these two instantly: Big Red and Sparky. The third rooster was a runt with beautiful black and orange feathers that glistened in the sun and fuzzy down extending all the way to his toes.

"That's a Cochin. They're known for their small size and furry slippers," the woman said. "I realized as I was leaving home—I don't want to move any chicken paraphernalia, either, so I brought along this gravity feeder, a water tray, and half a sack of oyster shell calcium. I'll sell them to you for ten bucks if you want."

"Done," I said. "But what's the calcium for?"

"It makes their eggshells harder. You won't need it for roosters, but when you get your laying hens, you will."

I called Anne. "Hey, Anne. I'm now the proud owner of three roosters. Do you think they'll be able to take care of themselves all right during the week when we're not here?"

"They should be okay. Chickens are pretty independent. Just give them a water source and get a gravity feeder—one of those metal hoppers you fill from the top, so the feed trickles down as they eat it."

"I've got one already," I said. "The boys are really gorgeous. I think I'm going to love hearing them cock-a-doodle-doo in the mornings."

"I hope your neighbors will, too," Anne said.

Deborah returned from the hardware store and was less than pleased with my new acquisitions. Had I failed to mention it to her?

"What in hell do we want with three roosters?" she asked.

"Well, we're living in the country, and we have a terrific chicken coop. Roosters will cock-a-doodle-doo for us and earn their keep eating bugs." She looked skeptical. "Couldn't we try it for a while?" I asked. "If it doesn't work out, I'll give them away to someone else."

I knew Deborah had bought into the project when she came up with a name for the smallest rooster: Little Sammy. She'd named him after her youngest nephew.

I built a simple bench, so I could observe the roosters while I drank my morning coffee. I'd bring a bucket of table scraps and fresh weeds, then sit and watch my roosters parading around, picking at the scraps and pecking the ground for worms and insects. They'd crow—and sometimes fight. It was clear the little Cochin was at the bottom of the pecking order. Big Red and Sparky would screech and lunge at each other with spurs flying. Little Sammy would cower in a remote corner of the fenced yard.

Scooter developed a crush on Little Sammy. She would pine away from the other side of the chicken wire, whining and mimicking the rooster's movements.

A few months after we adopted the roosters, Anne and Marianne invited us to see a play at the outdoor amphitheater in Volcano. We brought a picnic dinner and a bottle of wine, sat on the grass, and enjoyed the performance. Many people came to say hi to Anne or Marianne at intermission. Some were patients at the clinic in Jackson where Marianne worked as a nurse practitioner. It was clear they thought very highly of her. Others knew Anne through her landscaping business or because she'd lived in the area a long time. I felt envious of their connections to the community. We were still newcomers. It was challenging to build relationships when we were around only on weekends and spent most of our time working on farm tasks.

Two guys came over to chat with Anne and Marianne, and their conversation turned to chickens. The men had retired and moved to the area from Los Angeles and now had a small business selling fresh eggs. I mentioned I enjoyed having a few roosters.

"How would you like half a dozen hens to go with them?" Jack asked. "We're replenishing our stock of layers and would love to give some of the older girls to a good home. They still lay eggs, just not as many as they used to."

"What kind of chickens are they?" I asked.

"Mostly Cochins," Jack replied. *The same type as our Little Sammy!*

"I'd love to have those chickens," I said, "but I should check with my partner first. Call me next weekend. We can talk about it then." I gave them my number. Deborah had gone to use the restroom. I made a note to talk to her about this at an appropriate time.

We were out mowing and weed-whacking the following weekend when a pickup truck came up the driveway. It was Jack, with chickens on board. He hadn't called, so he must have gotten directions to our place from Anne. And I'd forgotten to talk with Deborah about layers.

"What's this?" she asked.

"Umm. Remember those guys we met at the play in Volcano? They have an egg business, and they were looking for a home for a few hens. They were supposed to call me to discuss the proposition, but it seems they jumped the gun."

Deborah rolled her eyes and said: "This is your thing—you take care of it!" She went back to weed-whacking. Jack offloaded the six hens we'd talked about, plus two more that must have been an afterthought. They were indeed all Cochins, small hens with luminous red, black, and brown feathers and furry feet like Sammy's.

"Thanks," I said, wondering what I'd gotten myself into. We'd gone from having three bachelor roosters to having three roosters and eight hens. The chicken yard now looked as if it might belong to a real farm. This would mean buying more feed, but I thought it would be fun having a few fresh eggs to gather on the weekends. And it was.

The spring weather remained reasonably cool. Deborah and I enjoyed omelets and soufflés filled with asparagus straight from our garden. She began to think the chickens might have been a good idea. But as the weather turned warmer, the layers started producing a dozen and a half to two dozen eggs each week.

We invited Anne and Marianne over for a feed of egg-based culinary delights. They arrived with two more chickens. "If you're going to have a flock, you ought to have a couple of these Araucanas," Anne said. "They lay the coolest eggs in a range of colors, mostly turquoise blue or green."

"They're probably the inspiration for Doctor Seuss's famous *Green Eggs and Ham* story," Marianne said. Deborah gave me a look, but how could we refuse a gift from friends, especially hens with a connection to literature?

Now we had three roosters and ten hens. As the weather grew warmer, the hens laid even more eggs. We arrived one weekend to find thirty-six eggs in the Hilton, with no way of knowing whether they were hours or days old. I took them into the kitchen and washed and cracked some to make an omelet. As I began to scramble the eggs, I noticed a couple of the yolks were lumpy. Yuck! I got on the phone.

"Anne, I think there are eyeballs in my scrambled eggs!"

"Well, there's nothing wrong with eating fertilized eggs, but you can't leave eggs outside in this eighty-degree heat for a week. You'll have to get someone to gather eggs a couple of times a week when you're away. And as for those eyeballs... if you don't want chicks, you should get rid of your roosters."

I called my neighbors Mary and Pam, neither of whom had chickens of their own. Both said they'd be delighted to walk over and gather fresh eggs during the week, so we worked out a schedule.

The two big roosters continued to fight and disturb the peace in the Chicken Hilton, so I posted a "Free Roosters" sign at the local hardware store. Big Red and Sparky were snatched up right away. I suspected they were headed for the dinner table and thought it served them right for being so bellicose.

Little Sammy underwent a remarkable transformation as soon as the other roosters were gone. He became a tyrant overnight. He created havoc in the hen house, dominating and nailing the poor hens every chance he got. They were losing feathers and began to look quite tattered from his excessive attention. One day, when I'd let the chickens out to peck around the lawn, the rooster flew at Scooter with his feathers ruffled and his spurs ready to slash. Scooter let out a yelp and ran between my legs for protection, puzzled by her beloved's behavior. Sammy then flew at me, managing to draw blood on one of my calves.

"Your days are numbered, buddy," I warned him. That night Little Sammy mysteriously disappeared, which saved me the trouble of advertising him. We wondered what had happened to him. We thought of it as divine retribution, until two layers disappeared the following night. We inspected the fencing around the coop and found a break in the wire—not big enough for a fox to slip through, but perhaps a skunk or a raccoon. We fixed it.

Now we were back to having eight hens, but with no roosters. Peace prevailed at the Hilton, and we had production under control. Our neighbors gathered eggs mid-week, and we enjoyed fresh eggs on the weekends, free of unpleasant surprises.

Later that summer, however, one of our visiting nephews went out to gather eggs and left the door to the chicken coop open overnight. By morning, all the layers were gone. We found a single freshly laid egg on the paint shelf in the barn, the last evidence of them. We imagined they would not survive long in the wild.

Deborah declared the chicken experiment over, which was okay with me. I'd given it a good try. It was a relief not to worry about keeping the birds in feed and water, making sure their eggs were collected regularly, and protecting them from predators. It made more sense to focus on other living things—our vines, trees, and garden plants.

Deborah had begun to suggest we should replant the vineyard, which would be no small undertaking, given we knew nothing about it. Such a project would take a lot of our time and attention, not to mention our energy and savings. Perhaps it was time to focus on becoming competent grape growers. Deborah got out her UC Davis viticulture textbooks. I dusted off the Xeroxed notes Dick had given us when we first bought the property. We began to study these seriously.

PART TWO
CULTIVATION

UNDOING THINGS

As our professional careers became busier and more demanding, we tried to make our farm weekends a bit more relaxing. We hired Joe one day a week to do the mowing and weed-whacking, so the place looked tidy and inviting when we arrived instead of when it was time to leave. We had him do minor repairs, too, as it seemed Joe could fix anything.

Deborah began a campaign to get rid of any outbuildings we were not using. Why spend our time maintaining useless eyesores?.

The Woodshed

First on her list was James and Norma's old woodshed, a simple structure between the trailer and the chicken coop. I had no problem with that small, scruffy woodshed. It was conveniently located across the driveway from the trailer's side door, making it easy to fetch a wheelbarrow of split wood to keep on the porch, close to the woodstove. The shed was no beauty, but it served its purpose.

"It might be practical," Deborah said, "but it's ugly. Why don't we get rid of it and convert the sheep shed beyond the barn into a woodshed? We don't plan to raise sheep, so we don't need a sheep shed. That building is bigger—and a lot nicer too. It even has electric lighting."

"Yes, but the sheep shed is a lot further away from the house," I pointed out. "We'd have to push wheelbarrows full of wood up the hill to get to the back porch."

"But we wouldn't have to look at the crappy woodshed from the house. Instead of maintaining two buildings, we'd have one improved one. Besides, we should be getting more exercise at our age, not less. 'Use it or lose it,' as they say."
Ever the physician, I thought. Who could argue against aesthetic improvements

and more exercise?

We converted the sheep shed into a woodshed, which involved shoring the foundation, reroofing it, and painting it. I had to admit it was lovely—clean, attractive, and well lit. It held a lot more wood, and we got more exercise managing the fuel for our woodstove.

The Chicken Coop

With the woodshed gone, we now had a direct view of the chicken coop from the trailer across a sweep of lawn. I harbored fond memories of my chicken tending days and nurtured a small hope there might be more chickens in our future at some point. Deborah saw things differently.

"You did your chicken thing. I think we learned we can't keep farm animals until we can be here full time—and that day still is far off. Meanwhile, there sits a useless building surrounded with unsightly fencing. If it were gone, we'd be looking out over a sweet patch of lawn all the way to the walnut tree." *Who needs more grass to mow?* I wondered.

"It's not just a chicken coop," I argued. "It's a Chicken Hilton!" I knew I had a point. The old woodshed was nothing more than a flimsy lean-to, but the Hilton was solidly built. It was constructed with true dimension lumber, not so-called "2x4s" that actually measure only 1½ by 3½ inches. Each stud in the chicken coop was truly two inches by four inches, and there were quite a few true-dimension 2x6s and 4x4s in the framing, as well. It had welcoming nesting boxes and comfortable roosts. It was in move-in condition.

"A well-built eyesore is still an eyesore," Deborah argued. "It's just something else to maintain—and for what purpose? We have enough to do around here."

I placed a simple ad in our local newspaper.

You would not believe the number of calls I received in response. Apparently, everyone was dreaming about having their own chicken coop, and the chance to get one for free was too good to pass up. After learning more about the building, most people's enthusiasm waned. They could not think of any practical way to move an object of that size and shape.

One woman insisted on bringing her husband to see it. "He can do anything!" she proclaimed. But the husband took one glance at the chicken coop, turned to his wife, and said: "Have you lost your mind? There is no way in hell I can move that thing!"

More calls came; more people lost interest. Except for one tenacious woman, who seemed very enthused about having the coop. "My husband can move anything," she said. I told her about the previous husband who had come to look at the coop. "You don't know my husband," she said. "He moves vending machines for a living. He has all sorts of tools, trailers, jacks, winches, and know-how." I invited them to come by and take a look before committing to the project.

"No need for that," she said. "We'll be there Saturday morning to take it."

I left the gate open on Saturday, and sure enough, a huge pickup truck soon arrived towing a flatbed trailer. It was the woman, her husband, and their two teenage daughters. The husband—a solid, sturdy-looking man—did appear capable. He looked around inside the coop and emerged to announce: "Yep, I can do this. Should take me a little over an hour."

The girls rolled their eyes as if to say there was nothing more boring than to watch Dad do his thing for an hour—on a weekend, no less. I guessed they were not planning to help since they were wearing clean white shorts and lacey tops, and there were no nicks in their coral nail polish. But they turned out to be resourceful, too. They pulled a couple of folding lawn chairs from the truck and set them up in the shade of the walnut tree. I asked if they'd like some iced tea, but Mom had refreshments covered. She brought out a cooler of cold beverages and set it between the girls. The daughters turned their attention to a stack of movie magazines while the wife and I supervised the work. I was curious to see how Dad was going to pull this off.

First, he assembled his tools and materials: a drill, a Sawzall, a measuring tape, some chalk, and a box of screws. He started by chalking a line to mark the center of the building, first across the middle of the ceiling and floor, and then up both walls. He proceeded to screw lengths of 2x4s along both sides of his chalk line, with about an inch of space between them. Once the reinforcing was done, he used his Sawzall to cut right through the edifice—flooring, siding, shingles, and all—along his chalk line. I felt shocked watching him. It seemed violent, unthinkable, to slash a building in half. When he finished cutting, the coop was in two freestanding pieces with no sign of sagging.

"There's the tricky part done," he said, removing his safety glasses and shaking sawdust out of his hair and beard. He detached the trailer from the pickup and backed the truck up next to the coop. He removed the tailgate, attached a steel ramp, and then got out a contraption that looked like a pile of thick braided wire with hooks and a winch. I asked him what it was.

"It's a come-along," he explained. "If you don't have one, you should definitely get one. They come in handy on a ranch all the time." I made a mental note to add one of those to my wish list.

He wrapped the braided wire around one half of the chicken coop and attached a hook to a metal bar he'd had welded onto the front of his pickup bed. Then he started cranking. The coop shuddered, and then half of it started to shift. He inched it forward until it touched the metal ramp, then he kept cranking until it shimmied safely onto the bed of the supersized truck. He removed the ramp, closed the tailgate, and reattached the flatbed trailer to the truck. He backed the trailer into place and repeated the operation, using the come-along to safely slide the second half of the coop into place on the trailer.

"Wow," I said, "that was impressive, ingenious. I never would have thought to slice the building in half. I guess now it'll be easy enough to reassemble at your place?"

"I could do that," he replied, "but I've been thinking it would lend itself very nicely to becoming an even larger coop. I think I might place the two halves a ways apart and stretch a nice, open, screened-in chicken run between them."

"Oh, honey, that's a great idea!" his wife chirped. The man spent twenty minutes tying down his cargo, so it wouldn't shift or topple over in transit. He packed his tools and only then took a sip of the iced tea his wife offered him.

"I told you he could do it!" she said proudly. The daughters gathered their magazines, folded their chairs, and put them back into the vehicle. Deborah and I waved goodbye as they lumbered down the driveway with their tall, heavy load, removing several branches off the adjacent oak and walnut trees as they descended to the main road.

"Well—that's done," Deborah declared. "Look how much better that area looks already. Our view is much improved!"

"I guess," I said wistfully. It did look different, a bit more parklike. But I'd been fond of the coop and thought I might miss it. At least it had gone to a good home, where it would be well used.

The Barns

You'd think with the woodshed demolished and the Chicken Hilton gone, we could relax for a while. But Deborah was so pleased with the changes she'd masterminded, she felt emboldened to think up more improvement projects. The main barn was a solid, two-story building constructed from sturdy posts, beams, and plywood. But it had a dirt floor—we could improve upon that! And if we were going to be pouring concrete anyway, why not cut into the adjacent bank and build a proper retaining wall? I had to admit such changes would result in a superior parking spot for the sweet Yanmar tractor we'd bought from Dennis. This was a bigger job than we could tackle, so we hired a local contractor to work on these improvements over several months as his time allowed.

Once the barn improvements were completed, Deborah was restless again. "Did you notice one of the sheets of metal roofing on the old pig barn has flown off, and several others are loose?" she asked. I had noticed the sound of corrugated metal flapping on windy days.

"It's an accident waiting to happen," she said. "Why do we need a pig barn, anyway? We don't have any pigs. Nor horses, donkeys, or cows. I think we should tear it down rather than repair it. That would be a lot of work and expense, and for what?"

"But it's a big building," I pointed out, "with plumbing, electrical, and water lines, not to mention the large beams, steel bracing, and metal roof. Dismantling it would be a huge project."

"Well then, let's declare a Women's Work Weekend," she said. "We can identify a long weekend and invite a bunch of our girlfriends up from the Bay Area—BYO tent, sleeping bag, work gloves, and safety goggles. We'll provide the meals and tools. They'll love it," she said. And they did.

I was impressed by the fervor with which professional women can demolish a pig barn. There is a special gleam in the eye of a Weekend Warrior when she is set loose with a crowbar or a sledgehammer in her delicate hands. Perhaps the women were thinking about the glass ceilings they kept bumping into at work when they started yelling and ripping into the structure. It was hard work, but they embraced it as some form of therapy, or an exorcism. There was a lot of cursing, shouting, grunting, and laughing as the building was dismantled. If we encountered a particularly stubborn section, we would involve the tractor, using its horsepower to shove or pull the resistant part into submission. Some of the lumber was set aside for reuse, and some went onto a burn pile. We separated stuff to sell to the scrap metal dealer from debris to haul to the dump. It took us most of two days to pull the pig barn down, but there was a great sense of satisfaction and quite a lot of cheering when the job was completed.

We cracked open cold beers and local zinfandel to celebrate. While Deborah cooked burgers on the grill, I moved our sound system down to the barn. Our guests danced gleefully on our new concrete pad until darkness descended and the stargazing began. Eventually, each one drifted away to her sleeping spot, feeling satisfied and refreshed.

"Hey—invite us back anytime you need something demolished!" our friends said as they waved goodbye and headed back down the hill Monday morning to resume their city lives.

I had to agree with Deborah. The Middle Age Spread did look better with the old, unused outbuildings gone. Still, I was left with a puzzling sense of longing for the animals that could have been living in the chicken coop, sheep shed, or pig barn, even though I understood we were in no position to give them the care they would need. Eventually, I found a way to scratch my vague, persistent itch. I painted a mural on the side of our woodshed, formerly the sheep shed. Now I get to gaze upon my menagerie—a pig, horse, lamb, and a hen with her chick—anytime I want to. They never fail to make me smile, yet they need no daily feeding or care, and they don't suffer when we're away.

NEPHEW SUMMER CAMP

Although we'd purchased 13.25 acres of land, our attention initially was focused on the area around the house and the barn. As we accumulated more equipment, it became possible to groom and explore more of our property.

Beyond the hill where the old pig barn had been, we rediscovered another outbuilding we had all but forgotten about. It was a long, narrow, simply built structure. ("You mean *shoddily* built," Deborah would say.) The framing was minimalist. It was closed in on three sides with thin sheets of warping plywood and topped with scraps of corrugated metal roofing. I recalled James telling us one of his relatives had constructed it, so he could park a vehicle there for a year while he went traveling. The building might have protected a car from sun and rain, but I'm sure the owner would have come home to find his vehicle ravaged by rodents. We'd learned how varmints like to chew engine wires (for the peanut oil that manufacturers apparently use to keep their plastic coatings supple) and build nests in glove boxes.

Deborah wanted the structure gone. We weren't using it; we didn't need it. I prevailed for a while, arguing we (or relatives or friends) *might* want to park something in the shelter or use it to store excess firewood or some such purpose in the future.

Around this time, we began a series of annual events we called "Nephew Summer Camp," devised to spend quality time with our nephews—whom we otherwise didn't get to see very often, as mine lived in Canada, and Deborah's in Virginia. The camps entailed lots of painting and farm chores, interspersed with swimming, biking, pony riding, and games.

My nephew Andrew and Deborah's nephew Ben attended the first camp. I had them help me sand and paint the old outbuilding, so it would look better from a distance. That way, it might avoid Deborah's demolition inclinations, and the boys would learn some practical skills.

Since there was no running water at that location, I had the boys carry over a couple of buckets of water, so they'd be able to wash their brushes. When the painting was done, we dumped the reddish water on the ground and moved on to the next project, sanding and painting a wooden wagon we used to haul brush or give kids hayrides around the vineyard, pulling it behind our tractor.

When our work was done, we went for a swim. We'd invented a game we called the "Fiddletown Whirlpool." This involved getting as many people as were available into the circular above-ground pool. We would all start running in one direction, pushing the water in a big circular swirl, first slowly and then faster and faster. When our legs began to tire, someone would shout, "Reverse!" We'd all turn and try to run in the opposite direction, which was almost futile. The force of the current we'd created carried us with it, no matter how we tried to jog the other way. We'd giggle and guffaw as the water swept us off our feet and carried us like flotsam and jetsam, around and around until it finally lost momentum and we could run in the opposite direction at last. I often wondered if the Fiddletown Whirlpool might burst our pool apart one day, sending 8,000 gallons of water down the hill to gush across Zack's property to downtown Fiddletown, into Dry Creek, through the Sacramento delta, and into San Francisco Bay. Fortunately, that never happened.

While we were enjoying ourselves in the pool, our next-door neighbor Dodd walked over with two of his ponies. We'd installed a gate between our properties, so his ponies could graze in our wooded area and back pasture. It was a good arrangement, free feed in exchange for mowing services. But Dodd seemed angry. He started talking about immature boys and their pranks using his school principal voice. We were puzzled, but when he turned the ponies, we could see they had large patches of barn-red paint on their sides and backs. He accused Ben and Andrew of slapping their paintbrushes on the ponies. The boys looked astonished and denied this vehemently. I told Dodd we'd recently painted the remote outbuilding. But I had supervised the work, and the boys had done nothing wrong.

Dodd strode away, looking skeptical. Later, he called to apologize. He said he'd found our work area and saw the wet patch where we'd dumped the buckets after washing our brushes. Apparently, the ponies found the patch and decided a nice roll and back scratch might be lovely and cooling. A good bath had put everything right, and Dodd promised to come over with his pony cart the next day to take the boys to his favorite fishing spot to make amends.

A couple of years went by, and we still hadn't found an appropriate use for the spruced-up carport. Deborah could not abide a useless building. So, for the next Nephew Summer Camp, she decided to introduce the boys to the fine art of demolition.

DREAMS OF OUR OWN

Once we'd demolished all the useless outbuildings and refurbished the remaining ones, Deborah's attention turned to the vineyard and orchards. "Why on earth do we have thirty pecan trees to water, prune and harvest...?" she asked one morning as I was innocently enjoying my coffee.

"Well, because they came along with the property we bought," I replied. "Someone took the time to select varietals, plant and nurture them, and now we continue to care for them."

"Yes, but according to my Ag books, pecans aren't even recommended for this agricultural zone. We spend hours weeding, mulching, and watering those trees. And what for? When we harvest the crop, we don't know what to do with the nuts. It doesn't make a lot of sense."

I had to admit she had a point. It was odd having thirty mature pecan trees when we used about a pound of them annually in our holiday baking. Deborah's from Virginia, but she doesn't like pecan pie. The closest commercial processing facility for pecans was hundreds of miles away in Fresno. Like many things growing on our land, the pecan trees produced too much for our needs but too little to be a viable commercial crop. We ended up giving most of them away— which in itself entailed a certain amount of work. Still, was she suggesting we should remove those thirty towering trees? They were graceful and elegant—each about thirty feet tall. The idea of chopping them down made me feel slightly dizzy. The effort would be daunting, and destroying such majestic living things seemed sacrilegious.

"I've also come to think those ten peach trees are a pain in the ass," she continued. "We have to spray them three times a year to prevent peach leaf curl, and they need heavy pruning every winter. They all ripen at once, and then you've got a food-processing nightmare on your hands. That seems crazy when we drive past lots of farm stands selling perfectly ripe seasonal fruit every weekend. We should support them instead of working our butts off here for inferior clingstone peaches that happened to grow from pits Norma once threw into an old chicken yard."

I had to admit what she said made sense. "And we have those three cherry trees," I added. "I love cherries, but the damn birds get them before they ripen."

"Right—and we drive right through those cherry orchards in Clements and Lockeford that must supply half the country with perfect, ripe cherries for many weeks every spring. I'm beginning to think we're working too hard—to maintain *somebody else's* dream. Maybe it's time to develop our own dream for this place. If we're going to keep working as hard as we do, it should be our own vision we're trying to realize, rather than someone else's."

That sounded reasonable, but I'm not always comfortable with change. Sometimes I'm okay with the status quo. Nonetheless, I agreed it would make sense to define our own vision for the Middle Age Spread. Maybe then I'd embrace it. Perhaps it would be so lovely I'd get excited about it—rather than dreading the task of destroying things.

We discussed what we'd learned in our first five years of farming. What we liked most about it, and what we didn't like so much. If we were to remove the pecan orchard and the peach trees, we'd have a lot more space to do something else. But what?

We decided we most enjoyed growing walnuts and grapes. Walnuts were relatively undemanding. We had only five trees, but they produced an ample supply of nuts that were useful, nutritious, delicious, and easy to store. We loved grapevines because they are beautiful, hearty, and vigorous. We enjoyed getting our hands into their canes and vibrant green leaves. They are friendly plants, a pleasure to work with, and they deliver delicious fresh fruit, dried raisins, and wine. Zinfandel alone can provide rosé, red wine, dessert wine, and port.

More than anything else we had growing on our property, our vineyard allowed us to get involved in the local agricultural community. Deborah had bought books and taken a couple of viticulture courses at UC Davis, but we learned a lot from talking with neighbors. We'd learned how to prune, sucker, cane thin, canopy thin, irrigate, and harvest from local growers. And now we were experienced at applying what we'd learned.

"Those two hundred fifty vines James planted have trained us well, and we've had fun working with them, but you have to admit the vineyard has problems," Deborah said. I had to agree. The varietals were all mixed up. Our "training vines" had never been grafted onto proper rootstock. James had just stuck cuttings into the soil and hoped for the best. Deer had munched heavily on them. We were sure it was only a matter of time before we'd be dealing with phylloxera issues.

I was still reeling from the idea of eviscerating the pecan and peach orchards. Now the vineyard was threatened, too? I'd fallen in love with our land because of its rich, productive diversity, endless possibilities, weather, views, and very essence. It was hard for me to think about deleting so many things from it. If we'd had a clear vision from the beginning, it might have been easier to buy raw land and start with a blank canvas rather than become fond of this spot and the things growing here, only to have to euthanize them.

I needed time to adjust, but eventually, I did embrace the idea of implementing our own vision for the Middle Age Spread. The pecan trees did *not* make sense. The peach trees *were* too much work. The vineyard *was* a mess. Thus, the Era of Removing Living Things began.

We hired a guy with a massive chain saw to drop and cut up the thirty pecan trees. We then spent months splitting firewood and stacking it in the woodshed that once had been a sheep shed—and where soon some unseen pests would begin their yearlong project of turning our carefully stacked pecan logs into sawdust. We burned mountains of small branches and hired another guy with a backhoe to dig out the huge stumps. We spent most of the late winter months burning those.

Next, the peach and cherry trees received similar treatment. This was a lot of work but come summer, we had a fresh batch of Nephew Summer Camp recruits to help out.

The result of our efforts was dramatic. Once the fruit and nut trees were gone, more than an acre of open space emerged, surrounding the scraggly vineyard, which looked more foolish than ever. It had been planted in three blocks, with rows running higgledy-piggledy in different directions. Some were six feet apart, some eight. It was a relatively easy decision to remove those vines, too.

We spent more time that year reading books about vineyard management, but it was hard to find good information about how to actually lay out and plant a new vineyard. Some of the best, down-to-earth advice was contained in the handwritten notes Dick had given us, a sort of *Idiot's Guide to Farming in the Sierra Foothills*. One of his treatises seemed particularly relevant, as we were unearthing lots of rocks while removing trees and vines. It was titled "Rock Removal and the New Vineyard." Here's what Dick had to say on the subject:

There are a couple of things you need to know when you are de-rocking and re-contouring a new piece of ground for a vineyard:

1. It is going to cost you more than you wanted to spend on it.

2. You will have more rocks to deal with than you thought you would have.

We found Dick to be dead right on both scores. He might have added a third point:

3. It will require more time and energy than you can imagine.

LAWSON

We met Ben and Katie at their winery, Amador Foothill, and liked them immediately. Katie was the first female winemaker we'd ever met, and they both struck us as warm, good people. We tasted their excellent wines as we chatted about Shenandoah Valley viticulture. They asked us about our property. We described all that was growing there. I must have mentioned pears because Katie said she loved them and had many treasured family recipes to use during peak pear season.

There were only two pear trees on our land, planted at the edge of the lawn beside the trailer. We'd asked James and Norma what variety they were, but the only answer we received was "canning pears." We called them Wonder Pears because they were oversized, delicious, and versatile. When the crop ripened, we had many more pears than we knew what to do with, so one day Deborah and I stopped by the house near the winery to deliver a sack of pears for Katie. They invited us in for coffee. Ben mentioned he'd just returned from a brief trip to San Francisco—to visit his eldest son's grave, located in the AIDS Memorial Garden in Golden Gate Park. Enough said.

Several months later, Ben called to say he and Katie were seeking accommodations for their summer intern. Someone told him we had a guest house on our property that might be available to rent. I said we did have a small guest cottage, but we'd never rented it, and it really wasn't suitable as a rental unit. It was a studio with a bathroom but no kitchen facilities.

"Hmmm..." he said, "that still might work."

Ben explained that every year he and Katie would hire a foreign student as an intern to work at their winery for the season to help with topping up barrels, bottling wine, harvesting grapes, and making wine. It was a terrific opportunity for someone aspiring to become a winemaker in their own country to see how things are done in California. The previous year, they'd had a young man from Italy named Luigi, and the year before that, they'd had an Austrian fellow named Andreas. This year they'd identified an Australian bloke from Adelaide named Lawson who sounded interesting. Typically, they would provide room and board in their own home for the foreign "Cellar Rat," but one of their kids had returned home to live with them for a while, so their spare room was unavailable. He wondered if the new intern might sleep in our cottage if they would feed him at their place.

We might have been concerned about a stranger inhabiting our guest cottage, especially because we were absent so much. On the other hand, we thought it might be good having someone around to keep an eye on things. It shouldn't interfere with our privacy or enjoyment of the farm since the intern would be working long hours and taking his meals elsewhere. Besides, we liked Ben and Katie, so we were inclined to help them out. We think foreign exchange experiences are great. In addition, I have a soft spot in my heart for Aussies because my dad was born in New South Wales. I have a lot of relatives Down Under. After talking it over, we agreed to put Lawson up in our guest cottage for a few months.

When Lawson arrived, we weren't sorry about our decision. We liked him right away. He was a handsome young man with dark curly hair, warm brown eyes, long eyelashes, deep dimples, a firm handshake, and a ready smile. We guessed he was in his early twenties, a charismatic "chick magnet," for sure. He had a wicked sense of humor. He enjoyed good beer and hard work. And he could play the didgeridoo!

"I've heard those things are really hard to play," I said.

"Yeah, they are. I'm not very good at it, to be honest, but I thought it would be interesting for people to hear—it's such a uniquely Australian thing." He tried playing it for us, producing a mix of eerie low moans and sounds like springs uncoiling. "I need time to practice, and I should be able to find that here," he said. "Thanks ever so much for having me. I'd be happy to do some chores for you if I get some spare time," he said. "Just let me know if there's anything you want done."

"Great," Deborah said. "We never seem to get to the end of our task list. We'd be happy to pay you something for doing odd jobs."

Lawson proved very eager and willing to earn extra cash helping us out on long summer evenings after his regular workday. We had him remove some old vines, repair fences, pull weeds. Between his work at the winery and the extra work he did for us, I don't know how he found time for anything else, but he did. He joined a gym in Jackson and went there four or five times a week to work out. He planted a small summer garden behind the guest cottage and hand-watered his squashes, melons, and tomatoes daily. He enticed a flock of wild turkeys to come and eat the grain he scattered around the yard for them. He even signed up for once-a-week square dancing lessons at the Fiddletown Community Center.

Soon, Lawson knew every pub in the foothills, from Angels Camp to Placerville. He knew which ones had lavish happy hours on weekdays or live music on weekends. While he never brought any women to our place when we were there, we did notice a collection of hickeys blooming around his collar line from time to time, and there were nights when he would not come home at all. The next day when we saw him, he'd say he'd had too many beers and thought it best to sleep in his truck rather than drive home.

"That was smart," we'd say. But we weren't born yesterday.

As Lawson got to know more people, he became less available to do work for us. He became best buddies with Rich, who also worked at Ben and Katie's winery. Rich was probably twenty years older than Lawson but loved to pal around with him, going for a few beers after work, going to the gym, and sharing odd jobs on weekends.

Rich and Lawson contracted themselves out to remove an old walnut orchard. That took care of whatever remained of Lawson's "spare" time. It was nerve-wracking for us, never knowing when he'd be coming or going. Now he was mostly gone whenever we were around. In a moment of weakness, we'd agreed to let Lawson use the kitchen in our trailer on weekdays when we were away. It seemed mean not to. He'd tired of eating his meals at Ben and Katie's, preferring to cook for himself. Now we'd return on weekends to find bottles of home-dried herbs in our cupboards or dishes and implements in the wrong place.

When we confronted him about the frying pan whose coating was ruined by metal scraping, he replied: "I didn't do it! Everyone knows you can't use metal on Teflon." It didn't occur to us other parties might have been involved.

One day we bumped into Lawson's friend Rich at Fat Eddy's restaurant in Drytown. Rich had brought some visiting relatives there for brunch. He was delighted to see us walk in. He brought his visitors over and introduced them to Deborah and me. "These are the people who live at Lawson's place," he said. We all had a good chuckle over his mistake, yet somehow, we *were* beginning to feel like the people living at Lawson's place.

On Labor Day weekend, Lawson informed us that his mom wanted to visit, but this would only be possible if she had a free place to stay, as her budget would not stretch far enough to cover hotels. He wondered if, by any chance, the guest room of our mobile home might be available for such a purpose. We asked when she would be coming.

"It has to be after the grape harvest is over because I'll be swamped until then," he said. "She'd arrive on October ninth and leave on the eighteenth." Nine days. That sounded short and sweet, so we said sure, no problem. Only later did we learn Mom would arrive on October 9 and depart on November 18.

"I assumed that was obvious," Lawson said in response to our astonished questioning. "Why would she travel such a long way to stay for only a few days? Her ticket's bought and paid for now—sorry if there was any misunderstanding...."

As Lawson's occupancy stretched into the fall, we began to tire of him. We'd reminisce about the time we'd previously spent alone on our property. Deborah and I worked far too hard at our city jobs. We needed those country weekends more and more to unwind and recharge. For the most part, we could ignore Lawson when we chose to, but once Mom took up residence in our home, things were different. Of course, we had to chat with Mom and take meals with her and Lawson in our home. She was a perfectly nice person who pitched in to help with cooking and cleaning, but we sorely missed our privacy. She was on an extended vacation. We were not.

We began to feel exhausted with company. Mom became perkier and more rested by the week from her free stay at our lovely country estate, her daily jogs to Fiddletown, and her naps in the hammock we could never find a spare minute to enjoy. But what could we do? We'd unwittingly agreed to this arrangement. Deborah reminded me the end was in sight. We should just "buck up." We would survive both Mom's visit and Lawson's stay.

In late October, I made a weekend trip to Fiddletown by myself. Deborah had to stay in the city to attend a conference, but I felt the need to get away to the hills. Upon my arrival, I announced to Lawson and his mom I was feeling particularly beat and just wanted a low-key weekend. Perhaps I was hoping they'd take the hint and go on a road trip or something, leaving me alone. But Lawson informed me he'd planned a Halloween party—at our place. He'd invited his new friends from miles around to come over and meet Mom and have a last hoorah before they returned to Australia. I looked out the window and saw numerous bales of straw positioned behind the trailer for outdoor seating. There were scarecrows and corn stalks for decoration. Mom proudly showed me the costumes she'd made for herself and her son. Lawson was going to be a devil, and she'd be a witch. *How appropriate,* I mused, uncharitably.

I felt like cooking something, just for the therapeutic value I get from baking or roasting things, but Mom was busy at my stove—heating apple cider and making hors d'oeuvres and casseroles for the party. I could feel my stress level rising and decided I better seek relief, try to do something relaxing. I took Scooter for a walk over to Al and Russ's place, fuming with every step. By the time I reached Al's A-frame, I felt furious about these people who had completely taken over my country home and destroyed my replenishing weekends. The guys sat me down, gave me a cup of tea, and let me vent for a while. Their outraged "Oh nos" and "You've got to be kiddings" helped soothe me a bit, but not much. I continued walking in the woods with the dog for another hour, still feeling ready to blow my top. My heart was pounding. I was sweating and stressed. This was most unusual for me. I wondered if I might be having a nervous breakdown or a stroke, or a heart attack. Eventually, I felt calm enough to return "home."

That evening, I tried my best to get into the party spirit. I sat on one of the straw bales chatting with Mom and observing the array of costumes everyone but me was wearing. Lawson had collected numerous ex-pat friends, both male and female. Many, like Lawson, worked at local wineries and wanted to make the most out of their brief stay in America. They worked hard and played hard. Europeans, in particular, seemed to go all out celebrating Halloween, displaying elaborate costumes and practicing creative tricks and treats. It was fun meeting people from Holland and Germany who were making the foothills their home away from home—people I would not have met without Lawson introducing me to them. I had to admit they had considerable *joie de vivre*. I got up to mingle, sipping decent white wines the guests had brought from the wineries where they worked.

I'd noticed a young Black woman drive up in a Porsche convertible earlier, and I was curious to learn who she was. I introduced myself and learned she was a dentist from Sacramento.

"Lawson is so lucky you let him stay here!" she exclaimed. "I just love waking up on your property, walking out the door to collect pears, pomegranates, and walnuts. Breakfast straight off the trees is to die for!" I wondered how in the world Lawson had met her and how many nights she'd spent overnighting on our property—freeloading off our trees. I wondered how many other guests at this party might have done the same thing.

I lost my taste for partying and retreated to the bedroom at the far end of the trailer. Scooter followed me to her dog bed. The music and dancing kept the walls vibrating until the wee hours. I put my earplugs in, but they didn't have much effect. The last few cars left just as the sun was rising, the Porsche among the last to leave.

When I rose, I wandered to the kitchen. I needed coffee. I bumped into Mom, who must have stayed up all night and looked fresh as a daisy. I mentioned something about noise and not sleeping well. She looked astonished.

"I thought they were quite orderly and considerate for a bunch of young people having innocent fun," she said. I stormed out of the trailer and took Scooter for another long walk, bumming a cup of coffee from Al and Russ along the way. When I returned home, I packed up and drove back to the city, not feeling the least bit rejuvenated from my weekend away.

Toward the end of his mom's stay, Lawson decided he should take her on a major road trip to see some famous American sights he hadn't had a chance to see yet himself. Yosemite National Park was an obvious choice. They talked about renting a car, but Lawson's pal Rich would not hear of it. He offered them the use of his family car. When his wife heard about it, she protested, but Rich insisted.

"It's just for a few days—and we still have the truck. This will really help Lawson out. He doesn't have much money, and it's his last week in America. It's the least we can do to show these foreign visitors some hospitality."

As Lawson and his mom were leaving for Yosemite, Rich's parting advice was: "Just be sure not to leave any food in the car. The bears in Yosemite are famous for breaking into vehicles for their meals."

Upon his return to Fiddletown, Lawson drove up our driveway with Mom waving hello through the roof. I hadn't remembered a sunroof on Rich's car...

"Who knew a single candy bar would count as 'food'?" Lawson said. The cloth roof of the car had been peeled back like a banana skin. The glove box hinges were broken, and the cassette player dangled uselessly.

"We took out all the sandwiches, chips, and sodas. We missed one candy bar in the glove box, out of sight. I don't even know how to tell Rich about this. His wife's going to go bonkers," Lawson said.

Rich was sad but philosophical about the accident. It turned out he had not insured the vehicle because he had not quite finished paying his neighbor for it yet. His wife went off the rails. She threatened to sue the Australians for their negligence, and she ripped into Rich.

"I *told* you not to do this! This all could have been avoided had they simply rented a car—which is not expensive and comes with unlimited mileage and full insurance!"

Mom tried to comfort Rich and his wife by saying she'd contact her car insurance company in Australia to see if they could help. But no one knew how long it might take them to get back to her with a response, and the chances of having an insurance company halfway around the globe make Rich whole again seemed remote.

Mom departed on November 18, as planned. Shortly afterward, we received a surprising telephone bill with several hundred dollars in long-distance charges. I asked Lawson about it. He had Mom call me to explain.

"I thought those calls were being charged to my calling card," she said. "I must not have been doing it right. I couldn't possibly have spent so many minutes on the telephone, could I?" I offered to fax the bill, which itemized the minutes and charges for each call to Australia.

"No, that's all right, I believe you," she said. "I'll send you a money order when I get my next paycheck." The bill was paid eventually, but not until after we stopped by the winery to ask Ben to pressure Lawson further about it. Ben had a bit of leverage. He had to write a report about Lawson's internship, so he'd get university credit for it. He threatened to hold that up until our phone bill was settled properly.

Lawson was scheduled to depart shortly after his mom did, but he was having so much fun in California he decided to postpone his departure for another six weeks. He asked if it would be okay to stay on in the cottage.

"No!" I snapped without a moment's hesitation. He looked a bit surprised and disappointed but said no worries, he'd bunk in with a mate over in El Dorado County.

"That would be good," I said. "I can help you move your stuff this afternoon if you like."

Soon after Lawson moved out, Ben dropped by with a case of wine to thank us for putting him up. We had twelve bottles of good wine, along with lessons learned.

Photo by Kay Ellyard

VINEYARD PLANTING 101

We tried to hire someone to plan and plant our new vineyard. There were competent consultants around, but the statewide phylloxera epidemic had them fully occupied. The experts were so busy planting or replanting vineyards all over Northern California they could not take on another project, let alone one as small as our two acres. We asked Dick to help us, and he reluctantly said he would, but months passed, and he never showed up. He'd meant well, but he was clearly overcommitted.

We heard about a new vineyard planting consultant in Calaveras County seeking new customers. We leaped at the opportunity, as did our neighbor Pam, who was trying to plant her new five-acre vineyard at the time. We called and asked Hector to come to Fiddletown to give us estimates for the work. Hector seemed knowledgeable as he described his approach and what supplies he would need. He discussed how best to lay out the vine rows to maximize sun exposure, and he knew where to buy the stakes, irrigation line, and drippers. We hired him.

Hector started on Pam's vineyard, and it soon became apparent he had very little expertise and not as much common sense as one might hope. Based on our tractoring experience, we could see he was placing the rows too close together, and he was laying out the water system in a way that seemed irrational to us. Sometimes he'd show up briefly to get the crew started, and then he'd disappear for most of the day to meet with other clients, leaving his workers without supervision. The laborers would dig holes to plant the future vines, but these were not always on the same side of the wooden posts they'd installed—apparently without using a level.

Deborah and I concluded that if we wanted a new vineyard, we would have to design and install it ourselves. We did more research. We consulted with our County Agricultural Extension agent for advice. We asked questions in the hardware store, local wineries, and irrigation supply warehouses. As usual we heard conflicting ideas and tried to pick out the bits that made the most sense. We decided to use a simple 8' by 8' planting grid, which I plotted on graph paper, leaving a twenty-foot margin around the vineyard for a tractor lane. We determined we could fit approximately 1,200 vines into our recently cleared, triangular, southwest-facing space.

We called the nursery in Modesto with a memorable phone number: 1-800-GRAFTED. They confirmed we could purchase 1,200 green-growing, bench-grafted zinfandel plants on 110R rootstock for delivery the following spring, so we paid a deposit. Now we had a deadline to motivate us.

Since the vineyard area had the shape of a sloping amphitheater, we decided it would be best to run the main PVC water line along the high side, which was the eastern edge, then cut down through the middle of the space to create a row of risers—one for each future vine row. Black poly irrigation tubing would carry water north and south along each vine row. This way, gravity would help us, and the water wouldn't have to run too far to reach any particular vine.

We dropped by Dick's place to ask his advice on where to purchase supplies. When he learned we'd gone ahead and ordered vines, he said he could help us in some ways, even though he didn't have time to do the planting for us. He was about to place a big order for stakes from Valley Orchard and Vineyard Supply in Lodi and offered to tack on another 1,200 stakes for us. We'd get a better price that way, and he'd pick up our order along with his own. When Dick's helper delivered our 1,200 wooden stakes in bundles, they made a formidable pile in front of the trailer. Now we had to figure out what to do with them.

We puzzled over how to install the stakes. How would we get the rows straight? We learned you don't just pound six-foot stakes into the ground. Instead, you first identify the location of each vine with short marker sticks (about ten inches long), so you can make sure the layout looks right before committing to driving in the big posts.

Dick had his own surveying equipment and offered to come out and "shoot the transect" for us, because starting with two straight lines at a perfect ninety-degree angle was key to vineyard planting. From there, we could mark out the rest of the rows with the help of our city girlfriends and some colored string.

Soon we'd placed short stakes at all twelve hundred locations where a new vine would be planted. It was thrilling to look over the area and envision how the new vineyard might look with its canes growing and waving in the breezes.

We asked vineyard managers in the area how they tackled the problem of ensuring the wooden posts were all pounded in to the same depth. Each person had a different answer. One said he would lay the stakes on the ground and snap a chalk line across them to indicate how deep they should be driven. Another did something similar using spray paint. Someone else said he would attach a safety pin to the shirt of each of his workers, so they would know to stop pounding when the top of the stake reached that level. We had a good laugh over the possibility of combining these approaches by lining up the laborers and spray painting a line across them as the indicator.

Around this time, we were able to get help from Lawson's former pal Rich to help us out. He didn't have experience planting vineyards, but he'd done plenty of vineyard management work, knew where to find laborers, and spoke Spanish fluently. He located a crew of workers who knew exactly what to do. They executed the hard work of pounding in the grape stakes perfectly. Now our field looked even more like the real vineyard it would soon become.

Our next bit of luck was finding Rudy, a retiree who owned a Ditch Witch, one of those miniature excavators with a narrow bucket that could dig trenches in a fraction of the time and much more tidily than career girls with shovels. As Rudy worked, we glued PVC pipes together and laid them in the trenches to be backfilled so only the risers at each of our forty-four vine rows remained visible aboveground.

Dick was kind enough to pick up more stuff we needed on another one of his supply runs to Lodi. When he dropped off the giant rolls of black irrigation line, it looked like miles of plastic tubing—because it was, we realized in awe. He'd also bought 1,200 unused quart-sized milk cartons we could use to protect our young vines from rodents, instead of buying expensive plastic "grow tubes." We plugged away at cutting and installing it until we had an irrigation line strung along each of our forty-four vine rows, secured to each wooden stake by a green agricultural tie cut in half and screwed onto the wooden post.

Around this time, we got a call informing us our young bench-grafted vines would arrive the following week. Yikes! We hadn't finished our preparations. Everything was in place except for the one-gallon-per-hour drip emitters. We'd need two of those for each vine—or 2,400 total—and each emitter would need a couple of feet of quarter-inch spaghetti tubing attached to it to deliver water to the base of each new vine where the developing roots needed it.

I took a day off to be at Fiddletown when the vines arrived. It was a gorgeous Friday afternoon when the nursery's box truck pulled up our driveway. The driver parked near the barn and raised the roll-up door. Inside was a small forest of shimmering, pale green, lush-looking plants destined for our vineyard. We unloaded them and placed them in the shade of an oak tree, knowing it would be another week before we'd be ready to plant them.

We hired Joe and called on more of our city friends to help punch holes in the poly line for emitters and cut and attach the spaghetti tubing. It was tedious work, and soon all of us had sore thumbs from wrestling hard plastic drippers into the water lines. Just as we were installing the last of these, late on Sunday afternoon, Pam came by to show us a new tool she'd found on the internet. It looked like a manual paper punch—but it would make a perfect dripper hole in the poly line exactly where you wanted it with a simple squeeze, rather than screwing back and forth a dozen times with the straight punch, as we had just done 2,400 times. Oh well, a gadget for next time.

Finally, the vineyard was ready for the new vines to be planted. We tested the irrigation system. It worked—except our water system seemed unable to put out enough water to pressurize our miles of new drip tubing and supply all 2,400 emitters at once. We figured out we could make it work if we irrigated half the vineyard at a time. We hated to leave those baby vines sitting in the shade another week, but it was getting late on Sunday, and we had to return to our city day jobs to pay for this venture. We asked Joe to rearrange our PVC piping so we'd be able to water half the vineyard at a time. He promised to keep an eye on the baby vines and water them as needed, and Rich confirmed he could secure laborers to help us plant them the following weekend.

Finally planting the vines was fun. We all pitched in to help, with Scooter in the thick of things. Several of our city friends came to help, Joe and Rich supervised, and a crew of about fifteen men and women did most of the hole digging.

Planting was not a matter of simply removing each vine from its plastic pot and sticking it into a hole in the ground. The field workers showed us how we had to dig a large hole, loosen the soil, place the new vine next to the post, and then slide a milk carton down over the plant to protect it before banking fresh dirt around the carton. Then, the spaghetti tubing would be placed inside the cartons so the water delivered through the drip irrigation system would not simply run off, away from the vine.

By the time we finished the planting on Sunday morning, we'd decided on a name for the new vineyard. We'd call it "DAMAS Vineyard." The word *damas* means "ladies" in Spanish, but it was also an acronym for the vineyard founders—Deborah and Mara and Scooter.

Once the vines were in, we retreated to the shade of the ancient oak tree to admire our work. We celebrated with a bucket of ice-cold sodas and beers, burritos, chips, and salsa. Scooter entertained the crew by showing off her tricks. We would yell out a number—one, two, or three—in English or Spanish. In response, she would deliver the correct number of barks. Of course, she was responding to our hand signals, not the words, but everyone thought she was a very clever, bilingual dog. At the end of the day, we felt exhausted but delighted. The vineyard was beautiful, and we had managed to plan and execute it mostly by ourselves—albeit with a lot of help from Dick and Rich and Joe and our friends—and, of course, the hired laborers. We couldn't have done it without them.

Those baby vines grew in leaps and bounds over the subsequent weeks and months. At the time, we didn't comprehend that, in just a few years, our vineyard would be producing tons of ripe zinfandel grapes—and we'd have to figure out what to do with them.

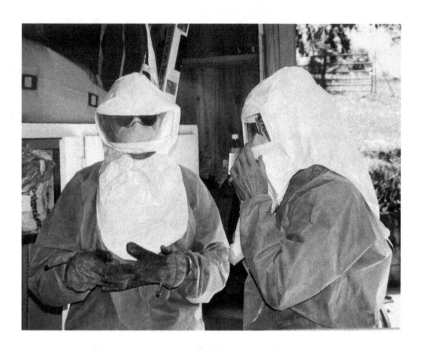

Photo by Linda Morris

THE SULFUR SISTERS

Once we finished planting the vineyard, we began to think about the future, when our vines would need training. We researched various wine grape trellising systems. Some experts believe vines are more productive when trellised to enhance their sun exposure. In the end, we decided to go trellis-free. Zinfandel has traditionally been "head-pruned" in Amador County, and we liked the look of the old vines, with their canes spreading out from an open center. They looked like free spirits compared with vines whose arms were stretched along rows of wire. Besides, trellising would have cost multiple thousands of dollars, and we were not enthused about looking at a lot of poles and hardware during the winter dormant period.

We don't regret that decision. Our head-pruned vines are elegant, and they certainly became plenty productive. If anything, we found ourselves constantly trying to beat back their remarkable vigor. However, we did discover a downside to head-pruning. As the canes grow longer, they droop down into the vine rows. They reach out and begin holding hands across the aisle, making it impossible at some point to drive the tractor through the vineyard any longer. With trellising, those canes would be fastened onto wires, keeping the lanes between the vine rows open, so the tractor could be used to mow or disc or sulfur much later into the season. In hindsight, we could have avoided these problems by planting the vine rows ten feet apart instead of eight feet apart, but we were not about to rip the vineyard out and start over.

The third summer, as the DAMAS Vineyard was just coming into production, we needed to sulfur the vines to suppress powdery mildew. In the right temperature conditions, mildew can establish itself in tight, damp places as the grape clusters begin to form and eventually lead to mold and bunch rot.

We bought an adorable Italian-made sulfur duster with a big yellow hopper for sulfur powder and a turquoise green fan-blower mechanism attached to the tractor's power take-off. That machine worked like a dream. It would quietly exhale a steady cloud of fine sulfur dust that settled like an embrace on each vine as the tractor passed. The problem was we only got to use it a couple of times in the spring before it would become impossible to drive the tractor through the vineyard. As the canes lengthened, they'd start to catch in the rough tread of the tractor tires and break off, ruining our beautiful pruning job. We couldn't stand that, so we'd suspend sulfuring.

Doing nothing was also hard on us, especially if there was unexpected rain or the weather turned warm and humid. We could almost hear the mildew growing, and we felt helpless to protect our beloved vines. We had a hand-duster we used to sulfur our small patch of table grapes but walking the entire two-acre vineyard and hand-applying sulfur to each of our 1,200 zinfandel vines didn't seem feasible.

I decided to try a new approach, taking a bamboo pole with me into the vineyard. I'd reach in front of the tractor to push canes away as I rode along the rows. I felt like an elephant trainer I'd once seen in India, riding on the back of a mighty beast, reaching out with a bamboo pole to touch its shoulders and guide it carefully through a crowd of people. Except that I was guiding my tractor through the vines, working to avoid running over and ripping off precious canes. This seemed entertaining and effective—until I accidentally jammed my pole into the ground as the tractor moved forward. It quickly sprang into an arc with so much tension that, had I not had the presence of mind to thrust in the clutch, I could have been catapulted over the fence and into the Moose Lodge parking lot. I'm sure that would have been highly entertaining to the men bellied up to the bar near those windows facing our property.

I reflected on my experiment and concluded it was too dangerous. It took too much of the driver's attention, and it was not easy switching the pole from side to side manually while driving. I tried a variation. I got another bamboo pole from the supply Deborah uses for string beans and cucumbers to climb in the summer garden. I rigged up the two poles like elephant tusks—one on each side of the tractor—to scoop up canes and guide them over the big rear tractor tire. I wired them in place, ensuring they would clear the ground enough to avoid dangerous snagging problems. This worked well, as long as the canes waved above ground level. If they were lying on the soil, the poles would miss them, and the tires would grab them and tear them off. I gave up in frustration.

Deborah and I had an errand to run in Ione, so we stopped at the hardware store there. We chatted with the owner about how we might rig some type of temporary fenders for our tractor, something flexible, not too heavy, yet capable of scooping up tender young canes. He couldn't think of anything offhand, so we wandered around looking over the stock. We came to a reel of copper tubing among the heating and air conditioning supplies. It was thin-walled, so you could bend it easily, yet it would retain its shape.

"Do you think we could bend this stuff into tusk-like protuberances?" I asked.

"Maybe," Deborah said. "We could turn the points up like ski tips, so they'd be less likely to jam into the ground. But how would we attach them to the tractor?" There were metal fittings of all sorts in the store, but those would require drilling holes into the tractor frame to accommodate screws or bolts.

"What about using duct tape?" I asked. She thought that might work. We asked a clerk where we could find the duct tape, and his eyes lit up.

"Duct tape!" he said reverently. "Now, you are some women after my own heart! I find most women don't give duct tape the appreciation it's due." He asked what we needed it for and marveled when we told him what we planned to do with it. He thought we were ingenious, inventing seasonal fenders from copper tubing, then attaching them to our tractor with his favorite product on earth.

"Between you and me," he confided, "I call it 'Jesus tape' because it has been my salvation in a million and one fixes. I worship the stuff."

We returned home, shaped the tusks, and Jesus-taped them onto the tractor. By the time we made them long enough to be able to pick up the lowest-hanging canes, however, their cumulative weight made them sag and droop until they rested on the ground. We could see that, even with their upturned ends, they would bend into a mangled mess as soon as they encountered any obstacle less movable than a very young cane.

The tractor sat useless in the barn again. After a time, I removed the duct tape and put about fifty bucks' worth of gnarled copper tubing on our pile of metal to be taken for recycling.

I gazed over our beautiful head-pruned vines, feeling desperate. The temperature and humidity were perfect for mildew formation. We could hear tractor engines laboring in other vineyards, where our neighbors were sulfur-dusting their trellised vines. We began to suffer acute trellis envy. Joe came by to replace the seat on our riding lawn mower and had to listen to us complain about not being able to get the tractor into the vineyard. When we told him about our various experiments, he held up the old riding lawn mower seat.

"Hey, here's an idea. You could weld this onto the front of the tractor. That way, you could have another person sit out front and push the canes out of the way." He was proud of himself for thinking up this remedy. I was enthusiastic about a project I could do with my recently acquired welding equipment, but I couldn't quite envision how this would work. We could install a seatbelt, to make sure the cane handler wouldn't accidentally fall beneath the tractor, but it could be dangerous to have feet dangling down around ground level.

Deborah proposed a solution: "I can swipe a set of stirrups from a pelvic exam table at the hospital, and you can weld those on, too. They'd make perfect footrests." We had a good laugh, but this plan seemed a bit far-fetched, even for innovative farmers like us.

Then Deborah had a real brain wave. Kay and Linda were heading up for a visit—reinforcements! "What if two of us were to jog ahead of the tractor. We could grab the longer canes and tuck them out of the way just before the tractor passed," she said.

"Are you crazy?" I asked. "That sounds like a lot of work. And what about the potential for someone getting hurt? It's not worth it."

"Well, we'd have to be nimble and quick, and we'd have to wear protective clothing, even if the tractor operator would try her best not to sulfur-dust the assistants. It would be better than a workout at some boring indoor gym."

Kay was game for this experiment. She and Deborah donned Tyvek "moon suits," gloves, masks, and special Tyvek hoods with clear acrylic face shields built into them. Linda and I laughed at the sight of them, looking like nuns from some very odd religious sect. We dubbed them the Sulfur Sisters.

"Let's get going!" Kay and Deborah said. They were beginning to perspire in those outfits, as laughing caused their face shields to cloud up with steam. I drove as they trotted ahead of the tractor. They were remarkably effective at pushing canes out of the way. I had to clutch periodically to avoid running over one of the nuns, but we were able to complete one more crucial round of sulfuring before the weather turned hot enough to reduce the potential for mildew growth.

We never repeated the Sulfur Sisters routine. It was entertaining but too labor-intensive. Instead, we had steel fenders welded onto the tractor, so canes would be swept aside, allowing us to use the tractor just a bit later into the growing season. Mostly, we came to rely on mildew control techniques like early cane thinning and leaf pulling, removing vegetation to promote air circulation around the grape clusters. But I look back with nostalgia on that Sulfur Sisters summer and chuckle to think about the men who must have been elbowing around the windows at the Moose Lodge, trying to get a better look at whatever the hell was going on next door. Perhaps they were able to raise some money for charity by setting up pay-per-view booths before the cypress trees we planted along our property line finally, mercifully, grew into a thick, tall hedge.

SHADOWS

One fall weekend, just after the light early winter rains had begun, Deborah and I were bucking wood and burning brush when Russ dropped by. We could tell he'd just come from the Moose Lodge by the smell of his breath. Russ adored booze as much as he appreciated a bargain, and he'd discovered that the Moose Lodge could deliver both—lots of low-cost drinks on demand. He could even walk home from there if he had to, which was often.

"You ladies must come over to visit again soon," he said. "It's been way too long, and you won't believe the improvements we've made recently. Al finally finished his art studio/storage area/who-knows-what room. The guest house is under construction, and the pool deck has been expanded. Everything's freshly painted. You won't believe how great the place looks. I can hardly believe it myself."

We were busy with our burning but promised we'd walk over with Scooter the following day. Russ mentioned this flurry of improvement projects came about because they'd been thinking about selling their property. Al had not been feeling well recently. It made him feel old. He'd begun to think it was too much to maintain a large property so far from their city condo.

"I know what Al's talking about," I said. "The idea that country living is cheap and easy is all wrong. Maybe you have to experience it yourself to learn this, although the names people give their estates around here provide clues—'Rancho Costa Plenti' or 'The Back Achers,' for example."

Deborah asked Russ how he felt about selling the land he and Al had owned for decades. He said he was willing to go along with whatever Al decided.

Once the work was done, however, Al changed his mind. He was feeling better, so he wanted to relax and enjoy their spruced-up estate rather than put it on the market. They'd even come up with a name for their property: Fiddlesticks.

"Well, now you can't get rid of it," I said. "It's like naming a child or a pet. Once you do that, you've taken ownership and bonded with it." Russ nodded in agreement. He said they'd begun talking about the possibility of living in Fiddletown full-time, perhaps for the rest of their days. Russ was even investigating purchasing grave plots in the Fiddletown cemetery. He happened to meet the man who managed the cemetery while sitting on a barstool in the Moose Lodge. The man had assured Russ there were plenty of available spaces and anyone with a Fiddletown address was eligible to purchase one. I suspected the price he'd been quoted—$500 for two plots—was also attractive to Russ. It was far cheaper than anything available in the San Francisco Bay Area.

"Can you just imagine?" Russ said. "He pretty much guaranteed me space in the cemetery when the time comes..." When Russ told Al about the deal on cemetery plots, Al agreed that being laid to rest in Fiddletown seemed appropriate. After spending so much time—not just building things but also marveling at and being inspired by the natural beauty of the place—it seemed fitting and proper to be buried there. The place stoked Al's creative spirit. He was working on a series of paintings representing the Wagnerian operatic cycle. He ordered lumber by the railcar to build things he imagined first—guest cottages, boardwalks, meditation sheds—and then would build and paint any color that moved him. Fiddletown was his muse.

Russ said he didn't want to get into "the gay thing" with the local cemetery overseer. He simply told the man he wanted to buy grave plots for himself and his "brother" Al, so they could be buried side by side.

"Oh, jeez," I moaned, "does that even have to come up? Can't a person just buy two grave plots—one for himself and one for the most important person in the world to him—without launching an inquisition? Not to mention, has he ever met Al? You two look like Mutt and Jeff—one tall and angular, the other short and chunky. You don't look one bit like siblings."

Russ shrugged. "You ladies can let us test the waters first. You won't be needing grave plots for a long while yet, I hope."

Deborah and I didn't know exactly how old Russ and Al were, but we knew they were older than us and older than they looked. Both confessed to having had multiple plastic surgeries to stay looking as young as possible for as long as possible. "Al is a show horse, not a workhorse," Russ was fond of saying, although as far as I could tell, it was Al who did the heavy lifting on their property while Russell was the "kitchen queen."

That night, Deborah and I discussed the concept of buying cemetery plots. It's a serious subject and one that deserves consideration sooner rather than later. Anything could happen. Why leave it for others to deal with when it would be better to state preferences ahead of time?

But there were so many questions: Cremation or cemetery burial? Canada or Virginia or Fiddletown? The City by the Bay or Sierra foothills wine country? A memorial? A wake? It was all too much to think about.

Quail with Pomegranate, Mint and Marsala

(from *Cucina Paradiso: The Heavenly Food of Sicily,*
by Clifford A. Wright, Simon & Schuster, 1992)

INGREDIENTS:

1 lg pomegranate	1 c. Marsala
1 T. chopped mint	Salt & Pepper to taste
6 quail or snipe	6 thin slices of pancetta
2 T. olive oil	10 T. butter
peel of 2 oranges, cut into 1/4-inch slices	12 fresh sage leaves

Remove seeds from pomegranate. Put them in a bowl and cover with Marsala. Sprinkle chopped mint on top, mix and set aside for 1 hour.

Salt and pepper the birds inside and out. Drain the pomegranate seeds and mint, saving the juice, and stuff birds. Truss the birds with a toothpick running through the body cavity opening and legs. Wrap each bird in a slice of pancetta and press tight. Preheat oven to 375 degrees.

Heat the olive oil, 2 T. of butter, 2 sage leaves in a sauté pan. Sauté the birds over high heat for 5 minutes, or until they are very brown. Lower heat, add remaining sage leaves and pomegranate seeds and a few T. of leftover Marsala.

Cook birds in the oven, uncovered for 7 minutes. Drizzle the remaining Marsala on the birds and spread 4 T. of the remaining butter over the birds. Stir pan juices around and spoon over the birds to coat them. Cook for another 5 mins.

Meanwhile, heat the remaining butter over low heat and sauté the slices of orange peel for 5 minutes, gently pushing them around in the pan. Remove peel and set aside.

Transfer birds to a serving platter and cover with the orange peel. Spoon some pan juices and any loose pomegranate seeds over the birds. Serve immediately. Serves 4-6.

COMFORT FOOD

Our 2001 harvest turned out to be Scooter's last. The joy of pulling our first serious crop off the vineyard that fall lost its luster after the "S" in DAMAS left us. She had reached the age of thirteen and began to decline. First, she lost her hearing, and she began to have trouble getting into her favorite chair. She lost interest in walking up the hills of San Francisco and began to have minor incontinence episodes. Signs of trouble. The more fragile she became, the more loving she became—sweeter over time like onions caramelizing.

She carried out her vineyard management duties during the harvest with Tux by her side. But a few weeks later, she collapsed and was diagnosed with inoperable kidney cancer. She started having seizures. Wanting to spare her further pain and discomfort, I consulted websites that advised: "When you start to wonder whether you are keeping the dog alive for your sake or hers, it is probably time to put her down."

Deborah was resistant, not sure if the dog was truly suffering or if she still enjoyed her limited quality of life. I wanted to spare her from more seizures. Soon, Scooter stopped eating. I thought that was a sign, but Deborah remained unsure. It was tough not to be on the same page during such a difficult time. Finally, reluctantly, Deborah agreed to have her put down.

We drove to Fiddletown, so Scooter could see the vineyard and her beloved cat one last time. She seemed very weak, but she was able to stagger around the garden and let Tux rub up against her. Anne recommended a vet who could come to our home to make this horrible thing a bit less awful. Scooter received an injection and died in Deborah's arms. The two of us blubbered the rest of the day, heartbroken and inconsolable.

I dealt with my pain by cooking, reading, and writing. Deborah retreated to the barn, where she built a Scooter-sized pine box. She carried it to the trailer and placed it next to the wood stove in the family room. We laid Scooter in the coffin on top of her favorite blanket and tucked her best toys around her. That evening, we held a wake. We called friends to tell them Scooter was gone, sipping Jack Daniel's to take the edge off our pain.

That night there was a powerful storm, different from any we'd experienced in Fiddletown to date. The wind howled and walnut branches whipped the metal siding as rain pounded on the tin roof. It seemed an appropriate display of cosmic energy as Scooter's spirit left us. In the morning, we screwed the lid on the small coffin and buried it in a pit we'd dug beneath our most majestic oak tree.

I would have loved to take time off to grieve, but we had to buck up and carry on. We both had meetings scheduled and work to do in San Francisco—and someone to pick up at the airport. Deborah's father, who'd been diagnosed with Parkinson's disease, was coming to stay with us for a time. Gene needed our help now; Scooter was beyond it.

Deborah had an important conference call to run, so I drove the truck to San Francisco, feeling utterly miserable. Tears streamed down my cheeks while Deborah professionally addressed her colleagues about the results of some important drug trial or another.

I trudged through the following months, disinterested in my consulting work and everything else. That curly-haired mutt had been at my ankle, both in the foothills and in the city, every day for thirteen years. I missed her terribly, with an acute physical ache. I saw her black shape in every dark shadow, still felt the impression she made on my lap when we rode in the truck together. These feelings diminished over time, but my heart would not feel truly healed for almost two full years.

We spent a few months focusing on Gene, taking him to appointments at the VA hospital where Deborah worked and knew many of the specialists. They tweaked his medications to optimize his daily functioning, and after a few months he was able to return home to Virginia.

We were not looking forward to the Christmas holidays that year. We knew we had to do things differently, or we'd be depressed and miss the dog who'd played a key role in our holiday rituals. We couldn't bear the idea of staying away from Fiddletown, especially when we had two full weeks off work. So we went but invited friends to distract us. We studied cookbooks arduously, hoping exotic meals might take our minds off our loss.

We'd sit around the woodstove during rain showers, making up menus and discussing which wines would go best with each course. We'd challenge ourselves to include as many estate-grown or locally raised items in our menus as possible. It had been a mild winter, so our garden was bursting with mixed greens and root vegetables at the time.

We cooked and ate many gourmet dinners, and we didn't skimp on lunches, either, although those were less elaborate affairs. We'd spend the mornings cutting wood or burning brush, then return to the house for a bowl of pork and beans. Not just any pork and beans, mind you. It was a pot of dried beans I'd harvested from our own garden, stewed with our summer tomatoes and a hock from a local, free-range 4H pig. The house smelled great when I baked crusty French bread to go along with that pot of beans.

A few days before Christmas, Kay and Linda paid us a visit. Kay, that angel of mercy, showed up at the door with a pot of coq au vin and baguettes she'd picked up from Acme bakery in Berkeley. Linda brought a giant bag of pistachios, homemade cranberry-orange bread, and champagne. It was good to see them before they had to scurry back to Berkeley for holiday rituals with their extended family.

Anne and Marianne came for Christmas dinner and stayed overnight.

On Boxing Day, our friends Marilyn and Janice arrived, bearing bags of fresh citrus, boxes of yummy pastries, and a selection of fine wines. Russ and Al came by with a sweet cake (hot from the oven) made from sugar, butter, and walnuts they'd picked from Gino's orchard when he decided to replace his walnut trees with grapevines. They invited us to come over for a bonfire, which we did, hunkering around it in a light drizzle. It was much more subdued than the gathering we'd had on New Year's Eve the previous year when the night sky was lit up for miles by a massive bonfire, around which about twenty of us sang and danced to celebrate the arrival of Y2K.

We were invited to the city for New Year's Eve festivities, but we did not feel festive, so we declined. We decided to stay home and sulk and cook and eat more fabulous things. We talked about options, but nothing seemed quite right until

I came across an ancient Sicilian nobleman's recipe for *Quail with Pomegranates, Mint, and Marsala*. We are not in the habit of eating quail because we love to see them running around the property, but the dish sounded delicious, and we had all the needed ingredients. There were still a few pomegranates hanging on a bush near the driveway. There was mint growing in the winter garden. We even had some Marsala left over from who-knows-what in the kitchen cupboard, so there'd be no need to drive to town for anything. When I announced my intention to make the dish, Deborah asked where I planned to find quail. I said I intended to shoot them. She chuckled and went back to her recipe browsing.

The following day, I walked around the entire property three times with the shotgun, returning empty-handed. The brush piles we refer to as "quail housing projects" were silent. Whenever I think about how cute quail are, they seem to be everywhere, but as soon as I think of them as dinner, they're nowhere to be found. I was searching the freezer for something I might substitute for quail when Deborah shouted, pointing out the window.

"Quail in the table grapes at eleven o'clock!"

Sure enough, there were ten or twelve of them running around. Deborah grabbed the shotgun, opened the kitchen door, and fired. Damn if she didn't hit a bird. It fluttered, then lay still as the rest of the flock scurried away. Suddenly, Tux swooped out of the asparagus patch, snatched the quail, and took off into the vineyard.

"BAD CAT!" I yelled. "DROP THAT BIRD!" But to no avail. Tux had vanished among the vines to enjoy his own special New Year's Eve supper. I cooked the recipe using chicken tenders I found in the freezer. It was good, but I couldn't help imagining how it might have been better with fresh, free-range, grape-fed California quail.

A TOUCH OF TUSCANY

The pain of losing Scooter eventually became blunter, down to something almost bearable. Diane and Shirley helped us heal—first by carving a custom headstone for Scooter and then pushing us into some new projects at the Middle Age Spread.

Diane and Shirley worked with Deborah at UCSF. They'd been professional gardeners previously but decided a career switch was in order as they approached middle age. Full-time outdoor work is hard on the body, and they knew they should be thinking about pensions and 401(k) savings plans. They stored their gardening equipment and went to work at UCSF, entering data for clinical trials, some of which Deborah managed.

The women missed getting their hands in soil. Once they learned about our country place, they became frequent visitors. At first, they'd sleep in their van with their two Jack Russell terriers, not wanting to intrude on our space. Once it became clear they were very skilled and hardworking and really wanted to help with farm work, we let them use the guest cottage Lawson had previously occupied. We found them amusing and resourceful, and we appreciated their help enormously. They seemed to genuinely love outdoor work. Diane, especially, loved to spend hour upon hour pulling up star thistle or digging up horehound and mullen, making piles of taproots as long as parsnips. The harder the job, the better. One day she asked us if we'd let her split wood by hand, just for the fun of it—but only after the needed tasks were done. She claimed the abundance of challenging work put the Middle Age Spread at the tippy-top of her "Fun-O-Meter."

One day in early January 2002, Diane and Shirley pulled up with a van full of cutting and grinding equipment we'd never seen before. We marveled. We had no idea they were also rockhounds who owned many tools for working gems and rocks, including engraving. They'd come to make a suitable headstone for Scooter's grave. They'd left the terriers with Diane's parents in Orinda. Perhaps this was out of respect, as Scooter had never been overly fond of those two small yappy dogs.

There were many chunks of granite lying around the property, stained the color of clay from the iron in our soil, so finding a good headstone rock was easy. Diane carried it to the barn, and Shirley proceeded to carve:

SCOOTER

Best Dog in the World

1988-2001

When they were done, we used our tractor to move it to the gravesite under the massive oak tree next to the vineyard. With the tractor in low gear, it felt like a proper funeral procession. We placed the headstone in position and laid some late-blooming roses I'd cut on the grave, which was now green with emerging grasses and tiny leaves of wild miner's lettuce. We stood silently, with our heads bowed. Deborah and I couldn't muster words; we just let the tears flow down our cheeks.

How many dogs are honored with engraved headstones? I wondered. *How many humans are so cherished, celebrated, and missed?*

It was Diane and Shirley who got the bright idea we should plant an olive grove. They weren't pushy about it, but they were jittery with excitement. They really wanted to do it. They offered to do all the research, so they could present a plan to us with cost estimates. All we had to do, if we chose to proceed, was buy the materials for the olive orchard—irrigation supplies and the trees themselves. They were eager to help with most of the labor involved in digging the trenches and planting the trees.

They went to work networking with their circle of friends and relatives who were professional gardeners or commercial farmers. They'd come to Fiddletown loaded with videos and tomes on the history of the olive and binders full of olive oil recipes they'd printed from cookbooks or downloaded from the internet. Small bottles of olive oil samples kept showing up in the trailer for tasting. Deborah and I do love olive oil and use quite a lot of it, so the idea of having our own estate-grown extra virgin olive oil was of some interest. We were just too busy between our city jobs and vineyard management to take on another big project.

But Diane and Shirley were in a complete twitter about olives and seemed to have boundless energy. They visited olive orchards, crashed olive grower meetings, and signed up for olive courses at UC Davis. If they passed a property with olive trees, they would turn up the driveway to strike up a conversation with the owners, picking their brains about how they'd accomplished it, what varietals they grew, and why. Soon, they presented us with a proposal for a planting grid and an irrigation scheme. How could we say no, when they'd done so much research and were so full of enthusiasm and energy?

In no time, the open space around our aboveground pool was waving with pink survey flags. Deborah and I didn't have any other plans for that area, so it seemed like an appropriate spot to plant olives. We had two other meadows we viewed as potential future vineyard expansion areas, so we wouldn't have agreed to grow olives there. But the area around the pool was somewhat steep and rocky, not prime for growing anything else.

The four of us did plenty of olive oil tasting and unanimously decided we liked the olive oil produced by McEvoy Ranch in Marin County the best. It turned out McEvoy also had a nursery where one could purchase young olive trees of the same Tuscan varietals they used to produce oil. Diane and Shirley found a way to visit the place and befriend the olive orchard manager. They learned a lot from her, including which varietals to plant in what proportions. We placed our order for fifty one-year-old trees.

In the spring, Diane and Shirley launched into digging holes for the trees, as Deborah and I (with help from some visiting relatives) dug trenches and installed the PVC pipes needed for the irrigation system. Diane was not satisfied with making a hole big enough to hold a young olive tree that would arrive in a one-gallon container, plus a wire gopher basket to protect its young roots. We would find her digging six-foot-deep, five-foot-wide pits, pulling out rocks the size of bread loaves so they would not interfere with tree roots in the future. As our nursery delivery date approached, she took an entire week of vacation to finish digging holes and driving in stakes to support the new trees. We insisted on hiring a couple of men with shovels to help her for a few days. Diane sent an email to thank us for the opportunity for such a fun week of hard labor. She added that, as much as she loved pounding stakes, the soil was rockier than she'd imagined. She had to come to terms with the fact she was not twenty-five years old anymore and added, "Thank God for laborers! I couldn't have finished without them."

"Hey, Diane," I replied, "Thank *you*! You and Shirley are amazing. You are welcome to work your tails off on our property anytime. I suppose you know it does seem a bit wacky, but we really do appreciate your interest and help."

BEES BY THE POUND

Once the olive trees were planted and thriving, Diane and Shirley turned their attention to a new project: bees. They wanted to learn to keep honeybees as a fun project of their own, but their enthusiasm was contagious. They enticed us with offers of honey and beeswax candles as a form of rent for keeping hives on our property. The house filled up with books and videos about bees, and mealtime discussions became seminars on the hows and whats and whys of bee tending.

We learned the worker bees are all female, but each hive keeps a few males around (called drones) just in case a new queen should emerge at some point and need fertilizing. When and if this occurs, a drone is available to fertilize the new queen (one shot only!), and then he dies, having provided for thousands of baby bees she'll deliver in her life span of about two years (versus an average of just thirty days for worker bees).

Diane provided regular progress reports. Her plan was to purchase one piece of equipment each month until she'd gathered the basics. This month it was a smoker; next month, hats with veils, etc. She wanted to plant lavender on the front slope, so the bees could make lavender honey.

There was much to learn and do. We passed many winter evenings assembling frames and supers for the hives, learning a new vocabulary as we went along. Shirley invented a contraption we used to give the thin wires that ran the length of each frame a brief shot of electricity—just enough to warm sheets of wax so they'd adhere to the wire better, providing a strong foundation with a honeycomb pattern imprinted on it. This would save the bees a lot of time and energy as they prepared to nurse the brood and store honey.

The hives had to be perfect to meet Diane and Shirley's standards. They ordered two ready-to-assemble hive kits, which soon arrived by mail. They replaced any parts made from fiberboard with solid pine. We painted one hive white and one yellow, then added strips of flashing to the edges to protect them from moisture. We shaped some soft galvanized aluminum over the top of the hives to protect them from the elements. These were Bee Marriotts!

Diane and Shirley discovered a bee store in Sacramento—a whole new wonderland of paraphernalia, including honey jar labels and candle molds. Of course, they had long talks with the proprietor and the many beekeepers who frequented the store. They contacted several beekeeper associations to see if a swarm of local, disease-resistant bees might be available. They had no luck with that but learned you can order bees by the pound and have them delivered by mail. You can order many different types of queen bees, too. (The best queens were reputed to be the gentle Tuscan ones.)

Finally, they felt ready to place an order for two fertilized queens (Italian, to go with our Tuscan olive trees) and enough "starter" bees to eventually populate two hives. It takes a minimum of around 25,000 bees to maintain a hive, and only higher numbers (such as 50,000 bees) would produce surplus honey for human consumption. The bees would be delivered in the spring, just as wildflowers began to bloom in the foothills. Our excitement cranked up a notch once the bees were ordered.

We surveyed the property to find a perfect site for the new hives. We were looking for an open area that would allow unobstructed bee takeoffs and landings, preferably near a water source and a tree that could provide some shade in summer. And the site couldn't have buckeyes nearby because buckeye pollen can give bees diarrhea. Once we found an ideal spot, there was another flurry of activity. We had to create a level building pad. We installed sturdy wire fencing to enclose an area about 20' by 20' to keep Dodd's ponies—and coyotes, raccoons, dogs, cats, and whatever else—out. They attached metal legs to the hives to keep them off the ground and set each leg in a can they could fill with water or oil or petroleum jelly to serve as a moat. This would prevent ants from storming the hives and stealing the honey.

The bees arrived one day in April. I found a notice in our post office box informing me there was a package to pick up. When I showed the postmaster my yellow card, she gave me a strange look. As she handed me two vibrating boxes she said, "I've never had to handle packages that buzzed before."

Each box measured about six by ten inches and four inches deep. They were framed in wood on four sides, with the other two sides open, enclosed only by screen mesh. Each box contained a pound of bees–or about 3,000 workers. These would soon become a population of tens of thousands because a fertile queen can lay up to 2,000 eggs per day during the spring hive buildup period. Mounted to the wooden frame of each box was a small plastic cage, about three inches long and a half-inch in diameter, with a sugar plug in the end. This sweet prison contained the fertilized queen bee, who would dominate life in the hive until her demise. She'd be the only one to mate and lay brood, with all the worker bees working furiously to raise and feed her and her offspring. It would take several days for the bees to chew through the sugar plug to release their queen. By that time, they would have become accustomed to her scent. They'd be bonded and loyal, ready to defend her and her offspring to the death.

We let the bees acclimate for a day and then followed the instructions for introducing them to their new hives. We opened the containers and shook some of the bees into the lower box of the new hives. They fell out in clumps and immediately went to work, checking the beeswax foundations we'd installed on the frames and orienting themselves to their new surroundings. We carefully detached the cage containing the queen and slipped it between two wooden frames, where a thin metal hanger held it in place. We shook the last of the bees out of the boxes, brushing out the stragglers with a whisk broom.

In the subsequent hours, they became very busy bees. They launched into their worker bee tasks: build comb, find nectar, store pollen, make honey, train defenders, clean house, and prepare the nursery for the thousands of grubs their queen would soon be laying. This was the same work their ancestors had been doing for centuries, while ignoring whatever shenanigans humans might be up to, even if those actions (politics, war, fire, suburban development, etc.) might threaten the hive in numerous ways.

We spent lots of time observing the comings and goings of the bees. I was surprised to find watching them a source of tranquility, no matter what was on the evening news. It was a kind of meditation. Those bees didn't seem to care about human preoccupations. They'd seen all manner of our behavior over the millennia—coups, love affairs, genocide, war. They ignored us and stayed focused on their mission: to build the strongest new hive they possibly could for their new queen.

This is the main lesson I took from the bees: life is short, so make the most of it. Do whatever you do as fast and hard and carefully and exuberantly as you can in the limited time available to you until you just can't do it any longer. And understand your life is just a tiny part of something much bigger than yourself.

Diane and Shirley clearly had Bee Fever, and I caught a case of it, too. I joined the San Francisco Beekeepers Association, which held its regular monthly meetings just a few blocks from our flat in the city. I installed a hive in our urban backyard. It was in an area with lots of backyard flower gardens and not far from Golden Gate Park, where no one used Roundup or similar chemicals. I could watch the hive through the sliding glass door while working from my home office. As my hive grew and prospered, I began to think of myself as a CEO with thousands of bees working hard for me.

That hive produced thrilling honey that tasted like liquid flowers. Until it suddenly died out. Beekeeping had once been relatively straightforward, but it became a lot more challenging due to the multiple insults of pesticides, cell phone towers, loss of crop diversity, and the importation of foreign bees. Our poor bees were soon plagued by tracheal mites, Varroa mites, and other problems. We had Colony Collapse Disorder to worry about.

I think our San Francisco backyard was a bit too damp and not quite sunny enough for the bees. When my city hive died out, I relocated the equipment to Fiddletown to try again. By then, Diane and Shirley's hives had died out too, and they'd moved on to new interests.

I faced issues with swarming the first summer in the foothills, and before I could re-queen the hive, more problems arrived. The hive was attacked by a squadron of vicious wasps intent on killing the bees at home tending the brood. After that, field mice moved in to chew wax and steal honey. My hive soon became silent again.

I decided I could not call myself a beekeeper if I couldn't keep my bees alive. I donated my equipment to other local beekeepers and decided it would be okay to have one less hobby. I'd refocus on orchard and vineyard management, instead. After all, we had young grape vines and olive trees to nurture now, along with the mature fruit and nut trees the previous owners had planted. There was always something to do.

Our hearts had had time to heal. We were thinking it might be time to get a new dog. One evening we were watching TV when a dog beauty pageant came on. Miss Pennsylvania won. We thought she was adorable, white with brown spots and patches and a solid brown head. We had no idea what breed she was, but Deborah did some online research and discovered she was a German Shorthaired Pointer. She began a search that resulted in us owning two of these dogs and fostering a dozen more over time.

HARVEST LESSONS

Deborah had taken some UC Davis viticulture courses, so we understood the need to concentrate on building a strong foundation in the first few years of vine development, focus on building the root system and a sturdy trunk to support good crops in the future. It sounded a lot like advice on raising humans. First, work on establishing sound health, a straight spine, and a strong physique for a long and productive life.

As we drove or biked around the Shenandoah Valley, we observed how other growers were caring for their grapes. We studied trellising, leaf pulling, and cane thinning practices. We'd stop and ask questions. There was one vineyard in particular that caught our eye. It was tidy and well-tended. The vines looked happy and vibrant. We learned it was zinfandel, owned by a Mr. Ferrero. We called him and asked if he'd be willing to come look at our newly planted vineyard and give us advice about training them properly. He was flattered to know we thought his vineyard looked the best of any in the Shenandoah Valley. He spent an hour one Saturday walking around our vineyard and sharing his thoughts. He warned us zinfandel is known for its vigor, especially when it's young.

"These babies will want to race into production. Don't you let them do it! You have to be ruthless. Cut off any fruit they try to produce for the first two years. You'll be glad you did." He gave us tips on head-pruning, showing us what to do with each vine: whack it off about thigh-high after its first year and then train the next year's canes into an open vase shape. Select six to eight evenly spaced canes and spread them out from the center like the spokes on a wheel for optimum sun exposure and air circulation.

We thanked him for taking the time to come out and share his wisdom and experience. "No—I want to thank *you* ladies for inviting me out here," he insisted.

"These days everyone wants to hire those whipper-snapper consultants from the UC Davis viticulture program. Nobody asks an old farmer for advice anymore."

As Mr. Ferrero predicted, our young vines were eager to fulfill their destiny. Many of them flowered the first summer. The flowers opened, were fertilized, and then formed tiny grape clusters that would fill out and become wine grapes if we let them. Instead, we dropped them all those first two years, as Mr. Ferrero had advised, encouraging the vines to focus their energy on building a sturdy trunk and strong roots.

The third summer (2000), we allowed our vines to produce a light crop. We cut off most, but not all, of the clusters. It was exciting to watch them plump up over the summer, and it was even more thrilling to experience our first veraison, when the grapes soften and turn from green to purple.

We were not winemakers, but my colleague Tom was. He'd been winning awards for his homemade wines for years. Just as our first crop was maturing, he decided to quit his environmental consulting job and take the plunge into commercial winemaking. He rented a winery space in Berkeley, and we reached an agreement. We would grow the grapes; he would make the wine. He would sell our zinfandel under his label, and we would get a share of the product back for our own consumption. We would split the bottling expenses. Bartering allowed both parties to ease into commercial wine production without a large cash outlay. We were excited to have our own estate-grown wine at last.

In early September, I made a trip to Canada to visit relatives. I was stunned when Deborah called and announced: "Tom says the grapes are ready to harvest. We have to pick tomorrow."

"But that's impossible. I'm in Canada. Can't it wait until I return?"

"Apparently not," Deborah said. "Tom says we have to do it now. The Brix is twenty-five, the grape seeds have turned brown, the juice is pink, and the taste is fabulous. He says if we wait, we risk having the crop devoured by birds or having the Brix shoot sky-high from raisining. That can make the juice taste 'jammy,' which is not a good thing."

Harvest Lesson #1: Do not schedule any trips in early fall.

Over the years, we'd learn our grape harvest could occur as early as the end of August or as late as mid-October. The grapes mature when they mature—a mysterious process influenced by climate, soil, weather, sunlight, moisture, and other factors beyond our control. The chemistry must be right—especially the Brix (percent sugar in the juice, which increases steadily as the grapes ripen) and the acid (which rises initially but then begins to drop as sugar increases). It's critical to find the right balance between Brix and acid, but even more importantly, the grapes have to taste good. As winemaker Scott Harvey once told us: "You can adjust chemistry in the winery, but you can't adjust flavor."

When everything comes together just right, you should pick without delay because anything can happen. A heatwave, a cold snap, a hailstorm, marauding birds, or gusty winds can desiccate the fruit. The crop will keep changing, but not always for the better.

So, Deborah and Tom and his friend harvested our first-ever crop without me. They filled almost three bins, about one and a half tons of grapes. Tom drove the bounty to Berkeley for crushing and processing. I was so disappointed to miss this important event I vowed never to travel in September again.

The following year (2001), we did little cluster thinning, allowing a fuller crop to mature. We anticipated a harvest of several tons of grapes, so we knew we'd need more picking help. Our Bay Area friends were enthused. We monitored the grapes closely—checking Brix, acid, seed maturity, and taste every week. Soon we felt confident harvest day was approaching. The Brix had been notching up steadily at a rate of about 2.5 percentage points weekly. Everything else was developing well, so we scheduled a Harvest Weekend based on our projections.

Our city friends showed up eager to work. They unpacked their cars, pitched their tents, and showed up in the kitchen for refreshments while Deborah and I made a final check on the vineyard. The Brix reading was okay, but the flavors had not developed as hoped. Many seeds had turned brown, too many were still green. We made the difficult decision to postpone the harvest.

We fed and entertained a group of friends for an entire weekend without getting a lick of labor out of them. When the grapes were ready to harvest the following weekend, our friends were busy with weddings or family camping trips. We had to scramble to pull together a crew of neighbors and locals to help out.

Kay and Linda were especially disappointed. They'd been looking forward very much to helping us harvest, but when it actually occurred, they were in Hawaii on a preplanned vacation.

Harvest Lesson #2: You cannot schedule the grape harvest; it schedules you.

The following year (2002), I tried a new approach, acknowledging we would not know for sure when the harvest would occur until only a day or two ahead of time. I created an elaborate calendar and had friends indicate when they were available to pick and when they were not. This way, we knew well in advance who would be available which weekend. Everyone was on board with this plan and hoped the harvest would occur on a weekend when they could participate. We felt assured we'd be able to muster a crew whenever harvest occurred. This strategy worked. On a Thursday afternoon, we tested the grapes and decided they were ready. We called for harvest that weekend. Since most of our friends worked full-time professional jobs, and the Friday evening traffic jam out of the Bay Area could be unpleasant, we thought it best for them to drive up on Saturday. That way, they could settle in and be ready to pick bright and early Sunday morning.

This seemed like a solid plan, but we soon learned it had a major flaw. We'd have to hold the Harvest Party on Saturday evening—before the harvest. The problem became apparent around 10 p.m. Our friends were in high spirits; the party was going strong. Everyone had fine wine to drink. When Russ got up and started tap dancing on the tabletop, I knew we were in trouble. Then Deborah brought out a bottle of Cognac and some cigars. Uh-oh!

Harvest Lesson #3: Do not, under any circumstances, throw the Harvest Party on the eve of the harvest.

I woke up early, but there was only one other early riser, my friend Marco. He joined me in picking grapes, even though he was suffering from a pretty bad headache and a stiff neck. The two of us poked at harvesting for what seemed like hours before other pickers began to show up. They were a sorry-looking lot.

The harvest that year was slow and painful, but we finished it. Our wrecked crew floated in the pool like zombies until they had to pack up and drive back to the city.

The following year, we used the email calendar and alert system again, but we insisted people drive up from the Bay Area either late Friday evening (stopping for dinner along the way) or very early the following morning. Thus our crew would be fresh to harvest on Saturday morning, and we could hold the Harvest Party on Saturday evening. Some folks arrived after dark on Friday, set up their tents by flashlight, and crashed. Others showed up in the morning with lattes in hand, ready to work. The one unfortunate factor was the weather. It was very, very hot that day. The crew was wilting as the temperature climbed to one hundred degrees before noon.

We got the job done, but our production had climbed to almost eight tons by then. Picking took longer and felt more challenging than ever—and, at times, not much fun. Once it was over, we had a leisurely lunch in the shade, and then people took the rest of the afternoon off for relaxing, swimming, wine tasting, or napping. It was too hot for biking. We waited until the air had cooled and then celebrated with a sumptuous Harvest Party dinner.

Harvest Lesson #4: Simplify your Harvest Party menu.

After a few years of trials and errors, we had the Harvest Party menu down: grilled pork tenderloins with Deborah's special rub, fresh Sloughhouse corn on the cob, and ratatouille made from our own garden veggies. I would bake a big loaf of Harvest Bread—focaccia with whole peppercorns, rosemary sprigs, and whole wine grapes (seeds and all). For dessert, it was home-made zinfandel sorbet and biscotti made with our estate-grown walnuts. And, of course, good wine to wash it all down.

I could make the ratatouille, biscotti, and sorbet in advance. Deborah could quickly and easily grill the tenderloins, slice them, and let everyone pick the pieces cooked to their preference. We'd have lots of helpers shucking corn, making it easy to boil or grill. We didn't need anything more. Nonetheless, our friends would show up with other treats, like appetizers, yummy cheeses, or killer chocolate to share.

Harvest Lesson #5: Hire professional help.

In later years, as the novelty of picking grapes faded among our city friends and we grew weary of the management challenges, we began to hire skilled pickers. They'd arrive at first light and work rapidly. They'd have most of the vineyard picked in a few hours. That allowed us to deliver grapes to Tom and other winery clients by mid-morning—about the time our urban pals used to start arriving. We'd then pick any remaining grapes with our home winemaking customers at a leisurely pace, with plenty of time for photo ops:

"Hey, look at this gorgeous specimen I just found. It has classic zin structure, with a big main cluster and a smaller shoulder bunch. Can you take a photo of me holding it?"

"I think this one is bigger, a bodacious double cluster—surely, it wins the prize! Please take my picture, and then let's have a group shot!"

Professional farmworkers would never engage in such foolishness. They'd run into the vineyard, drop an empty picking bin on the ground, cut grapes off the vine with both hands, race to the trailer with the heavy container on their head or shoulders, dump it, and then speed away to resume picking. Another cool feature was that they'd go home as soon as the job was done. No need to feed and entertain them.

Sometimes, we missed the atmosphere of fun, exhilaration, and camaraderie that pervaded those early harvest events but mostly we appreciated that harvesting became easier. It was enough to manage the equipment and drive trucks and trailers.

We somehow accomplish the grape harvest relatively smoothly every year, despite inevitable jitters and last-minute changes that always occur. We confirm the date, hire the crew, clean the bins, and purchase refreshments. We wash trucks, locate trailers, pump up tires, fill gas tanks, and make sure we have enough ball hitches and tie-downs. No one gets hurt, and we feel strong and capable after spending a day harvesting and delivering fruit to become delicious wine people can enjoy in the future.

There is nothing quite like sitting down to a desk job on a Monday morning, having harvested literally tons of grapes the day before. I would feel quite tired, yet like Superwoman at the same time. It would be satisfying to use my brain to analyze the social and economic impacts of a new proposed coal mine or dam or power plant while my body rested in a comfy chair.

GOING UPSCALE

We talked off and on for years about replacing the old trailer with a real house, but we never seemed to find the motivation to do so. There were times when we thought the whole idea of investing in a new home was absurd. We worked hard nurturing our vineyard and orchard and gardens, only to find ourselves tormented by neighbors, including Zack's shenanigans downhill and the Moose Lodge uphill, with its illegally parked motor homes and noisy outdoor horseshoe games.

One day, we went so far as to call our old real estate agent, Sue, to ask if she knew of any potential buyers who might be as crazy as we were. Ignorant city folks who might want to purchase a high-maintenance, non-profit enterprise next to an annoying fraternal organization licensed to operate a bar seven days a week. We didn't want a visible For Sale sign on our gate. It would signal to Zack and his pals that they'd won; they'd succeeded in driving us out. We said we were merely putting out feelers; we weren't sure about selling. Sue said she didn't know of any such crazy people offhand but said she'd keep us in mind.

For a time, I thought it might be fitting to construct a 2,000-square-foot home in the year 2000. Something substantial to acknowledge and celebrate the new millennium. But Deborah was not ready to build at that time. She felt cranky about the Moose Lodge noise to the north, the trailer camp and trash dump on Zack's property to the south, and California population growth in general. She cursed the worsening traffic to and from the Bay Area and occasionally spoke of "cashing out" and moving to New Zealand to escape sprawling population growth. It appealed to her there were more sheep than people in that country.

But then her dad died suddenly. Gene had been cleaning his refrigerator when he slipped and hit his head on the kitchen floor. No long months of intubations and interventions for him. Despite his Parkinson's, he'd lived many good years once Deborah started monitoring his medical care. She'd made sure his prescriptions were adjusted appropriately whenever he began to experience new symptoms or unusual confusion, allowing him to continue living in the family home he had built. He savored his meals. He went out. He was still dating. He enjoyed his life until the day he died in his own kitchen at home. Not a bad way to go.

Once the house sold, there was some cash to divide among his four children. Deborah used a portion of her share to pay three different architects to develop a concept design for a new Fiddletown home. We had clear ideas about what we wanted: a simple yet elegant home, no more than 2,000 square feet in size, with two bedrooms, two bathrooms, and an office. We wanted a great room with an open kitchen-dining-living area. And we wanted porches or patios on both the north and south sides with sliding doors to allow the air to flow through and blend outdoor and indoor spaces seamlessly.

When we reviewed the drawings, we could see how each architect had incorporated what we wanted into their designs. The desired elements were present but in forms that did not appeal to us much. The designs seemed too rustic, or too hard-edged and modern, or too sprawling. We paid a fourth architect, the son of close friends, for a concept design. Matthew was fresh out of college with a degree in architecture but limited experience. He was apprenticing with a firm that specialized in restaurant renovations. We asked him to complete the work by Christmas, so we could spend the holidays pondering the drawings. Our self-imposed deadline was to decide by New Year's Day whether to move forward with building a new home or not. And if not, then we would seriously consider selling our country property and doing something different in life.

We liked Matthew's drawings very much. We could actually imagine ourselves living in the home he'd designed, which had a Tuscan style to go with our grapes and olives. The spacious kitchen, great room, and outdoor patios would accommodate our friends and visitors well. The home suited the site we had in mind, and it fit our lifestyle. It seemed a structure worth building. We voted to move forward with the project and started looking for a builder.

We found a terrific local contractor who had lots of experience building luxurious yet understated homes with high ceilings and quality finishes. We also found a skilled heavy equipment operator. Once the rainy season ended, they got to work and quickly carved the building pad out of a hillside, cutting a small cave where the future wine cellar would go. In the course of excavating, we discovered a large cache of giant boulders, which they worked into the retaining wall below the house and the sloping garden above it.

We worked with the contractor to position the house exactly where we wanted it to maximize views of vineyards, orchards, and forested hills. We did not want to see Zack's house from any window. And if I had to wash dishes, I wanted to do so at a sink with a western view of the majestic ancient oak tree where Scooter was buried.

By fall, the concrete pad had been poured and much of the framing was done. When harvest day arrived, we decided spontaneously to stage our Harvest Party at the new home site. This involved gathering tables, chairs, and grills and setting them up on the clean concrete pad. We had enthusiastic volunteers to help, energized by working in the vineyard most of the day, picking and hauling grapes—and even crushing some of them in the barn with the hand-cranked stemmer-crusher Tom had given us.

As we were unloading and setting up tables, our friend Mike quipped: "I love what you've done with the ceiling." We all paused to look up. Indeed, the rafters framing the bright blue Fiddletown sky did create a marvelous effect. It was even more thrilling when the sky darkened and the stars came out.

Once the framing was completed, the roof went on and the stucco work began. Plumbers, electricians, and tile layers were all busy inside. A real house was taking shape. Some of the local craftsmen were talented stoneworkers who built a fireplace from rocks they found on our property. They also laid the flagstone patios and created rock stairways and retaining walls where needed outdoors. Our new home was coming together beautifully.

We were in the habit of ordering manure for our gardens in bulk from Ray, an old-timer who owned a horse ranch in Fiddletown. I guess we were among Ray's best customers because he jokingly referred to our place as "the shittiest farm in the valley." The manure was free if you wanted to shovel it yourself, or you could pay Ray a bit of money to deliver it, which is what we did. Ray and our vineyard advisor, Dick, had been among the last students to attend the little red schoolhouse in the Shenandoah Valley that had become a community center and an office for our Agricultural Extension agent.

There was a sense of excitement whenever Ray was due to deliver a load of manure—all that shit to shovel! And it always came with Ray's endless stories about growing up in the area. "When people ask me where Fiddletown is," Ray would say, "I tell them it's this close to heaven." As he said this, he'd be holding his thumb and index finger a scant millimeter apart. We'd agree how fortunate we were to be living in this part of the world.

When he'd finished unloading, Ray asked about the new construction beyond the barn, where he could see a tower poking up from a corset of scaffolding.

"You building a winery?" he asked.

"No," I said. "It's going to be a house."

"Upscale!" he said. "That thing looks like a palace, compared to the old trailer here. You won't be talking to plain folk like me anymore once you're moved in up there."

I offered to give him a tour of the site, and he accepted. The flooring was finished, but cabinets were stacked everywhere, waiting to be installed. Ray was wide-eyed as he stepped inside the front door. "Holy cow, what a view you have from up here!" he said. "It looks like something out of a travel brochure. And the stonework in here is amazing. It must have cost a mint."

"I'm awed by this place myself," I said. "I can't believe how great it's turning out to be. It's beyond my wildest expectations, to be honest."

"You two will be driving up the price of real estate around here," Ray said.

"Apparently, this is a small house. Our contractor says he's building homes twice this size or bigger all over the hills around here. He's working on one near Buena Vista that's ten thousand square feet," I said.

"On the one hand," Ray said, "I hate snooty people with too much money moving in around here. On the other hand, a lot of them may want to board horses at my place, so I guess I shouldn't complain.

"By the way," he added, "did you notice Steve changed the name of the Swap Shop again? Now it's Steve's Antiques and Collectibles. Everything is going upscale around here!"

After Ray left, I continued to ponder the word "upscale." What exactly is the referenced scale, who designed it, where does it begin and end, and how is it determined where we land up on it? It did feel as if the new house was pulling us up somehow, as if there was some invisible force at work. I could sense a change in the way construction workers and service people of various kinds treated me. Several times toward the end of the project, I'd be working in the house, cleaning or hanging pictures, while chatting with whoever was there installing countertops or shower stall glass. Only after talking with me for a while would they ask (with a distinct note of surprise in their tone): "Are you the owner?"

I'm sure they took me for hired help, dressed in my ratty old work clothes. I guess the owners of custom-built homes typically do not get their hands dirty or socialize with the laborers. One young furniture delivery guy stopped cold when he stepped into the great room. His mouth dropped open as he took in the craftsmanship and the views.

"If you don't mind me asking, ma'am...what on earth does your husband do for a living?" Doctor, I replied simply. He asked if we had any kids, perhaps thinking only people who did not have to pay for shoes and school supplies could afford to live in a place as special as this one. We'd joked for years about being "trailer trash," but in truth I never minded inviting friends and relatives to visit us in the old trailer. In fact, I felt considerable nostalgia leaving it. By then, we'd lived through thirteen years of joys and sorrows and memorable times in that spot. Still, bringing this new home into being gave us a real sense of accomplishment and satisfaction. It seemed the culmination of things we'd been building toward for a quarter century, a physical manifestation of love and labor that had seemed intangible until now. Even though we'd broken ground on our home only twelve months earlier, we'd begun to lay its foundation long ago.

I took a break from unpacking boxes to take our exuberant new puppy, a German Shorthaired Pointer we named Ulrich (Uli for short), for a walk to Al's pond. It was another spectacular Fiddletown day. Bright sun shone on the green hills, illuminating the canes waving in Gino's and Pam's vineyards. Patches of fog rose from Al's pond like smoke signals. I felt full of wonder at my good fortune, with the phrase "How green is my valley!" running over and over in my mind.

Uli was ecstatic, bounding through the grassy meadows and racing up and down hills, covering much more ground than I did. It occurred to me the dog would display exactly the same amount of contentment, whether he went home with me to the old trailer or the new house. I knew when we returned from our walk, he would crash with the same complete surrender, whether on his new padded dog bed by the fireplace or on a sun-warmed patch of dirt.

TONS OF GRAPES

We'd bought the Middle Age Spread without much forethought. We enjoyed learning about the area, the climate, and the people over time. We learned how to care for fruit and nut trees and grow all sorts of vegetables. We tended the land and fencing and buildings. We planted a new vineyard and developed an olive orchard. Somehow, we failed to grasp that our fertile land soon would be producing tons of grapes and olives annually. It shouldn't have surprised us, but it did—the way some couples get pregnant without realizing how this will transform their lives forever. After our fifth grape harvest, we had a routine down reasonably well. We'd developed a list of friends who could help. We had our system of email bulletins to keep interested parties up to date on the grape ripening progress. We had punch lists to help us stay organized. But each crop was bigger and more demanding than the last. We'd likely have to make some changes...

In early August 2005, I sent out the first Harvest Watch bulletin:

> *This has been an odd year, weather-wise. It was cold and rainy in March, but the winter rains stopped abruptly, and we had a dry, hot spring. Everything in the garden and vineyard seems to be ripening ahead of schedule. The vines look good, and veraison has begun. We anticipate the 2005 harvest will be two or three weeks ahead of last year's. Since we harvested near the end of September in 2004, we'll probably pick sometime in the first half of September this year. Please confirm your interest and availability to help.*

My message sounded calm, but as soon as I hit the "send" button, a wave of panic washed over me. Veraison was underway. In a month or so, we'd have tons of grapes to harvest, and this year we had no idea what we were going to do with them. For five years, our crop had gone exclusively to our friend and winemaker,

Tom. But our crop had increased, and his capacity had not. Tom made some delicious wines, but now we began to think he was in real trouble. His winery was still selling our 2000 vintage. *What happened to the subsequent vintages?* Even if he still wanted to take three or four tons of our grapes, we were estimating bigger crops now.

Our phone and email messages to Tom became more frequent and anxious, but we still had no replies. The silence seemed to grow louder with each passing day. We began to worry that Tom might be in a hospital—or worse. We tried contacting his colleagues in the winemaking business. They passed on snippets of information they'd heard from or about Tom: a hernia operation, some depression over the state of his business, something about a new job elsewhere.

My concern turned into anger. It seemed utterly irresponsible of him not to get in touch, with harvest bearing down on us. One way or the other, we had to know if he'd be taking our grapes this year. Deborah asked me, for the fourth time that day, if I'd heard from Tom yet. I had not.

"Let's face it," I said. "Tom is not going to take our crop this year. Those days are over." The last time we'd driven by his winery facility, there was a notice posted on the door indicating his ABC license had been revoked. At the time, we wondered if he'd forgotten to pay his annual permit fees. Now we feared he'd actually gone out of business.

I tried to convince Deborah, the family scientist, that she should consider taking over winemaking duties. I was sure she'd excel at it.

"I just can't," she insisted. By that time, she had a bunch of young medical colleagues who depended on her to write grant proposals and find research funding to support their salaries. Besides, she wasn't sure she had any talent for winemaking. "I think a winemaker needs to recall tastes and smells from one vintage to another. I can remember if I liked a certain wine or not, but not much beyond that," she said.

Can making wine be that hard? I wondered. I recalled our first dismal experiment and the resulting stinky goop only fruit flies adored. I knew it wasn't for me, either. I would simply have to apply myself to finding a new buyer for our crop. Time was of the essence.

Perhaps we could sell our grapes, like our neighbor Zack, to some huge commercial winery that would blend them into California table wine, but we couldn't stand that idea. All of our hard work, just to see our precious zin flow into a river of mediocre jug wine? Never.

I dug out a handful of business cards I'd collected at the Amador County Fair wine tasting event. Deborah had been away, so Kay and Linda and I had worked the event, pouring samples and asking if anyone might need several tons of zinfandel soon. A winemaker from Auburn expressed interest, but he wanted only organic grapes, and we'd been practicing integrated pest management in recent years.

An Armenian gentleman from Lodi said he used to buy grapes from a neighbor in our tiny valley. Those grapes were excellent, so he thought ours would be, too. He'd just placed an order for five tons of zinfandel but hadn't received confirmation. He said he'd call me if the deal fell through—but I knew that was highly unlikely. California was experiencing a grape glut at the time. I couldn't imagine any grower backing out of a five-ton sale.

I called every person I'd met at the fair who'd shown the least bit of potential interest. I left messages on dozens of answering machines. Only one party even bothered to return my call, Fiddle Farm, a small winery about twenty miles from Fiddletown. They produced only two wines, a barbera and a sangiovese. Both had won medals in the County Fair wine competition. Kay and I had found Henry and Ivan to be the most laid-back wine pourers at the fair. Henry, who owned the winery, was a round huggy-bear of a man with black hair, serious green eyes, and a big beard shot with silver. He was a classical bassist and his wife a classical violinist. Ivan was Henry's neighbor and his winemaking consultant.

"He's got the technical know-how; I've got the palate," Henry said. "Tasting is my main duty, and I take it seriously." Ivan was younger, in his thirties, fit, with a medium build, short blond hair, and eyes that sparked with mischief. Kay and I enjoyed kibitzing with both men as we tried to convince them, with a name like Fiddle Farm, they really should be producing a wine from the Fiddletown AVA. I pulled out photos of our vineyard and described our grapes. Ours were happy vines—and why shouldn't they be? They sunned themselves daily on gentle southwest-facing slopes. They were watered, weeded, groomed, and harvested by caring hands. Our vines were beautiful, our grapes exquisite...

"Other than that, above average," Henry teased. But it was true, I insisted. Our vineyard was planted in a perfect location, in a deep band of rich soil made from decomposed granite, and it was directly across the road from a renowned vineyard that had been growing exceptional zinfandel for a century. The Middle Age Spread had all the makings of a superb terroir. No one had made bad wine from our grapes yet—not even first-time home winemakers.

Both Henry and Ivan liked the idea of making wine from Fiddletown grapes, but when I reached Henry by phone, he confessed they were drowning in inventory. They were in no position to buy more fruit at that time. Perhaps in the future, but not then. They invited us to come out and visit their winery operation, anyway.

After I hung up, I walked around our vineyard, wondering what to do. We had the usual handful of home winemakers eager to buy a few small lots of grapes. But our vines were loaded with fruit. I returned to the house and made more calls and received more rejections. I left another frustrated message on Tom's answering machine. This time he called me back.

"First of all," he said, "I want to apologize for falling out of communication. I've been dealing with a serious depression. I got professional help, so it's mostly behind me now."

"I'm happy to know you're okay," I said, feeling genuinely relieved and sympathetic. I waited to hear more. Would he be making wine this year? Would he want to take grapes from our vineyard, or not?

"Your 2000 zinfandel was the only vintage I could afford to bottle," he said. "Glass, corks, capsules, and labels can get really expensive. It didn't make sense to bottle more wine when I still had the 2000 vintage to sell. I've had to declare bankruptcy. The winery will be closed by the end of this month."

I wondered about the wine from our other vintages when Tom answered my question. "I still have the rest of your wine in barrels at the winery. Four vintages, 2001 through 2004. There are sixteen barrels in all. If you and Deborah want to come and get the wine, you can have it. Otherwise, it'll go to my creditors, and they'll likely sell it off as bulk wine."

I was stunned. *My babies!* I thought. We'd worked so hard to establish our vineyard, nurture those vines, harvest and deliver the grapes. The idea of having the fruits of our labor, our own estate-grown zin, flow into a river of spaghetti red seemed impossible, outrageous.

I pondered what Tom was suggesting and finally asked, "Um, how would that work?"

PART THREE

CUSTOM CRUSHING

ORPHANED WINE

Deborah and I had never dreamed of getting into the commercial wine business. We had enough to do already—demanding careers, extended families, pets to care for, volunteer work, and property to maintain. Growing vines and sipping wines provided us with enough grape-related amusement in our lives. We did not need or want more. Truly. But sometimes, challenges arise you don't anticipate. They require a response. You can turn your back and carry on with life as is, or you can rise to the occasion and embrace a new adventure.

After a puzzling and frustrating absence, Tom had resurfaced. He called and offered to "give" us four vintages of our own estate-grown zinfandel. I'd asked how that would work.

"Well, I'd turn the wine over to you," Tom said. "I wouldn't charge you anything for making it. I'd be satisfied knowing it's in good hands—and I can't imagine anyone who'd care for it better than you two."

"How much wine are we talking about?" I asked.

"I have sixteen barrels of your zin," he said. "Made from four different vintages—2001 through 2004."

Sixteen barrels of wine! I tried to wrap my mind around that quantity. One wine barrel holds about sixty gallons. Sixteen barrels would be almost a thousand gallons of wine, which would weigh between four and five tons. Deborah and I owned one quarter-ton pickup truck, so transporting even a single barrel of wine would be pushing our weight limit. How on earth would we move such a load?

"You'd need a box truck," Tom said. "There's a place in the East Bay that rents them at a reasonable price. You'd have to get one with a lift gate because I don't have a forklift. I do have a pallet jack, though, so we could maneuver the barrel racks onto the gate, raise it up, then use my jack to position the racks inside the truck. I can have them on double-stacked metal racks, so we can load four barrels at a time. Four stacks of four barrels would fit perfectly inside a sixteen-foot truck. You'd have to tie them down well because you don't want heavy barrels of liquid rolling around when you're driving on the freeway."

I had a hunch that if we moved forward with this venture, I'd be doing a lot of the heavy lifting on my own. My consulting business was booming with new Caltrans freeway projects, but Deborah's workload was insane. She was starting the new Womens Clinic at the Veterans' Hospital in San Francisco. She also headed a clinical research group at the University of California, San Francisco. In addition, she served on a National Institutes of Health panel that reviewed drugs proposed for approval—which entailed attending quarterly meetings in Bethesda.

I tried to envision myself driving a lift-gate truck big enough to hold sixteen barrels of wine on double-stacked metal racks. I heard a wee voice in my head ask: "Are you crazy!?" At the same time, I recalled a single Chinese character meaning both risk and opportunity, suggesting where there is risk, there is also opportunity and vice versa.

"I guess I could manage it," I said, "but I'm not sure where I'd take the wine."

"You can't just take it to your barn or store it in your garage," Tom said. "Wine has to be kept cool, of course, but it also has to transfer from one bonded facility like my winery to another bonded facility." He explained a bonded facility requires licensing and is regulated by the government.

"Your best approach probably would be to team up with an existing winery in Amador County," he said. "Preferably one close to your vineyard."

"Most wineries have some excess capacity, so you can pay them fees to store your wine. They'd also have resources you'll need, like laboratory analysis, label approval experience, bottling equipment, and wine blending expertise."

I recalled Tom mentioning bottling expenses. We'd already spent most of our savings building the new house. Did we really want to invest more in glass, labels, corks, capsules, and bottling services? What if we were no more successful at selling wine than Tom had been? How could we know? We'd never tried such a venture before. We had no marketing plan. Where would we begin?

Tom said we'd have to establish our own brand, create a label, and apply for the necessary federal and state permits and licenses to sell alcohol. We'd need a Basic Permit from TTB, the federal agency regulating tobacco, firearms, and alcohol. We'd have to get the appropriate licenses from California's Department of Alcoholic Beverages Control. There's a Type 17 license for wholesalers—if you just want to sell to other businesses, like stores and restaurants. If you plan to sell directly to consumers, you need a Type 20 license. "And you'd have to get a Seller's Permit from the Board of Equalization because they'll want to collect sales tax from you quarterly." I scratched down letters as Tom spoke—TTB, ABC, BOE...He suggested we also check with Amador County to see if they'd require us to get a local business license.

"The other agencies try to control production and regulate the flow of alcohol—but mainly they want to collect taxes on sales," Tom said. The feds would do criminal background checks on us to make sure we weren't felons (or bootleggers). They'd take our fingerprints, and of course, we'd have to pay permit fees. Tom wasn't sure what the current fees were but thought they were about the same for a tiny family operation as for a big commercial winery like Mondavi.

"This is a lot to digest," I said. "Let me talk it over with Deborah. Give us a few days to do some research and make some calls. I'll get back to you soon." Tom promised to answer the phone from now on.

I called Deborah right away to tell her what Tom had proposed. "That's wild!" she exclaimed. "But I'm just going into a meeting. Let's talk tonight."

There were many things to fret about: what if the older wines had oxidized or tasted like Popsicle sticks from sitting in wooden barrels too long? What if no one wanted to buy our wine? Where would we find the time to deal with the permit applications and all the necessary paperwork to manage a new business? What pitfalls might be involved? We had no idea. But how could we not take this bull by the horns? The alternative—having the fruits of our labor flow into the jug wine trade—was simply unpalatable.

FIDDLE FARM

Henry had invited us to visit his Fiddle Farm winemaking facility in Ione. Deborah and I decided to go. We were hoping we could still convince him to buy part of our 2005 crop, and now we also needed to research bonded wine facilities in the area. On top of that, we had a load of junk to take to the dump, which was not far from Fiddle Farm.

We'd always thought the dump vicinity eerie with its thickets of manzanita, patches of barren yellow dirt, and old quarry ponds an unnatural shade of turquoise green. Once we'd unloaded our trash, we followed the directions Henry had given us. We'd never driven beyond the county dump before. Soon, we were in unfamiliar territory. We turned left at Buena Vista, a place on the map but little more than a four-way stop with a gas station/bar/convenience store on one corner. We continued along Jackson Valley Road and soon realized we were driving below a high earthen berm.

"What's that?" Deborah asked.

"I think it's a retaining wall for one of the reservoirs around here," I said. My hunch was soon confirmed by signs sporting images of fishhooks and motorboats.

"It would give me the heebie-jeebies living near a thing like that," Deborah said. "It's scary enough just driving below it. What if it were to fail? What would happen in an earthquake?" *Inundation,* I thought.

We soon found the address we were looking for. It was not a winery but a wide driveway entrance with a bank of mailboxes and an automatic security gate. I punched in the code Henry had given me. The metal gate slid back to let us in. We drove slowly along the gravel road. At first, we saw no signs of civilization, just clumps of manzanita and coyote brush. The landscape appeared monotone, as if a fire might have swept through recently—or perhaps everything was covered with the dust rising from the gravel roadway.

"Kind of eerie," Deborah whispered. "Shades of *Deliverance*..."

At last, we began to see hints of human settlement: a few outbuildings, a riding stable with horses, some sheep and goats grazing. We passed several ranch homes set well back from the roadway, with boats or RVs parked in driveways. Soon, we were cruising past a vineyard, clearly dead—*from neglect or wildfire?* we wondered.

"We don't have to do this," Deborah said. "Maybe we should just turn around now..."

"No, we've come this far," I said. "We might as well get the full experience."

We found the open gate Henry had told me to look for. He'd said there'd be an old yellow pickup next to it, but he failed to mention its windshield was shot full of holes.

"That looks like Bonnie and Clyde's getaway vehicle," I said. Deborah nodded. She was driving with intense concentration, maneuvering around numerous potholes. We saw a weather-beaten hangar in the distance, surrounded by a collection of old vehicles, refrigeration units, and other equipment in various stages of disrepair. As we drove toward it, two big dogs came howling to greet the truck. We heard someone whistle to call them off. We parked next to the hangar and entered. Henry and his neighbor, Ivan (whom I'd also met at the fair wine event), were sitting with a couple of strangers at a cable reel covered with empty beer bottles and sandwich wrappers.

Ivan introduced the strangers as Mark and Claire, a husband-and-wife team who worked at a local winery, where Mark was assistant winemaker and Claire worked in marketing. But the couple also had a personal winemaking project at Fiddle Farm. They were trying to launch their own wine label, so they were helping Henry and Ivan make wine in exchange for using their facilities. It had been their idea to enlist some "custom crush" clients to get the infusion of capital they needed to purchase more barrels and equipment. It became obvious that while we were trying to sell our grapes to them, they were trying to sell winemaking services to us.

I asked what role each person played at Fiddle Farm. Mark said Henry and Ivan had known each other a long time. Ivan's home was just down the road, where we'd noticed horses grazing. Henry wasn't very involved in the winemaking process, but he owned the building, which was licensed and bonded and therefore critical to their operation. He was also a gourmand with a sharp palate, so he was involved in wine tasting and blending decisions. Mark had earned an undergraduate degree in geography from UC Berkeley but found his passion in winemaking, learning the trade by interning at various wineries around Amador County. He and his wife met Ivan through winemaking and became friends. Now they worked together to produce wines—for Fiddle Farm, Mark and Claire's "Black Dog" label, and a private custom crush client from Marin County. Claire helped with various tasks, including researching supplies and prices and ordering whatever they needed.

"We call her our Barrel Nazi," Mark said proudly, "because she finds us rock-bottom prices on stuff we need." He offered us a tour of the facility, and we gladly accepted.

The main crushing room was filled with creatively engineered devices, including a big pulley with some 2x4s bolted into a square frame. This was attached to a hydraulic jack capable of lifting a half-ton bin of grapes and dumping the contents into a hopper. Their stemmer-crusher looked no more substantial than the one we had in our barn for home winemaker use. There was also a closet-sized office/laboratory area and two air-conditioned "cold rooms," where barrels and bottled goods were stored.

Mark invited us to taste some of the wines they were making. Claire brought six wine glasses into the first cold room, which contained a few dozen oak barrels arranged on metal racks. He said they were conducting experiments using different yeasts and oaking agents. Because French oak barrels were so expensive, they used "neutral" or spent barrels, adding chunks of new oak staves, carved oak chains, "teabags" filled with oak chips, and even oak sawdust. This would mimic the effect of aging the wine in genuine oak barrels. Ivan waved samples under our noses to illustrate what Mark was talking about. They all smelled good to me—yeasty, peachy, or full of dark vanilla.

Mark removed the bung from a barrel and used a "wine thief"—a long glass tube for drawing wine out of a barrel—to extract a sample. A wine thief is a simple tool: you slide the open, tapered end into the wine, place your thumb over the open top of the tube to seal it, withdraw, and—voila, you have extracted liquid from the barrel. As you release your thumb, the wine slips into an outheld glass for tasting.

Our first taste was of a syrah Mark and Claire produced for their own label. They'd purchased the grapes from our neighbor Pam.

"That's delicious," I said. "Cherries and white pepper, and maybe a touch of chocolate. I love it."

"Want to buy a few dozen cases?" Claire asked. "I could give you a barrel tasting discount—but it's good for today only."

"We think Fiddle Farm should produce wine from the Fiddletown appellation," Deborah said to Henry and Ivan. "We can sign you up right now for a few tons of our current vintage."

Henry waved at the towers of case goods that filled the second cold room. "We'd be crazy to buy any more grapes at this point," he said.

Mark was curious to learn what kind of palates we had and which style of wine we preferred. I guess we must have "oohed" and "aahed" at the correct times (and/or he was a very good bullshitter, I mean businessman), because after the tour and tasting, Mark said he'd be delighted to work with us. We enjoyed every wine he poured but apparently, we'd expressed preferences for the very wines he was most excited about.

After quite a bit of tasting, I thought everything was fabulous, including all the Fiddle Farm characters. Despite our misgivings on the trip here, the joyful goofiness and bold inventiveness of the Fiddle Farm crew made us feel certain it would be a kick to work with them. And the wines they produced were excellent. But clearly, this was not going to happen immediately. We were all choking on inventory. We had sixteen barrels of wine to move. We had to prioritize that. The idea of making yet more wine was completely ludicrous. Since they couldn't buy our grapes and we didn't want their winemaking services, we shook hands and left.

Au revoir, I thought, just as Deborah said, *"Hasta la vista!"* We both had a feeling we'd be working with these folks more in the future.

LICENSING

Despite some trepidation, we plunged into the wine business. Above all, this was a rescue mission. We could not abide the idea of four years of effort—our devoted crop tending and Tom's fine winemaking—coming to naught or benefiting anonymous creditors and bulk wine purveyors. So, we filled out applications, completed interviews, got photographed and fingerprinted, paid fees, and obtained the necessary licenses. We ordered business cards. I figured out how to file quarterly sales tax returns in case we should ever make any sales. We had to post a legal notice on our gate for thirty days to allow public comment. No one objected.

Deborah and I researched our options for a new home for our wine. After considering the choices available, we selected Drytown Cellars. It was only about ten miles from our vineyard, we were impressed with the people who owned and ran it, and their prices for wine storage and services seemed reasonable.

When it came time to transport the wine, Deborah was in D.C., so I was on my own. I drove to Berkeley to pick up the rental truck. Tom loaded the barrels and racks using the hydraulic tailgate and his pallet jack. We tied them down carefully. We exchanged hugs, and he reminded me to pull off the highway at any open weigh stations. I hoisted my hundred and twenty-five pounds into the driver's seat and placed a bottle of water and a bag of sunflower seeds within easy reach. I figured out which levers operated the headlights and windshield wipers, just in case. I turned on the radio and found my favorite station. Then I fastened my seatbelt, released the parking brake, and rolled toward the freeway. I glanced at myself in the rearview mirror. *What have you gotten yourself into now, girlfriend? Look at you: driving a honking big ole cargo truck loaded with five tons of inebriating elixir!*

Soon I was cruising down the interstate in the right-hand lane, among the car carriers, moving vans, refrigerated trucks, and propane tankers. I stayed in the slow lane because I wanted to avoid situations that might require me to brake suddenly. I was so used to zooming past weigh stations on the highway in a pickup I missed the first one. I examined the rearview mirror for signs of a pursuing patrol car, but none came. I admonished myself to pay closer attention. When I saw the next weigh station, I did pull off the freeway. Fortunately, the attendant waved my rental truck through, so I did not have to line up to be weighed at the scales, where there was a long queue of waiting trucks. After a few hours of driving, I could have used a restroom break, but I did not want to stop and leave my cargo unattended. I kept going.

It was early afternoon by the time I reached Drytown, located just outside of Plymouth. The winery had a forklift, so unloading was quick and easy once I removed all the tie-downs. There was some paperwork to do, documenting the bond-to-bond transfer, and then I was free to go. I gave each of our sixteen barrels a pat, telling them we'd be back to visit on the weekend. The owner, Alan, was surprised to learn some of the wine had been in the barrel for almost four years, but he seemed confident he could help us turn it into something drinkable. I drove into Plymouth to buy gas, a sandwich, and a soda, and then I was on the road again.

Driving the truck back empty was a completely different experience from driving it into the foothills with a full load. The wind made the metal freight box pop and ping, and every bump in the road made the empty van skip like a light-hearted schoolgirl. I felt relieved once I turned the truck in—without a single scratch or dent.

BLENDING

In no time, we realized the decision to take our orphaned wine to Drytown Cellars was a good one. The winery itself had a welcoming, homey feel. Perhaps it was due to the three friendly dogs roaming the facility. Or maybe it was Alan's unique goofiness. The man bristled with energy, shifting his weight from one foot to the other as he spoke, his blond curls bouncing as his blue eyes flashed. He practically lived in the barrel room, where he made wine, took naps, and practiced drumming for his gigs with a local rock band.

Alan rented us the climate-controlled warehouse space we needed to store our barrels properly. He had the expertise to help us with wine blending and finishing decisions. In addition, Alan had his own bottling equipment—a sturdy old German dairy line he'd converted to bottling wine instead of milk. (It broke down frequently but got the job done.) His wife, Suzanne, helped us get wine labels designed, approved, and printed.

"Well," I said to Deborah when the business cards arrived. "Looks like we're in business now. Here are the cards to prove it, and we finally have some bottled product to sell."

She shook her head in wonder. "Here we go, ready or not..."

We clinked our glasses—a mismatched pair we'd scored at the S&M Swap Shop—which held a sample of our 2001 estate-grown zinfandel. It had tasted a bit tired straight from the barrel, but the Drytown Cellars crew had found something to blend it with that perked it up.

"It's not bad," Deborah said.

"I think it's actually pretty good," I said. "Let's hope we can sell this stuff because we now own more bottled zinfandel than we can drink in a lifetime." We felt relieved that we'd managed to rescue those four vintages of our wine, if uncertain about what lay ahead.

Meanwhile, the 2005 harvest was nipping at our heels. Those grapes would be ripe in just a few weeks, and we still had no buyer. This was already a top priority, but now it became urgent. It began to keep me awake at night.

SAINT CHARLES

I made another round of calls seeking a buyer for our 2005 crop and came up empty-handed again. We had tons of wine grapes available and no offers. Shit!

Our friends Anne and Marianne dropped by on the weekend. They had an errand in the Shenandoah Valley, where one winery ran an art gallery and framing shop above their tasting room. They'd had something framed there, and it was ready to pick up. We went along for the ride.

The Spinetta Winery grounds were tidy and welcoming. There was a long hedge of lilac bushes, ample parking, and a shady picnic area. We entered the main building and tasted a few wines before heading upstairs to browse the gallery and pick up our friends' order. We learned about the winery's history while chatting with the staff. They produced wines under their own label, but they also made wine for bulk sales. It was a big operation. I asked if, by any chance, they might be interested in some locally grown zinfandel. One of the Spinetta sons said we should ask his dad, who happened to be working in his upstairs office at that moment. We climbed the stairs, taking a quick peek at the art hanging on the walls. While Anne and Marianne paid for their order, Deborah and I tapped on the office door at the rear.

"Come in!" a deep voice bellowed. We opened the door to see Charles Spinetta himself seated at his desk. We introduced ourselves and said his son had suggested we talk to him about some zinfandel we had available. He asked a series of questions about the vineyard, the vines (varietal and clone), and our management practices. He was a hard-nosed businessman, but he softened when he learned our sole buyer had declared bankruptcy.

"I do sympathize with your plight," he said, "but I have seen this happen over and over, city people coming up here and planting vines. Frankly, most of them don't know what the hell they're doing, and the vines are neglected. They don't do proper pruning or canopy management, and then they want to sell me grapes that are underripe or full of mildew and bunch rot. I simply can't do it."

Deborah and I understood how that could happen, but we insisted we pampered our vines. We did our research; we consulted experts. We worked diligently at vineyard management, hand-tending each one of our twelve hundred vines.

"Tell you what I'm going to do," Charles said. "I'll go look at your vineyard and your crop. It's not far away, and it's only a small amount, and it seems you ladies have suffered enough. But I'm not going to buy bad fruit. So, before I even take the trouble to make a trip over there, I want to see your pesticide application records. Because if you haven't even sulfured properly, there is no point in talking further."

We thanked him for giving us a chance. I told him I'd deliver copies of our records that afternoon. When I dropped off the paperwork, I gave Charles our gate code and my phone number. I invited him to inspect the vineyard at his convenience and asked him to give me a call to let us know his decision.

We drove back to San Francisco for a busy work week. I was in a meeting when Charles called. I saw the red message light blinking when I got home. I pushed a button to hear his message: "Well, ladies, your records were impeccable, so today I went over to your place. I have to say, your vineyard surprised me. To be honest, I don't think I've ever seen a vineyard so well-tended. You did a great job of cane thinning and leaf pulling. Those beautiful grape clusters were dangling like Christmas tree ornaments ready to be plucked. I saw no signs of mildew or rot, and the fruit tastes really good. I'd be delighted to purchase five tons from you. Give me a call when you can, so we can schedule harvest and delivery."

I listened to his message three times, dancing around the living room. I played it for Deborah when she returned home from clinic. Our crop was sold, hallelujah! From that day forward, we referred to Charlie Spinetta as Saint Charles. Our contract was only for one year, but his blessing made it easier to negotiate contracts with other reputable local wineries like Easton/Terre Rouge and Renwood in the future.

DELIVERING

We called our local labor contractor to hire a harvest crew. We arranged to borrow trailers and bins from neighbors to harvest and deliver five tons of zinfandel to the Spinetta winery the following weekend. The day before harvest, we pressure-washed the equipment, made sure we had the correct trailer hitches for each vehicle, and got the trucks into position. We were ready.

We went to bed early, but we hardly slept because it rained most of the night. It was not a hard rain; it was more like a persistent drizzle. It stopped before dawn, and we had sunshine and warm breezes the rest of the day. Nonetheless, we had to delay picking to give the vines time to dry out.

Rain around harvest time is never welcome because crews do not like to pick wet grapes, and moist grapes are more vulnerable to mildew and rot. Also, water can dilute both the sugars and the flavors in the juice.

Our hired crew harvested five tons of zinfandel the following day. My brother and sister-in-law were visiting, so we broke into two-person teams and took turns hauling grapes a ton at a time to Spinetta Winery in the Shenandoah Valley, only a few miles from our vineyard. When we arrived, Charlie's son Jim would use the forklift to remove each bin, set it on a large square stainless steel scale, and note the precise weight, providing copies for our records.

Saint Charles called a few hours after the harvest was over. They had just finished crushing the fruit. Unfortunately, the vines had taken up enough moisture from the unexpected rain to plump up the clusters and drop the Brix by a couple of percentage points. He said he could still accept our delivery, but a price adjustment would have to be made. The sugar content was no longer high enough to make good red zinfandel. They'd have to turn it into white zinfandel, instead. This news was disappointing, but at least we would be paid something, and our grapes would become wine rather than bird feed.

We still had about a ton of fruit left hanging on the vines. In another week, the Brix had climbed back into the mid-twenties, and the grapes tasted great. We called Henry at Fiddle Farm and offered him a price he couldn't refuse. He agreed to take our last ton, so we invited a few city friends up for a fun and easy harvest event. They happily agreed.

Once the picking was done, Kay and I volunteered to deliver the crop to Fiddle Farm while the rest of the crew cleaned clippers and picking bins and laid out lunch. Kay's impressions along the way were similar to those Deborah and I had on our first trip to Fiddle Farm. By the time we reached the pickup truck with the windshield full of bullet holes, Kay was sputtering: "Surely there's not a functioning winery back here, is there?"

I parked at the hangar and honked the horn. Ivan poked his head out the side door and waved to show me where to park the trailer. He raised the big metal door and emerged driving a forklift to move our two full bins inside for crushing. Henry was resting inside on a folding chair next to a small fan, trying to keep cool, with his knees spread and a pitcher of ice water on the small table beside him. Mark and Claire were tending to bins of crushed grapes arranged in rows on the concrete pad. Squadrons of fruit flies circled lazily, perhaps a bit inebriated from breathing the Fiddle Farm indoor air, redolent with fermenting grapes.

Ivan handed Kay and me long-handled tools with a metal square welded onto the end, inviting us to help "punch down the must" fermenting in the bins. Claire was using a wooden oar to accomplish the same task. Mark showed us how to use the tool to break through the layer of seeds, pulp, and skins that had risen to the top of each container, forming a thick cap. He explained it was necessary to do this at least twice a day, every day, to keep the pomace in contact with the juice. This helps extract more flavors and tannins from the crushed berries and allows gases to rise rather than stay trapped beneath the solid cap. As we pushed the dry mass downward, purple liquid would squirt up and flow over the pulp on top, re-moistening everything.

"This is kind of fun and therapeutic," I said.

"Good," Mark replied. "You can have all the free therapy you want. It can get tedious when you have to do it several times every day, for numerous bins and for multiple weeks after harvest. But it has to be done to keep the fermentation process moving along." When we finished the job, Ivan asked if we'd like to stay to witness the crushing operation as they were about to address the ton of zinfandel we'd just delivered. Of course, we did.

Fiddle Farm had an elaborate plywood structure around the crusher, providing ample space for sorting and inspecting fruit before they pushed it into the hopper. Kay and I climbed onto the scaffolding to work beside Mark and Claire, sorting grapes to remove twigs, leaves, and any clusters that looked underripe, defective, or damaged.

"These grapes are amazingly clean," Mark said. "Sometimes we reject ten percent or more of what's delivered. Most people pick too fast, taking leaves and unripe bunches in their rush. We refer to anything that's not fruit as 'MOG' or 'Material Other Than Grapes.' Your grapes look like they were picked very carefully. It's a real pleasure to get fruit this clean."

We fed inspected grapes into the hopper continuously until the entire ton had been crushed. Then we placed the must in two plastic half-ton bins to begin the fermentation process. Ivan moved them where he wanted them with the forklift, and Mark labeled them DZ (for Damas Zinfandel).

"We need to get back to our guests," I said. Mark invited us to come back and visit anytime—to help punch down the must or see how fermentation was progressing. Ivan placed our empty grape bins on the trailer and secured them for the trip home. As we were saying goodbye, something on the wall caught my attention. It was nothing more than an empty paper towel tube. Someone had run a string through it and attached it to a wooden post near the sink with a thumbtack. That image seemed to epitomize the Fiddle Farm operation: a low-budget, underfinanced, fly-by-the-seat-of-the-pants operation. Resources might be slim, but the people involved were talented, hardworking, fun-loving, and creative—and they produced excellent wines. Other wineries might be more efficient and better financed than Fiddle Farm, but there's something to be said for gleeful young energy, enthusiasm, and innovation.

We finished the 2005 harvest with a sense of relief and satisfaction. All of our grapes had found homes. The vineyard had been picked clean. And now it was time to focus on selling wine. Soon enough, another harvest would come around, and we'd have to decide whether or not to continue making wine under our own label.

If we decide to continue, I thought, *we'll have to find a new winemaker...*

FROM CELLARING
TO SELLING

With the 2005 harvest behind us, we turned our attention to selling the wine we'd received from Tom. Given the overwhelming array of beverages available to consumers, why would anyone buy a bottle of wine from a tiny, obscure vineyard in the Sierra foothills with no track record, no reviews, and no advertising budget? We could hire a distributor to sell for us. Still, they'd confront the same challenges and keep fifteen percent of any sales as their commission. We had no assurance any distributor would be inclined to push our wine when they had larger and better-known wineries to represent.

I tried my hand at making cold calls and visiting wine stores and restaurants in San Francisco. I was pleasantly surprised when people actually invited me in to hear what I had to say. Initially, sales were very slow. The proprietors were reluctant about stocking our wine. Their customers would not have heard of it, so they'd have to "hand-sell" or promote it themselves. This would be more work than carrying brands that are familiar to consumers, are advertised on billboards and TV, and have built a loyal customer base over the years. I could appreciate that.

As in any endeavor, personal relationships are key. Unfortunately, we didn't know anyone who actually owned a restaurant or wine store or beverage distribution company. But our pal Jake owned the corner grocery store in our San Francisco neighborhood. Jake agreed to carry and promote our wines. He cleared a good spot to stack cases of our wine and encouraged us to post photos and information about our vineyard. But Jake's small business suffered intense competition from the new Costco and Trader Joe's stores in the city, so we had to keep our prices low to lure customers. We wanted to keep the wine affordable to our friends, anyway, as none of them would pay $30 for weekday dinner wine. Nor would we.

The key to selling wine, we learned, was to introduce it to people we already knew. They did not buy our wine because they felt sorry for us. Nor did they buy it for its reputation, price, or quality. Our wine was quaffable. It was neither the best nor the worst on the market, neither the most nor the least expensive. What made it appealing was that they knew us personally. We discovered people love to buy wine with a story. Consumers can go to any market and have hundreds of wines to choose from. Or they can take a bottle of wine to a dinner party and proclaim: "I know the women who grow the grapes and produce this wine. I helped them harvest last year. It was so much fun. Their vineyard is beautiful!" You don't get that kind of a story with any bottle off any shelf.

So, our marketing strategy evolved to focus on our existing network of friends, relatives, neighbors, and colleagues—mainly in San Francisco but also in the foothills. Most of our sales happened through word of mouth or at tasting events we called our "wine Tupperware parties." We kept our prices relatively low, encouraging our customers to adopt Damas zinfandel as their "house wine." We developed a small fan club. We put out a periodic newsletter including information about what was happening in the vineyard and a current price list and order form. A few friends and relatives enjoyed our wine well enough to pay to have it shipped across the country.

We felt very fortunate when our estate-grown zinfandel was featured by several wine clubs, including KQED's Wine Club and Michael Chiarello's NapaStyle Wine Club. These successes resulted from my hustling, Tom's winemaking skill, and our pricing policies.

Since wine sales were going relatively well, we decided to continue our unplanned business pursuit and make more wine for our own label the following year. Our first thought was to work with the Fiddle Farm gang, but things had become awkward. Mark and Claire had split up, making it tricky for Ivan to continue working with them. Mark and Claire didn't want to bump into each other at the winery, so they found reasons to avoid the place. This made Ivan feel like he was stuck doing most of the work with less camaraderie and fun. We didn't want to be in the middle of relationships that had turned messy and tense.

Claire kept her marketing job at Monteviña, while Mark took a job as winemaker at Bray, a few miles down the road. We spoke with Alan at Drytown Cellars about doing "custom crushing" for us. He was amenable, and Ivan had started working for him, which seemed good—a familiar face. But we also appreciated Mark's winemaking talent and wanted to keep him involved in some way, perhaps as a consultant. But it was challenging because Ivan was disgusted about the demise of what they'd had going at Fiddle Farm and blamed Mark for the mess. Meetings were strained.

We muddled through the 2006 harvest season, selling some of our grapes to wineries and home winemakers and keeping just a ton or two for our own label. But it was awkward working with Ivan and Mark at Drytown, so the following year, we decided to move our custom crush business to the winery where Mark was working. It was a few miles closer to our vineyard, and it was simpler dealing with one personality rather than two (or more). Thus, Mark became our go-to winemaker for many years. We would follow him as his career took him to various wineries around the valley.

After a few years of participating in public wine pouring events, where all we had to offer was our estate-grown zinfandel, Deborah and I got tired of people asking, "What else do you have to taste?" We could provide a vertical tasting of three different vintages of our estate-grown zinfandel, but they were not satisfied.

"Don't you have any whites or rosés?" they'd ask. *Sesame Street brats,* I would think, uncharitably. *They want tons of fun and variety packed into every damn minute.* Yet I could see their point. Even I do not enjoy sipping zinfandel when the thermometer reaches a hundred degrees. It makes me feel as if my tongue is wearing a mitten. Bring on those chilled whites and pinks, please–especially in summertime or with a plate of shellfish.

To address this issue, we began a new program of experimenting with small lots of white and rosé wines. We'd buy grapes from neighboring vineyards to make these wines. We tried to keep at least one white wine and one rosé in our lineup. Thus, our fans got to enjoy some good viognier, chardonnay, and sauvignon blanc, along with our reliable zinfandels. Mark made an excellent white Rhone blend for us one year by co-fermenting locally sourced viognier, roussanne, and marsanne. That wine won a gold medal and Best of Class at the

Amador County Fair. Sometimes, Mark and his new wife were able to source excellent fruit for us through their industry connections—like an excellent chenin blanc we made from the Clarksburg AVA, reputed to be the best chenin blanc growing region in the country.

Our one failed experiment, which occurred in the early days of our white wine program, was a pinot gris Mark made from grapes we bought from another client of his. He convinced us those grapes would make fabulous wine, and they did—until secondary fermentation occurred after it was bottled. Our pinot gris unexpectedly turned bubbly, like prosecco.

Kermit Lynch has written about how this phenomenon is embraced gleefully in France as a pleasant surprise. It is a rare and welcome exception, something to celebrate, transforming "Vin Ordinaire" into "Vin Petillante"—through a miraculous accident of the natural fermentation process. Lynch scoffs at winemakers' efforts to do everything possible to prevent this phenomenon, saying this is akin to "beating a dog for wagging its tail."

Americans, however, generally are not fond of surprises, so our pinot gris was a tough sell. We ended up thinking its highest and best use was as a base for white sangria—with fruit juice, sliced peaches, and a splash of Cognac added to it. The slight spritz only enhanced the yummy concoction. Still, there is only so much call for white sangria. We ended up donating the last cases to a non-profit organization for their annual fundraising dinner, where they touted it as "sparkly pinot gris."

Perhaps the most memorable moment in DAMAS sales history happened in 2011 at the annual Amador County Fair, which hosts a special wine tasting evening annually to showcase the wineries that won medals that year. Deborah and I (with help from our friends Kay and Linda) poured our medal-winning wines among dozens of other Amador County wineries. A man from Placerville attended this event with his daughter, who had just become engaged. They were shopping for the very special wine to be served at her wedding. After tasting their way carefully around all of the booths (perhaps twice), they returned and declared our wines to be the best of any they had tasted that evening. We were thrilled and flattered.

We scored a big wine sale—not just the fifteen cases of wine (ten red, five white) to be served at the wedding feast, but also eighteen magnums (1.5-liter bottles) and three jeroboams (4.5-liter bottles) to be used at various lead-up events or future anniversary celebrations, plus hundreds of 375 ml bottles to serve as mementos for the wedding guests. Mark embraced the challenge of bottling that complex wedding order.

As life would have it, that wedding never occurred. The marriage was called off, but the family never asked for a refund or complained about having too much good wine on hand. Years later, we learned the tiny party favor–sized bottles had made their way to Burning Man. There, numerous thirsty adults enjoyed their first sip of DAMAS zinfandel under a desert sky. The only complaint heard was that the father of the bride had not brought along the bigger bottles of DAMAS wines.

Photo by Linda Morris

COMPETITIONS

Our wine business was ticking along. We were in a good groove with our winemaker, Mark, as his career continued to flourish. He seemed at the peak of his game when he was offered a position as general manager and winemaker at a brand new winery in the Shenandoah Valley. We'd become close friends by then. Mark took our custom crush contract with him to the new winery, Andis. We were grateful for that. Andis was even closer to our vineyard, and we enjoyed the staff and young energy of the place.

DAMAS wines were selling, even if they were not exactly profitable. We were covering most expenses, and we had good wine to drink and serve to others. Fortunately, we'd kept our day jobs. Life seemed good. What more could we ask for? A bit more fame or recognition, perhaps? I looked into entering wine competitions, thinking it might boost sales if our wine won a prestigious award. Or maybe it would be a waste of time since our production was so small. I asked our new contacts in local wine businesses for advice.

"You should definitely do it," one winery owner suggested. He waved at his wall covered with plaques and ribbons. "It really helps with marketing and visibility. And it helps our customers, too. There are so many wines to choose from it's impossible to taste them all. People appreciate information about how well my wines compared with others—vetted by professional wine judges, rather than friends with untrained palates."

"It's a load of crap," said another wine industry insider. "They just want your entry fees. You ship them a case of your wine with a check, and they send you a ribbon. It's meaningless. Over half of all wines entered in competitions end up winning awards. It's nothing but a money-making scam to benefit the organizers."

We weren't sure whom to believe. Eventually, we decided to enter one of our estate-grown zinfandels Tom had made into the San Francisco International

Wine Competition. We were astounded when our zin won a bronze medal! Our relatives and friends were very impressed. They mistakenly believed a bronze medal meant your wine took third place in a particular competition with thousands of entries—not that it had been awarded one of many bronze medals given in a narrow category like "California zinfandels under $20" or "Estate-grown zinfandels under 14% alcohol."

I asked people in the wine business what a bronze medal really means. "It depends..." they would commonly reply. "Of course, you'd rather win silver or gold, but at least your wine won a medal. That's better than nothing."

I overheard a well-established local vintner talking about her winery's medals that year. "We won gold and silver medals in most of the competitions we entered, and even a bronze in the San Francisco International. It's the one competition I don't mind winning bronze in because the judges are tough and the competition stiff, with thousands of wines entered from all over the world." We felt encouraged enough to enter a few more competitions—and won more medals, including a repeat medal in the SF International and a mix of awards in other state and local competitions.

In 2012, we decided to try an experiment. We entered our current wines (a zinfandel, a zin-barbera blend, a viognier, and a white Rhone blend) in several competitions. We filled out entry forms and mailed checks. We shipped various combinations of our wines to the Amador County Fair Commercial Wine Competition, the Orange County Wine Society Competition, the California State Fair Wine Competition, and the San Francisco International Wine Competition. Of the fourteen wines we entered in these four competitions, thirteen were awarded medals, as follows:

2012 Amador County Fair (3 entries):
- 2011 Viognier – Silver
- 2010 Zinfandel – Bronze
- 2010 DUO – Silver

2012 Orange County Wine Society Competition (4 entries):
- 2010 Zinfandel – Gold

- 2010 Shenandoah Blanc – Gold
- 2011 Viognier – Bronze

2012 CA State Fair (4 entries):
- 2010 Zinfandel – Silver (90 points)
- 2010 DUO – Silver
- 2010 Shenandoah Blanc – Silver
- 2011 Viognier – Bronze

2012 SF International Wine Competition (3 entries):
- 2010 DUO blend – Double Gold
- 2010 Zinfandel – Silver
- 2011 Viognier – Bronze

We were excited about all this bling: four bronze, six silver, two gold, and one rare and highly prestigious double gold medal*—and that was won in the reputedly tough San Francisco International Wine Competition.

"I guess this boatload of medals proves our wines are good," Deborah said proudly.

"I guess so," I said. "But don't you find it strange that our zin-barbera blend that won double gold at the San Francisco International Wine Competition and won silver in two other competitions was our only entry that won no medal at all in the Orange County judging?" She agreed it seemed odd. I thought it so strange I called the Orange County Wine Society to see if there might have been a mistake. The person on the phone assured me their reporting was accurate and the judges' decision was final.

"But how can the same wine earn a double gold in the prestigious San Francisco International Wine Competition and not be considered worthy of any medal at all in your competition?" I asked.

I thought I heard snickering in the background. "That's wine judging for you!" the person said and hung up.

---

* When most judges on a tasting panel think a particular wine is top quality, it wins a gold medal. Double gold means the judges were unanimous.

After 2012, we retained a healthy skepticism about wine competitions. We would enter the Amador County competition annually—and others once in a while—just for fun. We scored another double gold medal in a special tasting of wines produced in the Fiddletown AVA. Still, entering competitions never became a key feature of our business strategy. Given those 2012 results, we felt confident saying ours were award-winning wines. That seemed good enough.

COOPERATION AND COOPERAGE

Our involvement in a small vineyard and wine business gave us entry into the grape-growing and wine-making community in Amador County. We had to talk with labor contractors, potential buyers, custom crush facilities, winemakers, and wine storage facilities, seeking help from anyone flexible enough to work with a small venture like ours. And when it came close to harvest time, we'd reach out to our grape-growing neighbors to coordinate picking dates and equipment needs. We'd lend our Kubota tractor to help with Pam's harvest, and she'd lend us trailers and half-ton bins for ours. We owned only one trailer capable of carrying two full bins (a ton of grapes), so we'd ask Pam or other neighbors if we could borrow theirs. In turn, one of them might ask to use our forklift attachment to move bins on harvest day.

Neighbors like Dodd, Joe, Al, Linda Sue, and Terryl, who were not growing grapes or making wine themselves, would lend their trucks to help deliver our fruit to local wineries for crushing. We typically needed three trucks to pull three grape trailers. Each rig would travel to the winery to unload, return with two new empty half-ton bins on their trailer, and move into position in the vineyard to reload. This way, the crew never had to stop picking because there was nowhere to dump fruit. They are paid by the ton, rather than by the hour, to pick grapes so they want to go full speed. We kept the bins moving efficiently to avoid disrupting their rhythm.

When we built the new house we were not in the wine business, so we'd built a modest cellar just big enough to hold a personal wine collection. Now our cellar was stuffed floor to ceiling with case goods, and we still had to store wine off-site, usually at other wineries. We had to coordinate with the busy owners to schedule deliveries or pickups as needed.

These interactions built partnerships with neighbors and enhanced our sense of being part of a larger community. We began to feel we had stronger ties to our rural neighbors than we did with our city neighbors, who often seemed remote or detached. We lived physically much closer together in the city, yet we had less reason to rely on one other, fewer opportunities to get to know each other better and build relationships. Our rural life began to seem the richer one.

In the early years, we took our crop to San Francisco, where our winemaker and most of our customers were. After a time, our grape buyers and winemakers—and a growing number of customers—were in Amador County. We could imagine the possibility of living in the foothills full-time at some point.

While we cherished these new connections with the foothills community, there was one neighbor we consistently avoided—our downhill neighbor, Zack. We didn't trust the man, so we avoided interacting with him. This was tricky, as most of our immediate neighbors depended on Zack for something. He owned the only forklift in our small valley, as well as the only set of porta-potties mounted on a trailer for easy transport to work sites. We'd make do using the fork attachment on our tractor—not as good as an actual forklift, but useful in a pinch. We let workers use the bathroom facilities in our guesthouse rather than borrow mobile facilities from Zack. We'd heard that he believed porta-potties should never be placed in a shady spot. Instead, they should be placed in full sun to discourage workers from lingering in them.

"What's he thinking?" Deborah asked. "That one of the pickers might take a magazine into the shitter and spend an hour flipping through it? Or someone might take a nap in there? These folks work as a team and get paid for their joint effort, for heaven's sake. It's just a heartless prank." I thought there might be racism mixed in with his meanness since many of the laborers had brown skin.

One year, however, we could not avoid getting mixed up with Zack. Until then, we'd delivered our grapes one ton at a time to local buyers, who would remove bins from our trailers with their own forklifts. That year, we had a new buyer whose winery was further away and who wanted to send a flatbed truck to fetch all the bins at once once we finished picking. We needed a forklift. Deborah favored renting one, but I thought that would be too expensive. With the in- and out-fees, it would have cost a thousand dollars to have a forklift available for the half-hour we'd need it. Our handyman, Joe, had a decent working relationship with Zack. We thought he had a better chance of getting a positive response from the old curmudgeon than we did.

Zack agreed to provide forklift services for our harvest if we'd make a small contribution to a cause dear to his heart. He was in charge of the Moose Lodge then and asked us to write a check to help it keep afloat financially. It was a reasonable offer, although it galled us to support the annoying institution next door we mostly tried to ignore.

I thought this arrangement might provide an opportunity to improve relations with Zack. On harvest day, Zack drove his forklift up the main road to help us and our neighbor Pam, who happened to be harvesting some of her syrah the same day. His job was to take full bins off our trailers and load them onto transport trucks at the end of the day.

I found Zack resting between loads that day and gave him a plate of my homemade fig brownies. "Doris will want this recipe," he said, licking chocolate off his thumb. He was so pleased he invited me to join him for a beer at the Lodge after the harvesting was done. I accepted and said I'd bring the recipe when I returned later to meet him for a drink.

The Lodge was dark and cool when I entered. Zack was already seated at the bar with a cold beer in front of him. He ordered one for me, and we chatted amicably for close to an hour. Mainly, I listened to Zack as he cracked jokes and told me about his adventures in the Merchant Marine. I do admire people who have traveled extensively—and who can fix broken things. He didn't ask any questions of me, and I was content to hear his stories.

Just as I was wondering if I should order another beer, Zack's tone changed abruptly. He swiveled his barstool and looked directly at me. "Some people call me a racist," he said, "but I'm not a racist." He paused for the punchline: "I just hate niggers!"

I wondered if this was one of his jokes, but he proceeded to rant about how we should gather our guns and get "that man" out of the White House (Obama was president at the time). I decided right then I had no need to befriend this man. It would be enough to coexist with him.

"Jeez, would you look at the time," I said. "I need to head back." I thanked Zack for the beer, handed him a check made out to the Moose Lodge, gave him my fig brownie recipe for Doris, and scurried toward home.

There were twelve hundred vines waving their arms in an exuberant welcome as the western sky began to put on a dazzling show of sunset colors. *Just because he got here first doesn't mean he owns this place*, I thought. *I have just as much right to be here as he does. I've worked as hard as he has to earn my spot in this paradise. We've got to figure out how to share this place without resorting to warfare.*

SPARKS

No matter how much Zack might annoy me, I tried to keep in mind that we were joined at the aquifer. His well and ours were close together and drew water from the same mysterious network of underground caves and crevices. This made a certain level of cooperation imperative, as we could cause one another serious harm, should either of us decide to literally poison the well or run it dry.

I began to wave at Zach if I saw him from the road, but I would never stop to chat. I simply wanted to acknowledge our proximity and participation in the same rural community. I simply tried to be respectful and neighborly. Soon, however, events occurring on his property disrupted our life to the point that I felt compelled to call his home late at night to complain.

As Zack aged, he needed more help managing his farm work but was averse to hiring skilled ag workers. He had access to a supply of men down on their luck who would show up at the Moose Lodge periodically. He devised a plan to park some old trailers near his entrance gate to accommodate them. That way, he could offer such men shelter in exchange for labor. To my surprise, he even applied to the county for a permit for his labor camp. The county granted him one that was valid only six months of the year (for seasonal workers). He ignored the restriction and invited several men to live there year-round. He provided electricity through a network of extension cords and water from hoses. Who knows what arrangements were made for sanitation.

The men who lived in the trailers showed a strong preference for dogs that would sleep all day and bark all night. One night, when I'd lain awake for over an hour from a constant barrage of barking, I called Zack's home. I would have called his tenants directly because I knew exactly where the nuisance was coming from, but I didn't have their phone numbers. In addition, I reasoned that disturbances caused by tenants should be brought to the landlord's attention.

Doris answered the phone. I complained about the noise and got some retort about the need for ranch security and the right to protect one's property however one saw fit. I asked if she was sure the dogs were barking at burglars and not just raccoons, known to be nocturnal, or blowing trash and moving shadows. Silence. I suggested the four-legged security alarms should be relocated to the far side of Zack's supply shed, where their yapping might be muffled somewhat in consideration of neighbors trying to sleep.

Doris insisted the barking didn't bother them. I refrained from pointing out that people become hard of hearing at an advanced age. Instead, I mentioned how sleep deprivation might drive a neighbor to become so cranky as to want to shoot annoying dogs that can't be trained to quit barking at night. Then I hung up.

A few days later, Joe informed me one of the dogs from Zack's trailer camp had been killed. That's all he said. *Oh great,* I thought, *now they'll think I threw a poisoned meatball over the fence!* Anyone who knows how much I love dogs knows I could never harm one. In my view, it's almost always humans responsible for bad canine behavior. Several days later, Joe elaborated. The dog had been gored by a bull it had been tormenting. *Whew.*

Nevertheless, soon I began to sense palpable waves of malevolence emanating up the hill from our downhill neighbor. I wondered if my late-night phone call had crossed some line in Zack's mind. I respected people's right to the peaceful enjoyment of their property. Zack and Doris believed firmly in the right to do whatever the hell one wanted on one's property, and the neighbors be damned.

After that call, Zack and his boys no longer returned my wave when I drove by. Instead, they'd squint their eyes and send withering, hostile looks in my direction. I began to suspect they were hatching plans to punish me for my infraction. I would look out the front window or gaze downhill from the patio frequently, scouting the meadow for trespassers bent on retaliation. I occasionally imagined men dressed in camouflage slipping silently through our gate or cutting through wire fencing to do the Marine Corps crawl upslope, intent on harm.

"You're being paranoid!" Deborah insisted. "They may be idiots, but they're not *that* stupid." I wasn't sure. The atmosphere felt tense and sinister, poisoned somehow. I lost my sense of joy at waking up in such a beautiful part of the world. I began to feel uncomfortable, sometimes even unsafe, in my own home. I wondered if Zack would go so far as to contaminate that aquifer we shared—or start firing his guns in my direction (again?). When I confessed these feelings to Kay, she expressed dismay.

"Oh, Mara, something's got to change. You must get your sense of enjoyment of this magnificent place back. You just have to!" *Yes, but how?* I wondered.

One weekend, when Deborah was on the east coast, it was just me and the dog at home. I sat on the flagstone patio with Uli after dinner. Deborah and I often sat outside in the evening to watch the stars emerge as the last light faded. We'd laugh at Uli, running around looking like a headless dog, his mostly-white body still visible as his chocolate head merged with the growing darkness.

This night, however, I was tense. I watched. I listened. Though nothing moved, I experienced an intense sense of danger. My heart raced; the hair on my neck stood up. I locked all the doors and went to bed that night with the shotgun loaded and handy.

When I awoke the next morning, I gave Uli a pat and realized I'd gone to sleep with bullets in my pajama pockets. Something really did have to change. I wondered if I should reach out and apologize to Zack and Doris for crossing whatever line I may have crossed. Maybe I could explain that I'd inherited my father's Irish temper and could have a short fuse sometimes.

I talked with friends about it, and they agreed it was up to me to do something to change the situation that was making me feel a wreck.

"Send his wife a nice note," Pat advised.

"Take the old bugger a bottle of grappa," Marco suggested. "Even better, sit and drink it with him."

I pondered how I might best extend an olive branch.

Then came the fire.

Photo courtesy of Ledger Dispatch

THE FIRE

Zack had a large (10,000 gallon) metal water storage tank sitting on our property line, next to his pond and our well, near his work camp. The tank, like almost everything Zack owned, appeared to be secondhand. It was rusted, dented, and adapted from some other use. The cylinder now storing water looked as if it had once held petroleum products, and it appeared to be pressurized. The previous fall, it sprang a leak that shot a small stream of water into the air. As the months went by, we watched it grow steadily bigger. By spring, it had become so substantial that Deborah and I gave it a formal name: the "Jet D'Eau," after the famous water feature we'd once seen on Lake Geneva.

Zack ignored that leak through fall, winter, and spring. He waited until noon on a super-dry, 104-degree day in mid-August to get out his grinding and welding equipment to fix the leak. By then, the grasses surrounding his pond had grown tall and died, parched from the lack of summer rain. He turned off his water supply to repair the leak.

Of course, there were sparks! Of course, the dead grass caught fire! Flames leapt through the wire fencing into our lower olive orchard. With the wind blowing from the southwest, the fire moved quickly toward the oak forest separating our properties. At first, there was smoke, with low flames licking across the dry field. The flames gathered speed in the light wind as they found more fuel. They raced through the woods and up the hill toward our home. Soon, entire mature, drought-dry oak trees were igniting. They seemed to inhale hot air before exploding with a loud whoosh.

This happened on a Tuesday. Ordinarily, Deborah and I would have been in the city, at our desk and clinic jobs. For some reason, that week, we were not. We were in Fiddletown. I was working at my computer, and Deborah was on a conference call when suddenly, I heard her scream. Deborah is not a screamer, so this got my attention. I ran into the living room to see her pointing out the front window. "There's a fire!" she yelled. "And it's headed for our propane tank!"

She ended her call, and we hurriedly outlined an action plan. I called 911 while preparing to evacuate, gathering important stuff—pets, computers, cell phones, insurance files, photos albums—and loading them into the car. Meanwhile, Deborah rounded up hoses and attached them to numerous faucets so we could wet the area around our home.

When the dispatcher answered my call, she said the fire had already been called in. I heard fire engines screaming along the main road—down to Zack's driveway, where the fire had originated. I informed the dispatcher the fire was now racing uphill toward *our* home. The firefighters should come there to battle it from above, rather than chasing it up the hill from below. She said she'd try to relay that information. *Try?!*

I ran from the house, throwing the things I'd gathered into our RAV. Then I realized our front gate was locked! I raced down the driveway to open it as two more fire engines zoomed past with sirens blaring. I sprinted after them in my flip-flops down the hill toward Zack's driveway. By the time I reached our lower gate, the firefighters had already cut the padlock and were slashing through our cross-fencing, so they could drag hoses to where they were needed most. Several hoses had already been rendered useless by pulling them through hot embers, causing them to leak. I urged the crew to send firefighters to our upper gate, so they could fight the flames from there. They agreed to relocate some resources to our house site. I raced back up the steep, hot asphalt, reaching our open gate before them.

By this time, some neighbors had assembled. They'd seen the billowing smoke and rushed over to help any way they could. Deborah had one team spraying the meadow below the house. She had a second crew connecting garden hoses on the east side to cover the meadow between our home and the dense oak forest. She scrambled down our retaining wall to retrieve a sprayer someone had dropped, but something went wrong when she jumped off the last rock onto the short brown grass. She cried out and collapsed. When she rolled over, she was holding her left knee, her face contorted with pain. She couldn't stand, let alone walk. I ran to the barn to fetch our lawn tractor and cart. When I returned, several neighbors helped me lift Deborah into the cart and move her to the house, where we settled her onto the living room sofa with ice packs. On our way back out, I asked one of the paramedics to look in on her.

A plane arrived to drop bright pink fire retardant along the gully between our property and Zack's. A helicopter carrying a huge canvas bucket of water flew so close we could see the pilot's bright blue eyes. Five fire trucks parked on the sloping meadow immediately below our home. A crew of inmates from the Ione prison began cutting a firebreak in the woods with chain saws. They were finally making some progress at containing the fire, preventing it from sweeping further up the hill.

Once the situation was under control, most of the crew began packing up and leaving. Others stayed behind to monitor hotspots. The neighbors helped me get Deborah into the car, so I could drive her to the emergency room in Jackson. She complained an ER visit was a waste of time.

"All they're going to do is take an X-ray, which is useless," she said. "I need an MRI. I'm going to have to go to San Francisco for that." She'd spent her time on the sofa productively, discussing her knee injury with UCSF medical colleagues. She'd also called our health insurance company. She knew the hospital in Jackson was not authorized to do MRIs. She'd already decided to drive to San Francisco to have it done the following day. I insisted she get checked at the local ER, anyway, but the exercise turned out to be as useless as she'd predicted. At least they gave her a pair of crutches.

The next day, I offered to drive her to the city. She insisted on going alone, saying I should stay to take care of Uli and monitor the embers.

The *Ledger Dispatch* ran a story about the fire. It included photos showing Zack's welding equipment propped in the grass and the man himself, watching as the flames raced from his water tank toward our home. I wanted to know exactly what was going through his mind at that moment. I suspected it was something like, "Take that, bitch!"

He'd taken his sweet time to request aid. First, he'd called our local volunteer fire department number, but no one answered the phone there. Maybe he left a message; maybe not. By the time he called 911, things were out of control. Thank God we'd been home and able to spring into action. The fire had come way too close. We'd spend the subsequent few years watching scorched trees fall one by one, thankful the buildings and vineyard had been spared. It could have been worse.

Still, Deborah was seriously injured. She'd fallen in such a way as to shred the cartilage and ligaments in her knee. She'd spend the next six months on crutches, waiting for the swelling to subside enough to allow the needed surgery. After that, she'd spend another six months on crutches and in physical therapy, recovering from the surgery. It was a painful time.

Shortly after Zack started his fire, I learned our neighbor Dodd had accidentally started a grass fire on the other side of our property. *What the hell?*

We'd had some light sprinkles of fall rain, so Dodd decided to start burning the brush piles he'd assembled all summer. He went to the house for a short lunch break and didn't notice when the wind shifted. Conditions were just right to make the embers jump through the wire fencing and spread across the meadow on the north side of our home.

Fortunately, we were not around when this occurred. My nerves were still frayed from the previous fire. I would have freaked out as the flames ignited the dry pasture grass and raced toward our home again.

When Dodd saw smoke, he called Cal Fire immediately, and then he called us to let us know what had happened. He left a very apologetic message about it. Dodd and Mary were our friends; there was no reason to suspect them of malicious mischief.

When we returned to Fiddletown, I took a walk through the charred meadow. I noticed how easily and successfully the firefighters had created a firebreak this time. Using nothing more than ordinary shovels, they had cleared a narrow strip of our pasture, removing short, dry grasses to create a line of bare dirt. The flames had burned up to that line and then stopped, preventing a much bigger disaster.

Sometimes it takes so little to prevent a spark from becoming a wildfire, I marveled. *Too often, we let resentments smolder instead of taking action.*

I was impressed how such a simple strategy could be so effective. Might it be as easy to repair human relationships? Perhaps a minor gesture—like sending a note—could prevent disasters. Without such interventions, sparks can fly and flames spread, causing damage that will take years to repair.

I determined to try to mend my relationship with my neighbor. I vowed to try to hear barking dogs as a natural sound, like howling coyotes, yipping foxes, crowing roosters, or the croaking frogs. Natural country sounds. (This doesn't always work, but sometimes it does.)

I kept waiting for Zack to apologize for the harm he caused us (and especially Deborah), but time ticked by with no call. One day, I met with a fire inspector who told me their investigation concluded the fire had been caused by negligence. In that case, the person who caused it typically would have to reimburse the state for all the expenses associated with suppressing it. He'd heard, however, that one of our local politicians had called someone in the department to request the reimbursement requirement be waived.

"That hardly seems fair," I protested. As we stood talking at the lower gate, a car came down the adjacent driveway. Zack was driving it. It was the first time I'd seen him since the conflagration. I walked toward him, determined to give him a piece of my mind.

"What the hell were you thinking?!" I wanted to ask him, but as soon as he saw the look on my face, he jammed the accelerator and zoomed off, wheels squealing on the asphalt. *Chickenshit,* I thought, as I watched him speed away.

If the state won't make that man pay for what he did because he's a pal of one of our elected officials, I will. I convinced Deborah we should file a claim against his insurance policy for the damage his negligent act caused to our property and to her. Perhaps this had occurred to Zack by then, too. A few days later, he left a message on our answering machine: "Hi, Mara, this is your favorite neighbor calling. I'm sure sorry we had such bad luck with that incident. I'd like to get together with you and try to make amends. Thank you, ma'am."

When I called back, I got his answering machine. I left a message thanking him for calling *(finally).* I told him the worst of it all was Deborah's injury. I said we took comfort knowing no one would do such a thing intentionally. At least Deborah felt that way. The more I thought about it, the more I suspected his destructive act had been deliberate.

We filed a claim against Zack's insurance company for damage to our olive grove, loss of oak forest, and personal injury. The company's response was to cancel Zack's coverage immediately. Since the state had determined the fire had been caused by negligence, no other insurance company would take the risk. Zack had to carry on with his farming operation uninsured.

"That must have him smokin' mad," I said to Deborah.

"Yes," she said, "but let's wait and see what kind of settlement check they send us. I'm not holding my breath about it." Actually, the settlement was generous, but we'd have much preferred the fire had never happened.

THREE NOISY SEASONS

Zack loved running his bulldozer and riding his grader, but his heavy equipment seemed to run nonstop after the settlement. The sound of singing birds, croaking frogs, and chirping crickets was replaced by the roar of engines. Zack was busy rearranging the landscape, topping hills, damming creeks, and burying junk on-site. Why pay disposal fees?

"Zack's at it again," Deborah would sigh whenever she heard his dozer droning.

"Maybe Doris wants him out of the house," I said.

Soon, Zack moved his heavy equipment up the hill and began an aggressive grading program at the Moose Lodge. He and his helpers would run machinery up and down our property line frequently. It was very annoying, which may have been Zack's intent.

Our handyman, Joe, was a member of the Lodge, so we asked him what the grading program was about. He told us the Moose Lodge had gotten into financial trouble. "It's the time of year when property taxes and insurance all come due, and they can't seem to pay the bills. I hear they've taken out a thirty-thousand-dollar loan to stay afloat."

"Who in their right mind would lend that lodge thirty thousand dollars?" I asked. "It gets broken into regularly, and lots of booze and cigarettes disappear each time that happens. I can't see how they'll ever operate in the black." According to Joe, the leadership (Zack and pals) thought the solution to their troubles was to build an RV park to attract people to spend a night or two. More visitors would mean more meal and beverage sales. More profits.

"Don't they recall their conditional use permit restricts camping to fifteen RVs, four weekends per year? That'll never pencil out," I said. "They're not going to pay off a thirty-thousand-dollar loan with so few campers. Not to mention, did they look at the plan the county approved? No camping is allowed within fifty feet of our property line, but that's exactly where they're grading."

"I bet they forgot all about that," Joe said. "I better remind them." He agreed the RV park concept made no sense. "Nobody wants to drive way out here anymore. Everyone stays home watching Netflix. I predict the Lodge will go under within two or three years."

Wouldn't that be a dream come true, I thought, *but it'll never happen in my lifetime.*

Zack also had his helpers trimming the numerous eucalyptus trees that edged the property. He'd use the bulldozer to push the trimmings into a massive pile, which he torched on a particularly arid day. This occurred just as some neighbors we'd invited to dinner arrived at our home. Flames were soon shooting forty or fifty feet into the sky. We could feel the heat blast from our front door. Our guests were alarmed and urged us to call Cal Fire right away. I called the closest station and asked if the Moose Lodge had a permit for this burning. The man said burn permits had been suspended since the arrival of some early fall showers.

"But we've hardly had any rain yet," I said. "It's still parched out here, so dangerous." The man sighed and said he agreed with me. But there was a general perception fire conditions had improved slightly with the first light rain of the season. It was not his decision to make.

"Isn't there some limit on the size of fire one can ignite?" I asked.

"We rely on people to be sensible and use their judgment," the man replied.

"Well, common sense and good judgment are in short supply around here," I said. "Embers are flying everywhere. You should come see this fire for yourself before homes are lost." The man sighed again and hung up. The dozer ran for several more hours as the operator worked to extinguish numerous small fires ignited by embers falling on dry grass. We remained vigilant because he would not be able to get to any fires that might start on our side of the fence. It was not a relaxing evening. Our guests went home early.

A few weeks later, an ungodly wave of relentless, loud booming noises began to occur daily, from dawn until dusk. Zack had dusted off an old propane cannon he'd found in storage. It was the kind sometimes used to repel birds or bears from orchards or vineyards. He set it up in his vineyard, aimed it at our house, and programmed it to go off at the maximum volume and shortest interval possible—about every twenty seconds, from six a.m. until midnight. Over 3,000 booms per day.

Zack got a lot of phone calls from puzzled, angry neighbors. He told them he was doing this to protect his grapes from birds and he was permitted to do it under Right to Farm laws. Someone pointed out birds are only active during the daylight hours.

"Yeah, but deer are nocturnal," he replied. His vineyard was entirely deer fenced, but no one was in the habit of closing the front gate at night. *What a load of hooey,* I thought. No other vineyard in the area deployed such weaponry. Apparently, one farmer in the Shenandoah Valley had tried to use a similar device once, only to find his cannon filled with concrete the next day.

The constant blasts were irritating in the extreme. Neighbors called the sheriff, who came out and agreed it fell into the category of "excessive" noise. A deputy was dispatched to talk with Zack and his wife to persuade them to stop using the cannon to preserve peace in the community. They wouldn't budge.

Deborah and I had our lawyer contact the local DA about the noise pollution. Surely, it would be considered a deliberate disturbance of the peace. Our DA offered these words of comfort: "Around here, people have been known to shoot their neighbors over property disputes. Tell your clients to be careful."

One night, I felt particularly exhausted and went to bed early. I tried to sleep, but the cannon kept booming, three times a minute. I inserted my industrial-grade earplugs, but they only muted the booming a bit. I could feel the percussion of the explosions in my chest as if I were getting CPR. My annoyance increased until I got up, threw some clothes on, jumped into the pickup, and drove through the open gate to Zack's house. I pulled into his circular drive and laid on my truck horn until he staggered out of the house, dressed only in a T-shirt and boxer shorts. *Charming.* I rolled down the window and lambasted him about the noise, saying the cannon made no sense whatsoever.

"Do you actually think using it to save a few pounds or even a ton of grapes is worth pissing off all your neighbors?" I asked. "We all deal with hungry birds. We use mylar tape, scarecrows, fake hawks, whatever it takes. But not earth-shaking booms a couple hundred times an hour! You're disrupting the entire community!"

"Well, you started it!" he snapped angrily, pointing a plump finger straight at me.

He crossed his arms over his beer belly and put on a classic pout—a look I hadn't seen on any male since about fifth grade. *How old are you, anyway?* I wanted to ask, but his statement had struck me speechless. I drove home pondering what he meant, eventually concluding he must still hold a grudge over one phone call I made long ago.

Hasn't that man ever done anything that required forgiveness? Hasn't everyone? No one is perfect!

When I told Deborah about the encounter, she insisted I was imagining things. Zack couldn't possibly be using the cannon as an act of aggression or retaliation aimed squarely at me. She said I was being paranoid. She was sure I must have heard him wrong. I was sure I'd heard him right. I thought she was being far too kind after the suffering that man had caused her.

The calls from angry neighbors continued. The sheriff tried talking with Zack and his wife a few more times. They held their ground, but the sheriff's staff had found some language in the county code suggesting excessive noise should be limited to daylight hours. They'd received so many complaints that the sheriff threatened to take the cannon away entirely if Zack refused to comply with the limitation on hours of operation. After that, at least we could go to bed at night and awaken in the morning without the sound of cannon blasts. I started getting up extra early to sip my coffee and organize my thoughts before the booming shattered my concentration.

Deborah decided if we couldn't eliminate the problem, we'd have to adapt to it. She ordered two sets of Bose noise-canceling earbuds. They worked amazingly well. I could go about my farm chores—picking figs, weeding the garden, and harvesting tomatoes and cucumbers—almost oblivious to the blasts aimed my way frequently. Even the sound of all the grading at the Moose Lodge was blocked by this technological miracle.

Those headphones saved our sanity, but I felt sorry for our neighbors who didn't own them. One neighbor had been diagnosed with PTSD. Being bombarded by cannon booms daily did not help his condition. A local veterinarian, who lived in the hills above Fiddletown, had to tranquilize her dog because the poor thing had become a nervous wreck. Our own dog, Uli, was not himself, either. Some days, he would try to climb the ladder while I was picking figs, needing a cuddle or wanting to have his ears scratched. I felt sorry for him. I wondered how our neighbor Anna, who now lived in a trailer with her five kids near the cannon on Zack's property, was coping with the noise.

While our new earbuds worked well, I resented wearing them. Why should we have to—just to deal with the most unneighborly neighbor on earth? Of course, it was a relief not to hear the damn cannon, but I could no longer hear natural sounds, including the warning shake of a rattlesnake's tail. I could no longer chat with my lifelong partner during most of our waking hours. How was that reasonable?

The booming stopped once the grape harvest was over because the rationale for continuing it disappeared. Blissful, quiet winter ensued, followed by blissfully peaceful spring and early summer. But once the new crop began to ripen, the dreaded cannon resumed.

That summer, I decided to take a different approach. I was not going to let our crazy neighbor drive me out, but I would not stay around wearing ear protection, either. I decided to do some traveling. I realized this would be a perfect time to visit friends in Nova Scotia whom I hadn't seen since graduate school. And why not sign up for that exciting felting course in Umbria? That way, I figured, the very person Zack was aiming to punish would be absent for much of the noisy season. I'd be off traveling while he'd be punishing innocent neighbors, turning the community further against him.

The third summer, when the booms began in early August, I organized the neighbors and asked people how they felt about the noise. To a person, they hated it. Some were unaware of the source. Folks who lived outside our little valley thought it was mining blasts. Once they learned some sort of neighbor vendetta was being acted out, they began to speak out more forcefully about it.

One neighbor, who was about to retire, had planned to rent out a room to help make ends meet. She was livid. "Who on earth will rent a room from me, with that incessant booming happening?" she asked. "They'd have to be crazy—

or deaf. What can I do to help bring this insanity to an end?" I suggested she write a letter to our local elected officials, with copies to the local newspaper, the Planning Commission, the sheriff, the district attorney, our state Representative, and our Congressman. She did. Then she called me.

"Holy cow," she said. "I just looked up your credentials online. You're an expert, among other things, in community conflict resolution. Why did you put me in charge of writing that letter?"

"Because I've learned it's entirely different when you're the one being bullied," I explained. "I feel powerless. The community has to rise up to stop this thing, not me. I'm the target."

She'd written a compelling letter and sent it to all the places I'd suggested and more. She sent copies to our local Grapegrowers' association, the Vintners' group, the Farm Bureau, and even the *Sacramento Bee*. The booming stopped soon afterward, and it never started up again. Hallelujah!

We appreciated our peace and quiet more than ever. We vowed never to take it for granted again. Still, I wondered who actually persuaded Zack to stop. *Perhaps it was our local supervisor,* I thought. Zack was his friend and supporter, but maybe our elected representative was feeling the heat because so many of his constituents were complaining. And the published letter shone a light on the problem publicly. I decided to thank him personally for bringing the racket to an end.

Our neighbor Rick acted as a go-between. He supported our supervisor (whose politics were far from mine), but he also liked me despite my having supported a different candidate. Rick arranged a breakfast meeting in Plymouth, inviting the supervisor to meet me and talk.

I was the first to arrive at the café. A few minutes later, our supervisor pulled up in his black pickup truck and strolled toward the restaurant. (Rick would eventually show up twenty minutes late.) When Brian entered, I stood to greet him. We shook hands and sat at a table near the window.

"I'm going to confess I've always thought of you as a hyper-conservative, redneck asshole," I began.

Brian looked taken aback for a second but quickly grinned and replied: "Well, I've been called a lot worse than that!"

"I want to thank you for putting an end to my neighbor's cannon booming. I truly appreciate it. It was ruining the quality of life for so many people in the valley."

"I'd like to take credit, but it wasn't me," Brian said. "I tried to talk sense into Zack and his wife several times. He is one hard-headed son of a gun. He wasn't gonna stop using his cannon just because I asked him to."

"Well, then, who in the world...?" I asked.

"I'm not certain myself. It might have been some of the old farmers in the Shenandoah Valley who used their influence on him. Peer pressure. I heard they told him: 'Zack, you've punished those ladies long enough!'"

Further confirmation the cannon program was personal and vindictive.

"Well, whoever did it, I am relieved and grateful," I said. "I can be stubborn too. I'm not going to move away—if that's what my neighbor was trying to accomplish. But I admit it's been three unpleasant years."

"Well, I think it's over, and I don't think it'll start again. Zack realized he wasn't having whatever effect he hoped for." *Perhaps he realized his neighbor is as hard-headed as he is.*

The purpose of the meeting had been addressed, but Rick had still not arrived. Brian began explaining his way of thinking about local issues. He railed against government red tape, fees, rules, and regulations. Apparently, he, his father, and his brothers used to go to the El Dorado National Forest and harvest trees at will. Due to federal rules, state legislation, and environmental protection laws, you can't do that anymore. He seemed hellbent on getting the government out of people's lives and gutting such restrictions as much as possible. He seemed to think God created the earth to be plundered for human benefit, and the planet could heal itself, as it always had. He didn't believe climate change was man-made.

His worldview and mine were far apart, but at least we were sitting down and talking. *That's democracy,* I thought. Nonetheless, by the time Rick arrived to dissipate the tension with his jokes, I'd decided to work to elect a different representative next time around. That's democracy, too.

PART FOUR

EXTENDED MACERATION

MOOSE LODGE REDUX

By the summer of 2016, Deborah and I had begun to feel liberated from our career demands. I quit doing paid consulting work, though I became more active in local politics and volunteered for local non-profits working to protect the environment. Deborah cut back to working less than half-time for UCSF, mostly on research projects she could manage remotely. We decided to take the entire month of July off to celebrate. After considering many vacation options, we chose to stay in Fiddletown. The pool project needed our attention, and the summer garden was in full swing. There would be plenty to do—and more time to relax or participate in community events.

I joined a yoga class, a book club, and a local non-profit board. When our neighbor Pam asked if I wanted to be part of her morning walking group, I readily agreed. It was good exercise in beautiful surroundings—and a great way to catch up on neighborhood gossip.

One day, as we enjoyed a walk on North Quartz Mountain Road, Pam wondered aloud what might happen to the local Moose Lodge next.

"What are you talking about?" I asked.

"Didn't Joe tell you? The Lodge got shut down."

"What's that mean?"

"They lost their franchise. They're closed permanently," she said. Calmly. As if this sort of thing happens every day.

No, Joe had not mentioned it. I asked Pam if she was sure this had really happened. She said she had no reason to doubt Joe's word on the matter. He wouldn't make such a thing up, and he was a member of the Lodge, after all.

That place had been a thorn in our sides for decades. There always seemed to be some reason to be annoyed: loud music, raucous behavior, drunken conversations, foul language, illegal camping, booze-fueled road accidents. I had often wished the Lodge would just go away, but I never thought that might actually happen in my lifetime.

Deborah and I often felt we'd made a mistake buying land next door to a Moose Lodge. Particularly this one, which was run by a group of men with little regard for neighbors and a disdain for rules. They despised "newcomers," especially if they came from the San Francisco Bay Area, that bastion of gay and liberal nonsense.

For years, the Lodge was run by our neighbor Zack, the man whose welding and grinding on a hot summer day started a wildfire that burned several acres of our woods and caused Deborah substantial pain and suffering. The same guy who brought us three seasons of boom cannon abuse. Some days I felt surrounded by Zack, sandwiched as we were between his junkyard, boom cannon, and trailer camp downhill and the Lodge uphill.

I returned home from my walk with Pam and told Deborah the news. She insisted we drive over immediately to check it out ourselves. The building was locked, and a notice was posted on the door. It was a letter from Moose International stating that the Lodge had failed to live up to its charter requirements. As a result, as of June 22, it ceased to exist.

"I bet they stopped paying their dues to Moose International," Deborah speculated.

"Joe told us they were having financial problems," I said. "They sure ran the place into the ground in a short time. It's a bit sad, in a way."

"Don't be wacky," Deborah said. "This is fantastic news, but we need to find out what's going to happen next. I wonder if they plan to sell it."

The notice included contact information for a regional representative. I sent him an email expressing concern about security and maintenance issues and asking what Moose International planned to do with the property. I received a reply the following day, confirming the Lodge had been closed permanently and there were no plans to reopen it. The property would be listed for sale by the end of the month. *Wow!*

"Should we put in an offer?" I asked Deborah.

"I think we have to," she said. "What if some motorcycle club takes the place over, or folks who want to use it as a shooting range or a racetrack on weekends?"

We didn't want more headaches from bad neighbors.

"I agree we should try to buy it—as a buffer if nothing else," I said.

We found a local real estate agent named Rose to represent us. As soon as the property was listed, she called to let us know. The price Moose International was asking did not seem unreasonable. Rose said there'd been a few inquiries already. We speculated that one of the adjacent vineyard owners might want it for wine or equipment storage and for the additional well that would come with it. Who else would be interested in that odd piece of property with a utility line cutting across it and a charmless metal building surrounded by deteriorating asphalt?

We wanted to see the inside of the building, but it took Rose more than a week to obtain permission. The local Moose members apparently were not cooperative about cleaning the place or turning in their keys. The selling agent finally had to call a locksmith to change the locks.

Rose had the building opened when we arrived. We stepped into an entry hall dominated by a giant stuffed moose head with shiny glass eyes. A green extension cord hung from its antlers. (We later learned that the Moose members would practice their lassoing skills after a few drinks.) A sign-in sheet and suggestion box sat on a table by the door. A hallway to the left led to the restrooms. Beyond that was a large commercial kitchen where the Ladies of the Moose prepared Sunday brunches and communal dinners and the men oversaw Taco Tuesdays and Friday Fish Fries.

A stainless steel worktable occupied the center of the room, with a sink built into one end. A deep triple sink was mounted along the west wall, next to a commercial dishwasher. Along the north wall was a huge steel stove with two ovens, six gas burners, and a griddle. Next to that was a steam table capable of brewing bacteria in as many as six pots at a time.

"That vent hood is fabulous," Rose pointed out. "It even has built-in sprinklers in case you have a fire."

"Which looks easy to do, with all the grease coating it," Deborah said. Our foster dog was busy inspecting the building for signs of rodents. When she joined us in the kitchen, she began licking the cabinets, which were covered in grease, too. Yuck. I wiped the cobwebs off her ears and shooed her out.

"Look at this," Deborah said. "They left the deep fat fryer, still full of used oil. Looks like it wasn't changed very often."

"Don't open that refrigerator unless you're wearing a gas mask," I warned.

We explored the two rooms along the north wall of the lodge. One housed two upright freezers and numerous pantry shelves. The other was filled with tables, chairs, fans, and some office equipment that had seen better days. Someone had drilled a hole through the wall above the bar and strung a telephone cord at a height of about eight feet clear across the cavernous social room to reach the small office at the other end of the building. "Charming," Rose said, shaking her head in wonder.

"I don't know," Deborah said. "This building looks like one huge project—a negative, rather than an asset, to the raw land value."

"After seeing it, I tend to agree with you," Rose said. "I don't think this property is worth what they're asking for it." She told us she'd called the Planning Department and learned that when the Moose went away, so did their special use permit. This meant the parcel would be restricted to residential and agricultural uses, with no commercial activity allowed.

"So now you have this metal warehouse with a commercial kitchen on a five-acre parcel that can't be used for any commercial purpose. I don't see how anyone could turn this place into a home, so it will be a tough sell." Rose advised us to take our time and think about what we wanted to do. If anyone made an offer, she'd let us know immediately.

So we waited and deliberated. We wondered what we'd do with the property if we bought it. Deborah was inclined to tear down the building and rip up the paving, converting the land to some agricultural use, like grazing sheep or growing more olives or grapes. My mind swirled with ideas about converting the big building to some new use: workshop, warehouse, equipment storage, art studios, gym, community meeting space, or the olive press our county so badly needed. But that would mean investing in improvements.

Rose called a few weeks later to tell us someone had made an offer on the Lodge. She had no information about the amount or terms, but she did know it had been made by a couple who wanted to use the property as their home.

"I don't know who could be charmed by that run-down building," I said, "but I guess we'd better act. But how much should we offer?"

"You have to ask yourself how much you're willing to pay to control what happens next door in the future," Rose advised. "What's your privacy and peace of mind worth to you?"

We worried that whatever we might pay would only be the beginning. That property could be a sinkhole for money—dead trees to remove, fencing and security to add, and we'd have that big facility to maintain or tear down. Neither would be easy or cheap. After further discussion, we decided to offer the current assessed value (about half the asking price). At least that had a certain logic to it.

The following morning, I walked with Pam and told her we'd made an offer on the lodge. I asked her not to tell anyone.

"My lips are sealed!" she said. I told her that someone else had made an offer, and we were dying to know who. Pam said she'd keep her eyes and ears open.

The next day, she sent me a text message: "I found out who made the other offer." I called her right away. Pam had bumped into her neighbors Bev and Leon that morning as she was putting out food for some feral kittens. Bev told Pam that her cousin Collette and her husband, Dennis, had made an offer on the Lodge.

Collette was eager to buy the property to "bring it back into the family." (Their uncle had owned it at one time.) And she wanted to live directly across the street from her only remaining cousin, so they could spend their final years together. Collette and Dennis would graze their horses on the five acres and use the structure as their home.

"Well, that's interesting," Deborah said when I told her what I'd learned. "The best part is that they'll invest in property improvements, and we won't have to. Still, what a challenge to turn that building into a home. It has five toilets and a urinal but no bath or shower. How's that going to work?"

We learned from Rose that Collette and Dennis's bid was substantially higher than ours—close to the full asking price. But ours was an all-cash offer, whereas they wanted Moose International to carry their loan for five years. I couldn't imagine a fraternal organization would agree to that. But they did. We were happy for our new neighbors.

The following weekend, we heard a commotion at the Lodge. We didn't stop gardening to see what was happening, but later I called Bev to ask about it.

"Leon went over there with Dennis and Collette to look around and start making plans," she said. "You wouldn't believe it...a bunch of Moose came and tried to take away things they claimed they'd previously donated. The agent unlocked the door for Collette, and they stormed in. One man was trying to dismantle the outdoor play equipment; another guy was carting out a deep-fat fryer; someone had a TV in his arms. Zack himself was there trying to remove that ten-thousand-gallon water storage tank."

Collette told the mob she and Dennis had an accepted offer on the property, including all fixtures and appliances. If they had a problem with that, they would have to take it up with Moose International.

"Leon was starting to get into it with Zack, so I came over to talk nice to him," Bev said. "After all, he and Doris were once friends of my parents. I said, 'Listen, Zack, you know what the word donate means, don't you? It means to give. As in—I donated fifty bucks to the American Red Cross last year. Do you think I'm going to ask for it back a few years later? No!' He was not happy, but he did back down."

I was so thankful it was not me confronting angry Moose Lodge members. I probably would have called the sheriff or shown up with a shotgun, neither of which would have improved neighbor relations. Bev was exactly the right person to defuse that situation.

MORE CHANGES

A palpable tension hung in the air. There was a growing restlessness and increased factionalism in Amador County and across the nation. I chalked it up to the "silly season" that precedes any important presidential election.

Changes in our immediate neighborhood added to my sense of shifting sands. Our neighbor Dodd developed a rare form of cancer. He and Mary were considering moving to be closer to their children and medical care. Meanwhile, their next door neighbors the Boyers sold their place to people who hoped to clear trees and plant a vineyard. And Al and Russ had broken up. Al moved to Fiddletown permanently, leaving Russ with their urban condo.

New wine tasting rooms seemed to be popping up like mushrooms after a fall rain. We wondered if the area would become a wine-themed Disneyland in the future, with too many visitors causing traffic jams and inflating real estate prices.

The family that bought the property next door to the Thorpes applied to open a new tasting room. Their real estate agent told them they could build a tasting room on the property, but this was not correct. Commercial wine sales would require either a zoning change or a conditional use permit.

The owners applied for a zoning change, but the Planning Commission denied it. Next, they requested a use permit that would allow them to open a tasting room and host numerous events each year with up to 125 guests at a time and outdoor amplified music until 10 p.m. daily. The neighbors were not happy. We wrote letters opposing the plan and showed up at the Planning Commission meeting.

The new owner seemed surprised to encounter opposition. He insisted that permission to open a tasting room and host events was critical to his winery's financial success. At the public hearing, he made an impassioned speech about how he'd always dreamed of establishing a vineyard and building a winery and tasting room to pass on to his kids. He and his wife had made many trips to France and amassed a collection of architectural pieces they envisioned incorporating into a boutique, French Chateau–style tasting room. Deborah and I exchanged a look, thinking French Chateau decor in a tasting room tucked behind the old Moose Lodge and next to a commercial wine production facility seemed a waste of style.

Our Planning Commissioners are firm believers in individual property rights, yet they denied this application. Not because neighbors were concerned about light and glare or traffic and noise. They worried more about the location. To get there, you'd have to drive down an unpaved, shared-easement driveway to a gate set a quarter mile back from the county-maintained road, which was one of the more hazardous in the area.

"I can't imagine people who've been tasting wine or celebrating a wedding all afternoon hitting that narrow, twisting road," one of the commissioners said. The others agreed, resulting in a unanimous 5-0 vote against the permit.

The owner appealed the decision to the Board of Supervisors. Once again, neighbors submitted letters, pleading to consider community impacts and warning about setting dangerous precedents. There was only one small family-run tasting room in the vicinity at that time. It had trouble attracting visitors from the main Shenandoah Valley wine route, where most of the county's tasting rooms lie. Approving another tasting room in this remote location might encourage applications for more. It could launch a modern-day rush to attract tourists and dump tipsy drivers onto our inadequate roadways.

I attended the public hearing, which meant driving six hours round-trip from San Francisco to Jackson to add my three-minute testimony to the record. I arrived at the County building a few minutes before the meeting began. Many people were milling in the hallway. I greeted a few neighbors, then entered the hearing room to claim a chair. Bev, Leon, and Collette were already seated. They waved me over to join them. Collette gave me a copy of the handwritten note she'd sent to the supervisors protesting increased traffic next to the property she and her husband were in the process of buying. Her horses were her "babies." She didn't want them upset by dust and cars and noisy strangers whooping it up at private, loud, outdoor winery events.

"Of course, we're upset about that stupid tasting room proposal, but there's something else bothering me. The county wants us to pay more than twenty-five thousand dollars in school and traffic impact fees—even though our kids are grown up and gone. It's just us two adults and our horses now. We won't affect schools at all. And how can they think we'd affect roads when the Moose used to host hundreds of people for their parties?"

There was more. The county wanted them to bring the forty-year-old metal building up to the current code. They'd have to submit drawings by a professional architect and hire an engineer to do energy calculations "for new 'low-E' windows, whatever that means," Collette said. "It's overwhelming, to be honest."

People began swarming into the room and taking seats. Many wore fluorescent green "YES!" stickers to show their support for the tasting room permit. Collette wondered if the owner had hired professional protestors, but I recognized many of them as local ranchers, grape growers, and winery operators. Apparently, they were upset about recent Planning Commission decisions placing onerous restrictions on new wine tasting rooms. They felt it was time to make their voices heard. They believed agritourism would save our local economy. The more wine tasting rooms, the better.

The meeting opened with the Pledge of Allegiance. Everyone stood. Men covered the "Yes!" stickers over their hearts with their tractor hats while chanting about one nation under God, with liberty and justice for all. The supervisors invited the property owner to speak first. He made an emotional pitch, asking the supervisors to let him realize his dream of a family-owned winery with a French Chateau–style tasting room. I could hear sighs of sympathy from the people seated around me.

Next, the Board asked the consulting engineer to elaborate on the construction plans. The consultant described the proposed tasting room as being located "down in a hollow," where it was unlikely to bother neighbors. He insisted the access road was no worse than others in the county where wine tasting rooms are already located.

Leon was first to jump to the microphone when the hearing opened for public comments. He said he had a long family history in Fiddletown and had returned to enjoy a peaceful retirement there. But now, outsiders were creating raucous businesses to entertain tourists. He complained about the roar of bulldozers clearing trees, the pounding of grape stakes, the industrial truck traffic, and loud winery machinery. To illustrate how readily sound travels in our neighborhood, he turned to the proponent and said, "Your grandkids call you 'Bubba,' don't they?" The man nodded. He then turned to the owner of the small tasting room on our road. "And you have two dogs named Lucy and Moose, right?" That man nodded, too. Leon turned back to the Board and said: "What I want you to consider is this: what about *my* retirement dream and the dreams of my neighbors?" I nodded at Leon as he passed.

Next, a woman sporting a bright green "Yes!" sticker took the microphone. She said she wished people would return to being tolerant. "We need to learn to get along as neighbors, live and let live like we used to do." I saw other people with "Yes!" stickers preparing to stand, so I jumped up to speak next. When I reached the podium, the Board president reminded speakers of time limits and suggested we be brief and get to the point. I said no one was trying to deny the property owner any of his rights. He had the right to clear land and plant vines, and he was doing that. He had the right to build a winemaking facility, and he was doing that, too. But with his parcel's zoning, he did *not* have the right to conduct commercial sales or hold events with outdoor amplified music. If his real estate agent told him he could do these things, shame on the agent. But why punish the neighbors by allowing such activity in an inappropriate location? I thanked the decision-makers for their consideration, though I did not detect one iota of sympathy. None of the supervisors made eye contact with me. It appeared their minds were already made up. I left the podium feeling discouraged.

When I sat down, Bev whispered: "That was very well-spoken!" Then she added: "My cousin is too scared to get up and talk, given this room full of Yes! people. We have to get going anyway to take Leon to his oncology appointment in Sacramento. I'll call you later to find out what happened." They slipped out of the room.

For the next hour, a string of Yes! people spoke passionately in support of the project:

- "You could not meet a nicer family."
- "Why should his dream be denied?"
- "Give the man a break!"
- "These are the sort of people we want in this county, willing to stick their necks out and invest here, start a new business."
- "Allow the man his tasting room so his small operation has a chance to pencil out."

Occasionally, a neighbor would remind the supervisors about the effects such a facility would have on our quiet residential community nearby. But we were outnumbered and portrayed as impediments to progress. The supervisors closed the hearing and approved the new tasting room permit with little discussion, allowing it to operate seven days a week until 10 p.m. daily. The neighbors had felt so sure the request would be denied that we'd failed to ask for limits on hours of operation. We felt smacked down, bulldozed, steamrolled. As the meeting adjourned, the owner and his engineer rushed to shake hands with each supervisor. I spotted Zack and his helpers dressed in khaki shorts, hunting vests, and MAGA hats. They stared at me, smirking in victory. I left feeling nauseated, with the glares of those men burning into my back.

When I told Deborah what had happened, she was shocked and dismayed. We ate dinner watching the depressing national news. Afterward, I drew a bath. I felt coated with all the crap tossed around in the hearing room and wanted to soak it off. As I finished filling the tub, I heard the phone ring. A few minutes later, Deborah tapped on the door.

"That was Rose. The other offer on the Moose Lodge has been withdrawn, so ours is back in play." I closed my eyes and sank beneath the bubbles.

Art by Terryl Tagg

THE FIDDLERS' JAM

We left the city mid-morning Friday and headed for the hills. We were not going to miss the annual Fiddlers' Jam! While we were on the road, Rose called with an update.

"Someone from Moose International called me this morning to say they thought your bid was too low. They asked if I could get you to write another offer. I told them: 'No, that's not how we do things around here. My clients made an offer. You need to accept or reject it, not ask for a different offer.' They agreed reluctantly and said they'd respond early next week."

Deborah and I talked about what might happen next. Collette and Dennis had offered an amount close to the full asking price. Our offer was about half that. Maybe the Moose would try to split the difference.

"Let's not spend a lot of energy speculating," I suggested. "I'd prefer to enjoy the Fiddlers' Jam weekend. We can react to the counteroffer once we have it." Deborah agreed.

Al drove up in his black pickup truck with his new friend, Billy, whom we adored. They'd met at a San Francisco dog park. Billy was quite a bit younger than Al and devilishly handsome yet polite and down to earth. Al had invited Billy to visit Fiddletown, and he'd fallen in love with the place and Al.

Al handed me a carton of eggs. "Something from my girls—for you girls!" he said. We love those free-range chicken eggs as much as Al enjoys our fresh produce. We strolled to the garden to pick a basket of heirloom tomatoes to go.

"Wasn't that public meeting the worst thing we've had to endure in a long time?" Al asked, referring to the recent hearing about the proposed new winery close to us.

"It was awful," I agreed. "I haven't seen county politics up close and personal like that since the Moose first proposed an RV park on our property line."

"I remember those days," Al said, "but this meeting seemed even more deplorable. We never had a chance for reasonable consideration or accommodation. I left feeling strongly that *those* are simply *not* my people. I don't feel part of the community around here at all."

"But you *are* part of this community," I said. "It's just that we seem to have two separate communities living side by side. In fact, this county is a whole lot like America—split down the middle, with people on the two sides so far apart, it's hard to know how to bridge the gap. We have to figure out how to get along as neighbors because if we can't do that here, there's no hope for the country."

"I suppose you're right, but some days I just want to go home to the ranch and pull up my drawbridge," Al said.

"I wanted to speak against the project," Billy added, "but I felt so much hostility from the crowd in the room that day I simply froze up. What I was going to say was simply: 'Growth is fine, but it should happen at a reasonable pace—like cells dividing. When it happens too fast, it's called cancer.' But we could see their decision had already been made, so we decided to go home and feed the animals instead. That would be much more calming and productive."

The following day, I drove to the light rail station in Folsom to pick up Ellenmaeve (or "Ellie"), our Swedish-Irish WWOOFer[*]. She was coming for her third visit to our farm. Ellie was keen to start work the minute she arrived, so we had her sift compost for our raised garden beds. But I told her it was a special weekend and insisted she take time off on Saturday to hear live music in downtown Fiddletown. We'd also been invited to two evening parties. One was an after-Jam event at Rick's home in downtown Fiddletown, and the other was a twenty-fifth-anniversary celebration for Rosebud's, a restaurant in Jackson we supplied with wine and fruit.

"That sounds right fun—a taste of real Americana!" Ellie said.

We usually have WWOOFers stay in our guest cottage, but it was occupied that night, so we put Ellie in our guest room in the main house. We'd agreed to put up the musicians from Sunnyvale who had come to perform at the Fiddlers'

---

[*] The WWOOF program sponsored by World Wide Opportunities on Organic Farms matches people interested in learning about organic farming methods with host farms willing to mentor them. The WWOOFer provides farm help in exchange for room and board and education.

Jam. I introduced myself when they arrived, taking them a bottle of estate-grown zinfandel to enjoy with the sandwiches they'd bought at the Pokerville Market.

"Who's the artist?" the man asked as he admired the paintings in the cottage.

"Me, I guess, if you can call that eclectic stuff art," I said.

The petite woman who'd claimed the rocking chair said: "Of course it's art! The paintings and felted pieces in here are lovely—and inspiring."

"I recognize you," I said. "I've seen you at previous Fiddlers' Jams. I assumed you were local." She was of Asian ancestry, so she stood out in Amador County. There'd been a substantial Chinese presence in the foothills during the Gold Rush, but not now.

"My name's Judy," she said, extending her hand. "I'm not a musician, but my husband is a fiddler. I'm a clogger. I like to dance while he plays. We're retired now, so this is what we do for fun. We've attended quite a few Fiddlers' Jams over the years." They offered to come to the house to play a few songs for us that evening, but our friend Vicki had invited us to her B&B for dinner. I promised to come hear them play at the Jam.

On Saturday morning, we took the dog for a long walk on North Quartz Mountain Road. Ellie was pleased to discover a road that seemed like vintage Amador County: rolling golden hills dotted with oaks and grazing cows, without a grapevine in sight. We saw rabbits, turkeys, deer, and a huge, mellow bull resting in the shade of a heritage oak tree.

"This is such glorious country," Ellie said. "The weather seems perfect all the time. I don't know why anyone would ever want to leave this place." We told her she should come in spring when the hills would be as green as Ireland. Ellie had trouble believing that, as she had only seen Fiddletown in the summer or fall months, when the landscape turns golden due to the lack of rain.

Deborah dropped Ellie and me in town just as the Jam was starting. We could hear Giorgi, a local violin instructor and our own "Fiddler on the Roof," playing the Star-Spangled Banner from the community center roof. We strolled past the traffic barricades and along the row of craft booths dotting Main Street. When we reached the main stage, I saw the couple who'd spent the night in our cottage setting up to play. They waved. As soon as the music began, Judy, dressed in a long gingham dress with a white apron and bonnet, started to clog in front of the stage, hammering the heels of her laced leather boots on the asphalt. As she danced and spun, she tried to get audience members to join her. She'd dance up to one person after another, but most wanted to stay seated. She tried to get me and Ellie involved, but we were not in a dancing mood yet. Judy did succeed in getting some spectators up to dance, including a pack of freckled, giggling boys.

As the sun became warmer and the music louder, I pondered recent events. There were times when I could feel intense ill will emanating from neighbors toward me. Recently, it was for opposing one man's tasting room dream. Other times it was for daring to complain about night noise or light intrusion. Sometimes, it seemed as if simply being a woman, or gay, or from the Bay Area was enough to set people off.

Why can't we get along more harmoniously? I wondered. Americans were more divided than ever. Civil debate seemed impossible as the political atmosphere grew more toxic by the week. I felt a profound uneasiness almost daily.

I spotted Zack's wife, Doris, seated on her walker at the far side of the stage. Anna, her caretaker who lived in one of the trailers on their property, was also there with two of her five kids. Anna waved when she saw me, and I waved back. Doris glanced up but didn't seem to recognize me. She was holding Anna's hand, enjoying the music in the shade of a mature oak tree that grew at the side of the road. Her hair had turned white since I'd last seen her. She reminded me of my grandmother, who'd passed away decades ago. She didn't look very threatening. I wondered if the time had come to extend an olive branch and try to repair relations. Perhaps this was as good a day as any to forget past hostilities and begin a new dialogue.

Judy danced up to me again. This time she stopped clogging and went down on her knee in front of my chair as if she were about to propose marriage. *Oh no,* I thought, *she's going to beg me to get up and dance.* Instead, she grabbed my hands to command my attention.

"You are someone exceptional," she said. "I think of myself as a nice person, but you are a hundred times nicer than me!"

"Oh, stop," I replied. "I'm not that nice a person. I seem to have a fiery streak, an impatience inherited from my dad, and a hot temper that can land me in trouble."

"Nobody's perfect!" she said. "But you are amazing. Last night, I looked carefully at your paintings and wall hangings in the cottage. They told me that you have a huge heart. Truly. Maybe the biggest heart I've ever encountered."

My heart *was* aching at that moment. "Maybe I should see a doctor," I said. "Maybe my heart is enlarged."

"Seriously," she repeated, giving my hands another squeeze. "You are such a loving person. Thank you. Thank you just for being you!" She got up and clogged away toward the stage.

I glanced over and saw Doris still looking directly at me. The air filled with sweet music and a strong dash of goodwill. *It's now or never,* I thought. *Get up and be the extraordinary person Judy believes you are.*

I walked over to Doris. She took my hand and asked me how I'd been.

"Okay..." I replied hesitantly. It was hard to sum up exactly how I'd been lately.

"Are you still commuting from Sacramento?" she asked, perhaps confusing me with someone else.

"No, we drive between San Francisco and Fiddletown," I said, "but not as much as we used to. We've been spending more time here lately."

"Well, that's good. And you've been well? You look well."

"I have been well. Thanks for asking," I said. "I heard you and Zack had a tough winter, though, with bouts of pneumonia and hospitalizations. I hope this year will be easier on you."

"Thanks—what's your name again?" Doris asked.

"Mara," I replied.

"What was that?" she asked again.

"My name is Mara," I repeated. I wondered if I should add that I was her uphill neighbor who tended to lock horns with her husband and complain about noise, but I decided to leave well enough alone. Perhaps later, she'd remember me, or Anna would remind her.

"You're fortunate to have Anna taking care of you," I said, meaning it.

"Oh, I know it!" Doris replied. The sun had shifted. The oak was no longer shading her. Her white hair suddenly seemed ablaze in the sunlight.

"I'm about to leave," I said. "If you like, you can have my chair. It's under the big umbrella over there, right in front of the stage." Doris waved me off, saying that Anna would take care of her. Anna winked at me and nodded in confirmation.

Ellie and I strolled back past the craft booths and entered the clapboard house where musicians waiting for their turn on stage gathered to jam. Someone would start plucking out a tune, and soon, a dozen or more stringed instruments would join in, with a washboard player or two scraping out the rhythm. The old floor planks jumped from the tapping feet.

When we felt ready to head home for lunch, Ellie and I walked to the shuttle bus stop. I asked the driver if he could let us out at the last driveway before the Moose Lodge.

"Sure," he replied, "I do that for you every year, don't I?" I was pleased that he'd recognized me. I dropped five bucks into his tip bucket when he reached our gate.

After lunch, Deborah, Ellie, and I spent a few hours ripping out summer crops, turning garden beds, and planting seeds for winter greens. Ellie worked in shorts and a tank top, reveling in the sun after her summer spent in gloomy Galway. Later, we took a swim and then dressed for the evening parties.

It was a challenge finding the venue for the Rosebud's celebration. The family farm was in the Jackson Valley, on a road passing several old gravel quarries and manzanita thickets. We passed the place several times before noticing pastel balloons tied to a tree next to a dirt access road. We turned in and saw dozens of cars parked in an open field. People were streaming from their vehicles toward a cluster of trees. We could hear live music and smell barbeque.

"I'm so glad you could make it," the hostess said as we approached and introduced our guest. Mary looked radiant—her short light hair framing her smiling, freckled face. She suggested we get a glass of wine and do a quick self-guided farm tour. "I'm going to start our little program in about ten minutes," she said, "and dinner will be served right after that."

We walked into a deer-fenced area containing hundreds of blue food-grade barrels that had been sawed in half, filled with topsoil and manure, and planted with vegetables or flowers. Some of the summer squashes had grown to the size of baseball bats. Ellie couldn't resist pulling a few weeds. We could see the chicken, turkey, and lamb sheds in the distance. When we heard a bell clanging, we joined the crowd gathered beneath the canopy of oaks.

Mary thanked everyone for coming to celebrate Rosebud's twenty-five years in business. She called out several of her restaurant's partner suppliers, including the ladies from DAMAS Vineyards. Mary explained that she and her husband both had government jobs at one time. Mary had been a social worker; Robert maintained a public camping facility.

"I realized from my counseling experience that people were looking for more, something meaningful and nurturing in their lives," she said. "So we decided to quit our jobs, start a farm-to-fork business, and engage in something I like to call 'spiritual commerce' or business with deep, meaningful community connections." They started growing food and opened their restaurant on Main Street in Jackson. Mary thanked her kids (who all helped run the business) and her staff, asking each to stand and take a bow. Her son, the chef, was also a guitar player whose band was warming up to play during dinner.

When the bell clanged, we lined up for the barbeque buffet feast. Deborah and I filled paper plates with ribs, pulled pork, and coleslaw. Ellie was delighted to find some vegan baked beans and raw salads. We shared a table with people who raised goats in the valley.

We returned to Fiddletown, arriving at Rick and Lin's house (on Main Street right next to the Cowboy Church) just as his party was winding down. There was a table loaded with wine bottles, most of which were empty. Another table was covered with potluck dishes that had been savaged by hungry guests. We didn't stay long but had a chance to catch up with a few neighbors we hadn't seen in a while. We learned that two of Armando's daughters had graduated from high school and now were going to college. Soli told us he was planning to retire in a few weeks. His wife had quit nursing to take up her passion, music.

"That's her singing at the keyboard right now," he said proudly. She was singing a Van Morrison tune, and she sang it very well.

As I retired that night, I marveled at how different one Fiddletown day can be from another. One day you can feel spurned, abused, despised, and excluded.

The next day you can feel embraced, valued, and included—basking in the warm companionship of musicians, artists, cooks, neighbors, and friends...fellow travelers on this country road.

Our new neighbor would get to build his winery, but the Lodge was gone. Zack was aging rapidly. He seemed too tired to fight much anymore. The country was in turmoil and the presidential race uncertain.

When I asked Carlos what he thought of all the changes and uncertainties and asked how he thought the election would turn out, he said: "Vamos a ver!" We'll have to wait and see.

REAL PROPERTY

The presidential campaign was turning even uglier, but we paid it little attention because grape harvest was in full swing. Our former winemaker, Tom, came to pick up a load of grapes to take to a new winery in San Francisco where he was working. The facility was only a five-minute walk from his home—but he worried he might be evicted soon. His place was in an industrial warehouse that had been carved into multiple units. He'd built a living space within a former woodworking shop. He loved his living situation; however, it wasn't legal. Tom had no lease or contract—just a verbal agreement renewed annually by telephone with an absentee landlord who lived in Tennessee. He knew he could be evicted on short notice, and if that happened, he wouldn't be able to stay in pricey San Francisco. He was due to talk with the landlord at the end of October to see if he'd extend the deal another year. If not, he'd have to scramble.

"I have a super-sweet deal, but it's a house of cards," Tom said. "I wish I owned a Moose Lodge!" Meanwhile, there were grapes to crush and wine to be made. Tom departed with a couple of tons of our zinfandel, and we delivered the rest to Andis, where Mark would make wine for our label.

Rose phoned as we were finishing Sunday brunch. "I thought you'd want to know I got a call last night from someone who wants to make an offer on the Moose Lodge," she said. "I told them I couldn't help them since I'm already working with a client who's made an offer." Rose told us the interested party was in the wine business and wanted to turn the Moose Lodge into a production facility. Crap. What if they'd also want a tasting room and event center? We didn't want that. Rose said she'd let us know as soon as she heard from Moose International.

She got their call on Monday afternoon. They wanted us to pay $5,000 more than our previous offer. We'd feared they would ask for much more than that. They also made it clear that the sale was "as is." They weren't going to fix anything that might be broken, and the pool table had been promised to the Moose Lodge in Placerville.

"Well, that's a deal-breaker," Deborah quipped. We jumped on the counteroffer and made a date to sign the paperwork. Rose said we'd have to make a small deposit, which she referred to as "earnest money," to open escrow at the time of signing. She also scheduled the well and septic inspections and asked us to meet her for those events.

When we arrived, Rose opened the building. It was obvious people had been inside. The pool table was gone, and most of the folding tables and barstools had been removed. Several ladders, trashcans, and mops were strewn around as if someone had planned to do some tidying up. Rose was indignant. We were not. We hadn't particularly treasured the missing items.

"Less crap to haul to the dump," Deborah said. However, we told Rose we'd also seen people dumping on the property. She insisted we take a walk and inventory the trash. There were some rolls of chain-link fencing, several long pieces of drainpipe, three defunct hot water tanks, and several piles of brush. Rose took photos and said she'd insist the seller clean up the mess before close of escrow. She also called a locksmith she knew and asked him to come over to rekey the locks again. She suggested we have our handyman install a big chain across the driveway entrance to discourage trespassers.

Once the well test was completed, the inspectors let us know they'd found no problems. The flow rate was good. The pump itself was quite old but still worked fine. The septic crew finished their checking and said the system was operating the way it should. They were going to recommend we make only minor repairs that might cost a few hundred bucks. With that, the last box on our escrow checklist could be checked.

We returned to the house to find Joe waiting for us. He'd been on jury duty all week, so he came to see if there was anything pressing we needed him to do. We thought it was time to let him know we were buying the Lodge.

As soon as we mentioned it, Joe blurted out: "I knew that! Leon told me!" Since Joe had been a Moose Lodge member himself, we hoped he might know some essential things, like how to operate the heating and cooling systems.

He thought he could figure it out, no problem. His curiosity was piqued when I mentioned the big safe in the office. He was confident he could weasel the combination out of Zack, something I was sure I could not do.

I mentioned Rose's suggestion about installing a big chain across the driveway. "Don't do that!" he blurted out. "I mean, I'll do whatever you want me to, but you don't own that property yet. If the seller wants to stop vandalism and dumping, they should be putting the chain up, not you. And it needs to be done properly, with bright tape and orange safety cones, so anyone driving up there at dusk won't miss seeing it. If you just put up a chain and someone drives through it, you could be liable for damage to their vehicle."

I conveyed Joe's concerns to Rose, and she agreed with him. She also pointed out that if we installed a chain, someone would have to unlock it once a week to let the trash service in to empty the dumpster. She said she'd talk with the selling agent again. Meanwhile, she reminded us we should be shopping for property insurance.

We'd used the same insurance agent in San Francisco for over thirty-five years. Steve sends us birthday cards every year. When I called him to tell him we were buying a Moose Lodge, his response was: "A what?" I explained. Steve thought owning a big clubhouse was cool and said he'd talk to his underwriters. When he called back a few weeks later, he said no one he knew would insure it. Even though it was zoned for residential and agricultural use, the place was really a big, industrial building in a rural area. Recently, a few costly fires had occurred involving reportedly vacant buildings in remote locations. They were not vacant; they stored explosive materials like fireworks, fertilizers, or fuel. Now, California underwriters were very wary. "Sorry," Steve said.

I called several other agents, requesting a quote on coverage for a former Moose Lodge, but found no takers. I contacted the few insurers in Amador County, figuring they would be more familiar with the area. One even had a former Moose Lodge member on staff. At least they'd be familiar with the building. Even so, they could not find any US company that would insure the property. The only quote they could get at all was from Lloyd's of London, as if we'd purchased the Queen Mary or crown jewels. Lloyd's wanted over $1,600 a year to insure a building that Deborah wasn't even sure she wanted to preserve.

Some days she talked about tearing it down, but I thought the building had intrinsic value. I wasn't sure what its highest and best use might be, but it seemed full of promise. I wanted to preserve it. I was reassured when an insurance estimator said it would cost half a million bucks to replace that building at current labor rates and the cost of materials. Since Lloyd's of London was the only offer, we accepted it.

We approved the well and septic reports and asked Rose if she could speed up the close of escrow. We were eager to install a proper gate, fencing, and security cameras as soon as possible.

On a cool and cloudy Saturday morning, we drove to Jackson to do errands. Our first stop was the title company to sign the final sale documents. Rose told us that escrow would close by mid-week. We shook hands and then hugged before departing.

Once we had legal possession of the property, Joe and I went over together to look around. Zack had told Joe that there might be building plans and other documents hidden in the ceiling above the office. Joe was keen to investigate. He asked me to hold the ladder for him as he lifted the panels in the false ceiling to look for important papers. We did find treasures in the attic. There were some oversized site maps and building plans, as well as a photo album that showed the construction of the Lodge from site grading and pad pouring through framing and finishing. That was useful. The best was a booklet on the Women of the Moose's rights and rituals. A guide to Moose-ette etiquette. There were also piles of mouse and rat poop among boxes of old accounting records, battered sombreros, wicker Easter baskets, and Christmas decorations.

"Better put mouse traps and rat bait on your shopping list," Joe suggested. "And gloves and dust masks."

The empty building felt full of ghosts. There were hints of its former life in the shape of framed awards, ceremonial flagpoles, dinner menus from special events, photo albums, and unsorted snapshots thrown into desk drawers. I pulled out a Polaroid of Zack and Doris presiding over a fancy dinner party. I tacked it to the bulletin board, so they could gaze over the hall a while longer.

Joe opened drawers and cabinets with great curiosity and seemed thrilled when I gave him a paper turkey to decorate his Thanksgiving table. He found an old toolbox behind the bar. I let him keep an old metal level and a few other tools too heavy for me to use. I was anxious to dump the boxes of old financial records straight into the dumpster, but Joe insisted on peering into every envelope in case someone might have hidden cash there.

"Don't look at me like that," he protested. "My own father hid cash in the walls of his house. I was lucky he told me about it on his deathbed. I never would have found it otherwise." Joe noticed there were two safes in the office, a large freestanding one and a smaller one installed in the wall. He broke into the wall safe using only a screwdriver. He found an Allen wrench and a quarter inside. He'd obtained the combination to the big safe from Zack.

"Could be a million dollars or a bunch of booze in there," he said.

"Yeah, right," I scoffed. We held our breath as he tried the combination. It opened on the first try. There was a blue zippered money pouch inside. Joe handed it to me, so I could have the honor of opening it to see what was inside. That pouch held precisely $1.40 in change.

TWO AMERICAS

When our dog, Uli, met a sudden demise from cancer, we were devastated. We felt too heartbroken to get to another dog immediately but fostering seemed a good way to honor his memory. That way, we could enjoy furry cuddles without making a big commitment. We fostered a series of dogs on behalf of NorCal German Shorthaired Pointer Rescue. America was the eighth foster dog Deborah and I invited into our home for periods ranging from two weeks to six months. All of them were GSPs, like our Uli.

America's owner had surrendered her. We knew little about her, except that she'd spent most of her seven years living in a kennel at a hunting club. She arrived with an oozing lump on her jaw the size of a tennis ball. Perhaps the owner feared it was a tumor and didn't want to deal with it. Our vet diagnosed it as a burst salivary duct. Once the fluid was drained, the lump never returned. I wondered if someone had kicked her in the chops.

America was not familiar with indoor living. We had to teach her basic house manners. We practiced her "recall" so she would come to us when we called. We were surprised to learn she needed no tuning up on that. She would turn on a dime whenever we called her name, which made us think she'd probably been trained with a shock collar. Obey or get zapped.

We fed her, took her on long walks, and gave her plenty of loving, but she never became the snuggler our Uli had been. She was under-socialized and didn't fully trust humans, so she remained aloof.

The rescue group asked us to test America with kids and cats, so they could match her with the best permanent home. The cat test was easy because we had a couple of barn cats. The dog did not even notice them during her first week with us. She had no experience navigating stairs, so the cats were safe where they slept in the top of the barn.

On our first trip to San Francisco, America had to learn to use stairs to get to our top-floor Victorian flat and down into the backyard. When we returned to Fiddletown the following week, she immediately applied her newfound skill to zoom up the barn steps, where she tried to ram her shoulders through the cat door. I checked the "NO" box next to the question about cats.

The child test was trickier as most of our neighbors had no children. The only kids around belonged to farmworkers. I didn't want to ask Carlos to expose his three preschoolers to a rescue dog we knew little about. Then I thought of Mark, our winemaker. He and his wife had kids. They also had a Lab mix named Apollo, so we could test America around another dog at the same time. I called Mark and proposed that he bring the family over to meet America.

"We're on!" Mark said without hesitation. "I love spending time with you guys. And using the kids as guinea pigs? Yeah, we do that all the time!" We set a date.

Mark and his wife arrived on a Sunday afternoon with their seven-year-old son (their daughter had another commitment) and Apollo. As soon as they arrived, America turned snarly. We couldn't tell if she was growling at Mark, his son, or the dog—who all exited the same side of the car at once. The family ignored America's growling. They simply didn't believe such a cute, spotty dog could be aggressive. They thought she was bluffing.

Ryan and Apollo ran off to play in the vineyard, and Mark produced a cooler of adult beverages. We brought some snacks to the patio and spent a couple of pleasant hours chatting in the shade of the arbor. America took up a defensive position under the table and would growl whenever Apollo approached. When that happened, he would simply trot off to find Ryan again.

Mark mentioned they'd been thinking about getting another dog to keep Apollo company. They liked America. She was about the same size and weight as Apollo and very cool looking, with her chocolate head and patches. Mark suggested America might be the right fit for their family. Lynn and Ryan nodded their heads in agreement. I pointed out that she snarled at Apollo every time he came near. "Well, yeah, but there hasn't been any real fighting," Mark said. "Apollo is so mellow, nothing bothers him. If America doesn't want to play with him now, he'll try again later. I'm sure they would work things out. That's what dogs do."

They seemed ready to load America into their car and drive home with her. I explained that our rescue group had a multi-step process for placing dogs in permanent homes. The foster home couldn't just hand a dog over to any interested party. It was about finding the best and most suitable home given the dog's unique temperament and needs. Anyone interested in adopting had to fill out an application. Once the application was reviewed, a volunteer would contact them to set up a telephone interview. If that conversation went well and the home seemed like a good match, an in-person meeting would be arranged. And there would have to be a home inspection before the applicant could adopt one of our dogs.

"That sounds more elaborate than the process for adopting a child!" Lynn said. They were disappointed they couldn't take America home but said they'd fill out an application. A few days later, I got a call from our foster coordinator. She'd received their application. "I know these are friends of yours," she said, "but I see some red flags. First, the fencing around their home is incomplete—it doesn't meet our requirement to be a minimum of five feet high and completely secure. I know that might not be possible to do around several acres, but they'd have to make at least some part of their yard GSP-proof. The second thing is more critical. Were you aware they have three indoor cats?"

No, I was not. I called Mark to ask about the cats. He confirmed they had three. "But we don't like them very much," he said.

"What's that got to do with it?" I asked. "Whether you like them or not, I don't think it would be good for a dog to stalk or kill them in front of your kids."

"Well, they have a cat door. I just figured the cats would be out when the dogs were in, and vice versa."

"What about at night?" I asked. "Won't they all want to sleep indoors?"

"Probably," he said, "but then they'd mostly be sleeping."

"America wouldn't sleep a wink with cats in the house. She sees them as prey. She's a hunter. She would hunt them."

I asked why they kept the cats if they weren't fond of them. "They're part of our goofy household; that's just how it is," Mark said. "We're not going to turn them away. We always seem to have a mash-up of personalities and temperaments in our home—humans, dogs, cats, rats, birds, fish, you name it. We've always been able to work out the dynamics somehow." I told Mark to expect a call from a phone screener and prepare to answer hard questions about fences and cats.

The phone call took place a few days later. Mark tried to convince the interviewer that his family could provide a secure space for the dogs and that all the pets would "work things out." Our rescue group wasn't willing to take the risk. Their application was denied.

Mark called me to complain. "Jeez, we are a great home and family here, and we want to rescue a great dog. I can't believe they rejected us! I'm not sure anyone has ever rejected us for any reason until now. Do they think we're hillbillies or something? I know we can provide a good home for America!"

I tried to explain that our rescue group tries to find the best home for each of our dogs, given their particular needs and quirks. I had nothing to do with these decisions and no power to interfere. I suggested he call the foster coordinator to appeal the decision if he wanted to. He did. She held firm on the decision.

In my weekly foster report, I felt obligated to mention that America had growled when Mark's family arrived for a visit. I noted it was hard to tell whom she was growling at, but by then, she'd also snarled at our handyman, Joe, and his young grandson. She seemed to fear males. The rescue decided to have her evaluated by a dog behavioral specialist. Meanwhile, they listed her on the website as not adoptable to any home with kids younger than teens. Ryan's age alone would disqualify Mark's family now.

I took America to her appointment with a behaviorist, who spent two hours evaluating her. She said she'd submit a written report within a week. I asked if she had any immediate recommendations about the type of home that would work best for America.

"Well, I'd say no small children is the right call for now, at least until she's had more socialization." After further thought, she added: "If you ask me what the ideal home for America would look like, I'd say it would be a couple of women with fenced acreage and no kids or other pets."

"Bingo!" I laughed. She knew nothing about my home situation but had hit the nail on the head.

Months went by, but there were no further inquiries from potential adopters, so America stayed on with us. She was an easy dog to care for, undemanding. She was not destructive in any way, except for digging up the odd gopher hole. She sat patiently for her meals. She slept soundly through the night. She entertained herself well outdoors. She became increasingly settled and eventually wormed her way into our hearts. She was a good girl and clearly loved us and our land. How could we send her away?

When we adopted her, the rescue group was delighted, and our friends were happy for us, too. "The way things have been going in this country lately, we're glad you're doing what you can to rescue America," someone quipped.

Ah, yes, that other America. The superpower mired in nasty, divisive politics. If only the "fix" for that mess were as simple as providing food, shelter, and love to a pet.

Even though it was prime election season, there were few campaign signs to be seen in Amador County. Most were for Trump and for the proposed breakaway State of Jefferson. The only Clinton sign I saw said "Hillary for Prisoner." I feared that if we put up a Clinton sign, it would be shot full of bullet holes in short order.

"Well, then how about putting up a sign for 'Anybody but Trump'?" Deborah suggested.

"Aren't we in enough trouble already?" I asked. "We opposed the new tasting room, and now we're buying the Moose Lodge, making a lot of old boys mad. Do we really want to do something else to draw attention or provoke the wrath of our neighbors?"

"Why should one faction control the political dialogue in this county?" she asked. "What kind of a country do we have if only one side feels safe posting signs to support their candidate?"

What kind of country indeed, I wondered, but I didn't see the point of provoking people whose cooperation we might need in the future—for something as simple as figuring out the heating and cooling system at the lodge or how the kitchen fire suppression system worked. I reminded her we shared the same aquifers with some. We weren't living on an island.

In the end, the only sign we posted at the old lodge said: "Private Property, No Trespassing." Even that would be enough to annoy certain parties whose emotions were running raw.

ROLLING

The fall weather was lovely, warm, and dry, but the forecast predicted rain and a substantial temperature drop in the coming week. It was time to address our usual winterizing projects. I was anxious to get things done, not only because of the forecast but also because we had to prepare for the olive harvest soon.

I climbed onto the roof of our caretaker trailer to roll a coat of elastomeric sealant, a task I'd done several times before. The last time it was done, I'd declared I was too old to be running around on rooftops, so we hired Joe's son to do it. I bought a product that was supposed to last seven years. At the time, seven years seemed a long way off. But those years had flown by at warp speed. This time, I decided to pay more to get the formula guaranteed to last twelve years. The next time the roof would need recoating, I'd be seventy-seven years old. Surely, I would not be climbing on rooftops then. If this was to be the last time I'd do this job, I wanted to do it well.

I was meticulous about the prep work. Rust spots had begun to freckle the metal roof, so after pressure washing it, I sprayed on a base coat of a liquid that promised to kill rust. Next, I used four cans of spray enamel to provide extra protection on the worst spots. While congratulating myself for the thorough job I was doing, I felt a wave of fondness for the old trailer. So many memorable events had happened under this roof. And now, it sheltered our helper Carlos, his wife, and their three kids—all born after the couple moved in. I tried to walk softly on the roof, cognizant of Lola and the kids living their rich, quiet life below.

The sky was clear, the sun warm on my back. A gentle breeze was blowing. The view over Gino's vineyard was spectacular. I grew comfortable with the way the trailer roof buckled and creaked under my weight with each step. Some motorcycles roared up the road and turned into the Moose Lodge parking lot. They'd be disappointed to find it shut down, those bottomless Bloody Marys and cheap weekend and holiday brunches no longer available.

When I finished the roof rolling, I cleaned and put away my tools and took America for a walk. On the road to Al's pond, Mark called with somber news. Lynn wanted a divorce! He asked if I could meet him at the winery the next day to talk, but Deborah and I had to go to San Francisco for a few days. I promised to come over when I returned.

I went home and baked cookies in response to my instinct to stockpile some comfort food. I'd been experiencing a sensation of the ground shifting beneath my feet lately, the world tilting strangely through turbulent times. I wondered if spending hours on the supple metal roof had enhanced this sea legs feeling or if it was the ominous news from Mark.

We returned to the foothills Friday evening. On Saturday morning, I made egg salad sandwiches, which I packed along with pickles, chips, and my homemade cookies. I drove the short distance to the winery where Mark worked to join him on his lunch break.

Mark had told Deborah on the phone that he was contemplating a move to Arizona to be closer to his family. Minutes later, he texted me in great excitement, saying he'd just bought a plane ticket to France. I hoped he wasn't flying off the rails. We'd heard rumors that he was drinking heavily.

Mark admitted he'd been drinking too much. "Sometimes, I feel as if I just need to burn Lynn out of my heart," he said, "but I realize that's not an effective way to go about it. I'm trying to do better every day." There was no wine on the lunch table. He'd brought water from the kitchen instead. That seemed a good sign.

Mark was clearly distraught. He said he couldn't stand going home after work. "I used to come home to the laughter of children and the smell of dinner cooking. Now the house is cold and empty. It feels dead. I hate it there." He sought my advice, but I had no experience with these things. He was clearly in pain and wanted to be in a better place, but how? I suggested he go slowly and not make any sudden moves he might regret later. Time does eventually heal. He was young, handsome, and talented. Surely, his future was still bright. I asked about the ticket to France. Mark said one of his summer interns, a young woman from Bordeaux, had invited him to come for a visit.

"Don't worry—it's not romantic," he said in response to my look. "She used to work in a Cognac distillery over there and she's offered to show me around. C'mon—when's the last time I had a real vacation? And when will I ever have another chance to get a personal, guided tour of the Bordeaux region?"

Maybe a holiday break would do him good, I thought, *but to a wine region?*

"What's this talk about a move to Arizona about?" I asked. Mark assured me that he wanted more than anything to stay in Amador County and continue working at the winery he'd played a vital role in establishing. But Arizona was where his parents and sister lived. If he had to move, he'd prefer to be closer to them rather than further away. "Moving away is not my first choice, but lately, I've felt the need to have a Plan B in place, in case I get fired or something."

The first storm of the season arrived, so welcome after the dry foothills summer. The rain began overnight, interrupting our sleep with thunder, lightning, plopping raindrops, and rattling screen doors. We awoke to a silver sky filled with puffy gray clouds stampeding toward the northeast.

I felt excited about the day. I wanted to turn the last batch of summer tomatoes into marinara sauce and make eggplant parmesan with the excess eggplants from our garden. I also planned to dry figs, roast pears, process apples, and do something with all the tomatillos Carlos had given us.

As I tiptoed into the closet to dress, I could hear America rolling around on the rug, scratching her muzzle on the carpet. She followed me to the kitchen and went straight to the door, ready to check the garage for varmints before heading outside to do her business. As I approached to open the door for her, she broke into her happy dance, her tail stub vibrating like a hummingbird. She spun in several quick circles, leaping and prancing with excitement. Then, she sat very still and stared at the door, encouraging me to open it faster.

I better take her for a walk before the rain starts again, I thought. I put the coffee on, got a rain jacket from the hall closet, and reached for my cell phone. When I picked it up, it pinged. There was a new message waiting. I found my glasses and saw that it was from Mark and that he'd left it in the middle of the night: *The winery fired me. Talk tomorrow?*

Oh no, I thought as I replied with a simple "Yes." I fed the barn cats and walked America. When I returned, Deborah was up checking the weather forecast. "It looks like another big storm's coming in," she said. "It's supposed to start soon and rain all afternoon." She asked if I could help her throw seed and straw on some bare spots around the property. I said sure. My kitchen projects could wait.

We finished just as plump raindrops started to fall around us. It wasn't cold yet, but I gathered wood from the garage and lit a fire in our recently cleaned fireplace, anyway. The first fire of the season, to celebrate the first rain of the season. An annual joyous ritual.

I donned an apron and worked in the kitchen for hours, wondering where Mark was, how he was doing, what he was thinking and feeling. I figured he'd call me when he was ready to talk. When he didn't, I tried calling him. No answer. I texted him. No response. Finally, Mark called in the early evening. I was relieved to hear him sounding sober.

"My life is totally collapsing!" he said. He told me he hadn't felt well the previous day. He'd slept poorly, so he'd decided to take a day off. He was trying to nap when his boss showed up at the door with termination papers. After he left, Mark stumbled back to bed, but the doorbell rang again. This time it was a police officer serving him with a restraining order.

He asked for advice, but all I could offer was sympathy. It was stunning to see how quickly a life can unravel. I asked Mark if he wanted me to come over, but his parents were flying in from Arizona in a few hours, so he was busy cleaning house. Good.

Later, I wondered what would become of the wine he was making for us, but I knew this was no time to ask about it. Mark probably didn't know, anyway, since he was no longer employed by the winery where our wine was now resting in barrels. Hopefully.

AN OLIVE HARVEST

My brother Ross and his wife, Audrey, arrived from Canada in early November to help with the olive harvest and to farm- and dog-sit while Deborah and I made a quick trip to the east coast to visit her family. They arrived just in time for dinner.

We had planned to harvest olives that weekend but had to postpone due to rain. At least Ross and Audrey would still be around the following weekend. Deborah and I would be back from our trip by then, and the weather forecast looked promising.

The four of us drove to the Moose Lodge on Sunday morning in a light drizzle. We officially owned the old Lodge now, but someone else (Moose International, I presume) was still paying for the utilities. Ross figured out how to get the TV working and discovered that the cable subscription was still active, too. "You could have one heck of a Super Bowl party in here," he said. "BYO everything—even your own chair to sit on!"

We tackled some much-needed cleaning. America ran around inside the empty lodge hunting critters while we worked. We threw out numerous bins and boxes of stale crackers, broken cups, twisted forks, flattened bottle caps, rattraps, rusty chairs, cracked mirror tiles, used coasters, and stinky ashtrays. We sorted out piles of stuff to send to thrift shops—cups, bowls, vases, seasonal decorations, and lots of empty picture frames. When the dumpster was full, we knocked off and drove to Sutter Creek for a good sit-down lunch.

The weather was clear when Deborah and I returned from our trip. We were able to harvest the olives that weekend with help from Carlos and his friends and relatives. Everyone worked together, and the mood was festive. Carlos coordinated the picking while Lola prepared food for everyone. Ross and Audrey helped manage our olive inspection station at the mouth of a sixteen-foot rental truck, where we sorted the olives to remove any that were bird-pecked, bruised, or damaged by olive fruit flies.

By noon, we'd been standing and working for about five hours, but the crew wanted to finish picking before stopping for lunch. Finally, at around 2 p.m., the job was done. We'd harvested over a ton of olives. Now we could relax and celebrate. I paid the crew while Lola ladled out bowls of spicy pozole, and Carlos passed around ice-cold beers and sodas. Chips and salsa were on the tables, along with bowls of chopped onion and cilantro.

After relaxing a while, the pickers went home. The rest of us cleaned and stored bins, made sure the olives were tied down securely, and parked the truck in the shade of the massive valley oak in front of our house. We reviewed plans for delivering the olives to the mill. I would drive the rental truck with the full bins of olives. Ross and Audrey would follow in our pickup. Deborah had to work, so she would take the car and the dog to San Francisco, where we'd meet up for dinner.

Our olive convoy left Fiddletown at 7 a.m. We drove along freeways, through farm towns, across irrigation canals, and past reservoirs nestled among California's golden hills. We passed several old and tired-looking wineries as we climbed into the hills above Hollister. Then we turned into a valley filled with tidy rows of vines and olive trees. Suddenly, we felt as if we'd arrived in Italy. The Pietra Santa winery and mill was stunning, with its elegant brick walls, stained glass windows, and welcoming rows of palm trees lining the driveway.

We arrived just in time for our 11 a.m. milling appointment. The mill master told us the oil would be ready to take away around 2 p.m., so we drove back to Hollister to find a restaurant.

After lunch, we retraced our route into the hills to pick up our estate-grown, extra virgin, cold-pressed olive oil. I couldn't resist running my finger under the spigot delivering the unfiltered, vibrant green liquid into our five-gallon containers. It was heavenly, very peppery, and lively. "It tastes like an angry green goddess," I declared.

We left Hollister around 2:30 p.m. with 44 gallons of extra virgin olive oil. (The yield varies year to year from our hundred trees. It can range from 30 to 75 gallons, lower in drought years.) This was precious *Olio Nuevo*, as Italians call freshly pressed olive oil, which is cloudy, pungent, and intensely delicious. After a month or two, the oil settles and clarifies. It remains delicious and excellent for a year or two. But it mellows over time, becoming more subtle or subdued, no longer as vivacious, peppery, and thrilling as Olio Nuevo.

We'd repacked everything (bins, olive oil, bracing boards, tie-downs, and tools) into the small pickup truck so I could return the rental truck in Gilroy. After that, we were back on the US 101 freeway heading north—just in time to experience Silicon Valley rush hour traffic. I reminded myself that, as much as we liked the Pietra Santa facility, we had to find a mill closer to Fiddletown for future harvests.

We reached San Francisco around 5:30 p.m., too tired to deal with unloading the truck. We parked it in the garage, safe for the night. We tidied up and walked out to a neighborhood restaurant for dinner. Afterward, Ross and Audrey went straight to bed, as they'd arranged for a 4 a.m. taxi to take them to the airport for their flight home. Deborah and I stayed up sorting mail and monitoring news on the kitchen TV. We were stunned to witness the election returns as Donald Trump became the next president of the United States.

Mark called around noon the following morning. I thought he was calling to discuss the election, but no. "I'm going into rehab!" he announced. Apparently, someone in the wine community had confronted him and had the hard talk, telling Mark it was time to get into a rehab program. Mark agreed he needed help. He'd visited a reputable facility in Napa and had been accepted to start the following week.

"I wanted to let you know I'm about to disappear. Once I go in, I can't have any communication with the outside world for a while. I didn't want you wondering what happened to me," Mark said. "It's not cheap, but I know I need to do this."

"I'm proud of you!" I said. I envied him the opportunity to unplug from the world for a month or two. Deborah and I decided a news blackout would do us good, too. We'd focus on farming, exercise, creative writing, and studying Spanish instead of obsessing over the news.

SECURITY

When we returned to Fiddletown, Joe reported that he'd seen more people driving up to the old Moose Lodge, despite the "No Trespassing" signs he'd posted. That was the last straw for him. He devised an ingenious security system consisting of a long hunk of yellow rope and an upturned half-ton wooden pear crate he'd found in his barn. The rope was tied to oak trees on either side of the driveway and attached to the crate with a simple wire twist. To enter, all you had to do was release the rope, lift it over the top of the box, and drop it to the ground. Then you could drive right over it without having to move the container. It was so Joe. Simple, yet ingenious. Now, people had to stop at the barricade and read the signs. That seemed to discourage further trespassing.

"Jeez, maybe we can skip installing a gate and fencing," I said to Deborah. "Our goal was to keep people out, and Joe's contraption does the trick. What more could we want?" She shot me a look. "Okay, it is a bit makeshift," I admitted.

"Weren't we supposed to get bids from some gate installers and fencing companies?" Deborah asked. I'd called several of them, only to learn they had jobs booked into the New Year. And neither of the two I'd met with on-site had provided a quote. I called and learned one had a family emergency and the other had gone out of business abruptly.

I asked Joe if he had any spare time for fence work. He said he was too busy and didn't have anyone to help him stretch wire. He agreed to install a metal gate across the driveway, but said we'd have to find someone else to install the wire fencing. At least with a proper gate in place, people would be discouraged from motoring up the paved driveway.

I was taking measurements for the gate when Carlos drove past on his way home from work. He stopped to chat when he saw me. He told me that work for his brothers and friends was slow. Usually, grape harvesting lasts through November, and then there is a short holiday lull before vineyard pruning starts in January. However, in this drought year, the harvest came early and was over faster than usual. He suggested this would be a good time for any new projects we might have in mind, like clearing land or planting fruit trees or grapevines. If we had any work to do, he knew men who were available to do it.

"Do they know how to install fencing?" I asked.

"Of course!" Carlos replied. "Ranch fencing, barbed wire fencing, deer fencing—we can do it all." We hired Carlos and his friends to install posts and a thousand feet of fencing to connect the new gate to the ranch fencing that enclosed the other three sides of the property.

Thanksgiving came and went. The weather turned cold, and then it began to rain in earnest. A series of storms rolled through Amador County, each dropping three or four inches of rain. Once the red earth was saturated, the ponds rose, and the seasonal creeks surged to life. The fruit and nut trees clung to their colorful leaves, determined to wait for the first frost before letting them go. The men had finished installing metal posts along the road front, but it was too wet to stretch rolled wire. That would have to wait until the weather dried and the concrete set firmly.

We returned our attention to cleaning the lodge. I was itching to scrub sticky surfaces but discovered we had no running water. We checked shutoff valves and called Joe for advice. He guessed our pump had burned out. *Yikes.*

I called several well companies, but they were all busy working on other emergencies. Finally, one company sent someone out to look at the problem. It turned out to be the very guy who, twenty-nine years earlier, had installed the well at the lodge with the help of his cousin. He showed me their names written in permanent marker inside the control panel. He identified a short. "It might be in the control panel but could be in the pump itself." He told me the average life of a well pump is eight years, and this one had been running for almost thirty years.

I was not optimistic. The lodge sometimes hosted 250 guests for dinner parties. That meant using the pump heavily, with all the necessary dishwashing and toilet flushing. I feared we were looking at a big repair expense.

The electrician removed the old control box and installed a new one he had in his truck. When he flipped the breaker, the system came to life. We gave each other a surprised look. We could hear water running and see the gauge on the pressure tank ticking up. "Looks like you dodged a bullet," he said. He charged me $300 for the part, plus a small labor fee. I thanked him for fixing the problem, reflecting on the irony of standing in a former Moose Lodge with its long bar and some stools still in place but nary a drink to offer the man.

I bumped into Leon at the post office later that day. I asked if Collette and Dennis had any second thoughts about withdrawing their offer on the Moose Lodge. He rolled his eyes and groaned. "I was real unhappy about that," he said. "I spent a lot of my own time visiting county offices to research that property. I made drawings about how you could build it out to turn it into a home. Collette didn't tell me they'd withdrawn their offer. She told Bev, but not me. Sometimes when I get mad, I just open my mouth, and that F-word flies right out." He asked if we owned it now. I confirmed that we did.

"I'd like to have had a chance to buy it myself," he said, his dark brown eyes reflecting his disappointment. "We could've sold our place and bought that lodge. I could've made it into my dream home, and then I wouldn't have to be building more workshop space. I'd have it all right there under one roof. I'd be sittin' up on top of that hill in my big new palace, with a commercial kitchen and scads of workshop and storage space..." he said wistfully. I asked how he could downsize from his twenty-three acres to a five-acre parcel. "I don't need more'n five," he said, noting that much of his land was unusable oak forest or hilly terrain. I mentioned something about the lodge property being a tad ugly, with that utility corridor slung across the middle and several defunct coolers abandoned on the roof of the building.

"It's not ugly to me!" Leon said, looking surprised I might think so.

Our friend Tom called to ask if, by any chance, he might be able to store some belongings at the lodge if he had to. His dicey housing situation had become even shakier, and he felt the need to plan how to respond if he were asked to move his stuff out on short notice. I said that would probably be okay;

we had lots of space in the building. I asked where he would live if his current arrangement fell apart.

"I should think about that more than I do," he said. "I need a Plan B. There's no way I can afford to stay in the Bay Area if that happens. To be honest, it would make sense to buy a place like your Moose Lodge. That could be ideal for me—part home, part workshop, and part winemaking facility. I could continue my hobbies, minimize my expenses, and maybe even earn some income from custom crush work, too."

Tom is a superb winemaker and a good friend. We didn't think he could afford to buy the lodge but leasing it to him might offer a solution to our annual winemaking challenges, as well as meeting his needs. It would be lovely to have him as a neighbor, but it would be complicated to make the Moose Lodge habitable. We'd encounter the same issues that Collette and Dennis had: impact fees and code requirements, as well as property taxes, insurance, and utility bills.

Tom and Leon weren't the only ones dreaming about potential uses for the old lodge. Once word of our buying it got out, people came forward with all sorts of ideas about what to do with it. Someone inquired about opening a restaurant there. The Fiddletown non-denominational church asked about renting it for Sunday services and special events. Some local growers were eyeing the commercial kitchen as a place to prepare value-added products like jams, pies, pesto, or tapenade to sell at local farmers' markets. Several neighbors were kicking themselves for not snagging the building for additional wine production space or temperature-controlled storage.

Our friend Vicki waved off all such ideas. "Do NOT even think about involving ANY other persons in whatever you do over there," she advised. "I assure you, you'll regret it if you do. When it comes to land, more is better. It will enhance your property value in ways you can't even imagine. The point is to control it yourselves. You don't need to do *anything* with it. It's a perfect buffer as is. That's what you want it for, nothing more!"

I thought Vicki was right, but that didn't prevent ideas from floating around in my head. The lodge had potential. It could become a music venue, art studios, a community supper hall, indoor food and craft fair space, farmworker housing, an emergency evacuation center, a yoga studio, a kennel for rescue dogs, or a marshaling area for firefighting crews. It could house a community radio station, a major composting operation, an after-school tutoring program. Such ideas would sometimes keep me awake until I'd recall Vicki's advice. It was a perfect buffer. That was good enough for now.

BACK TO BUSINESS

Deborah and I made an appointment to see the general manager at the winery where Mark had worked. We needed to discuss our orphaned zinfandel—the wine Mark was making for us when he got fired. It felt odd entering the familiar winery knowing he was no longer there.

Mark was not one to sweat the details, so we had no written contract. Nor did we have a receipt to prove we'd delivered over a ton of zinfandel to the winery three months earlier. I knew we had because I had driven the truck and trailer there myself. We weren't sure if the manager even knew our zinfandel was in their winery. What if the answer was no? Or, what if the answer was yes, but she insisted we remove it immediately? Where would we take it? How would we finish and bottle it?

The conversation could have been very awkward, but it was not. Jenae began by expressing her and the owners' sincere best wishes for Mark, his recovery efforts, and future success. We asked if they'd hired a new winemaker. She said no; they'd decided to try a new approach instead. They'd hired consulting winemakers from Napa to visit and give them advice periodically. Based on their recommendations, the winery would be purchasing a lot of new oak barrels that year.

Jenae said she was aware of our wine project, although there was scant paperwork on it. She'd found an agreement we'd signed the first year we made wine there, but that had expired. We confirmed that we had not updated it annually, as we should have. All we had was a verbal agreement with our friend Mark. As for custom winemaking costs, Mark told us he'd talked to his boss and got us a really good deal, but he never wrote down exactly what that deal was. Now I couldn't recall the estimate he'd given us.

We hoped Mark had pressed our wine and put it into barrels somewhere in the winery. Jenae suggested we look for it. She led us into the chilled warehouse where Mark's former assistant was busy topping off barrels. He pointed to where he thought he had seen some barrels marked "DAMAS." We were expecting to find two, but there were three. Mark had always treated us generously. "Rarely does any grape delivery yield a perfect round number of full barrels," he'd said. "There are always partial barrels of wine around. For some clients, I round up; for others, I round down. And if I have a leftover bit of something outstanding, I throw it into the DAMAS lot."

Jenae asked if we'd like to taste our wine. Yes, please. She grabbed some glasses and a wine thief, and we sipped samples from two of the three barrels. We recognized the unique character of our own grapes in both. One was a bit livelier and fruitier than the other, but both were sound and showed promise. Whew.

We asked if it might be possible to keep our wine at their facility until it was ready to bottle. Jenae said she didn't see why not. We shook hands on that. I promised to look for any emails I'd received from Mark about our wine and share them with her. Jenae said she would do the same. She promised to send samples of our wine to their lab for analysis. She also assured us their cellar assistant would take care of racking, barrel topping, chemical adjustments, or anything else that might be needed.

"Well, that's a relief," Deborah said as we drove home, echoing my thoughts precisely. Our wine was safe; the winery would take care of it. One less thing to worry about.

By the time we arrived home, Jenae had already forwarded some of Mark's handwritten notes. There was a single page documenting the delivery time, date, and weight of grapes received from DAMAS Vineyards. A series of entries on subsequent dates noted readings on the wine's temperature, Brix, and pH during fermentation. He'd recorded the name and quantity of yeast he'd used to inoculate the must and the date he'd pressed and put the wine into barrels. At the top of the sheet, he'd scratched a cost per case number that did indeed seem like a super good deal. It was just over half of what we'd previously paid for custom winemaking services. We figured the scribbled note was not worth much, and it hardly seemed fair to the winery. But now we felt confident we could come to a reasonable agreement on winemaking fees. There would be bottling expenses to pay, of course. At least we had a basis for estimating our costs for this vintage. Having pleasant people to work with was a bonus.

FELIZ NAVIDAD

A few days before Christmas, Deborah and I were sweeping debris off the driveway in front of the lodge. "What's wrong with people?" Deborah fumed. She was cursing the neighbor who was clearing land for a new vineyard. The grading work had resulted in a large amount of eroded topsoil being deposited across the entrance. As we wielded shovels and brooms, our neighbor Armando drove by in his pickup truck. He pulled over when he saw us.

"Hola! Feliz Navidad," he said as he strode toward us, wearing his signature tan fedora. Armando had heard we'd bought the old Moose Lodge. He asked what we planned to do with the equipment in the children's play area behind the smoking porch. We told him Zack had asked if he could have it back, claiming he'd donated it years ago. We agreed because we didn't want the equipment, anyway. It looked like a maintenance headache and a liability to us. Some swings were broken, and some timbers seemed full of splinters that could hurt kids.

"We're happy to have Zack haul it away," Deborah said. "I guess he intends to set it up at his place, so Anna's kids can use it."

"Actually, Zack asked for the equipment on behalf of me," Armando said. "Since Anna does not own her land, as I do, we will put the playground at my house. Anna's kids visit their cousins often, so they can use it whenever they're at our house."

"Are you sure you aren't planning to have more *bambinos* of your own?" I teased, knowing the answer to that question was NO. Armando and his wife already had four daughters when they decided to try—just one more time—for the boy Armando had always wanted. Instead, they had a fifth girl, who now was almost school-aged.

Armando threw his head back and laughed, his green eyes sparkling with mischief. "Well, I would like to have more kids, but my wife—she's too old now."

Armando asked if he could remove the equipment sometime when Anna's oldest boys were available to help. We said that would be fine and asked when that might be. He said he wasn't sure because he was thinking about taking his family to Mexico for a Christmas visit with their relatives. If they went, he'd be in touch as soon as they returned. We wished him a Merry Christmas.

The next morning, when Deborah and I were having coffee and checking messages, there was a knock on our front door. It was Armando, holding out a package wrapped in aluminum foil. "Josefina said to give you this," he said. "It's some homemade tamales—two kinds—and a jar of her tomatillo salsa I know you like." We'd tasted that salsa at a recent party in downtown Fiddletown. I told Josefina that it was the best salsa I'd ever tasted, and I meant it.

"How cool is that?" Deborah asked, sniffing the tamales after Armando departed. "We better invite someone over for supper. There's too much here for two people."

I asked Carlos if he was available to help clean the lodge now that the water was back on. He said yes, it was a perfect time for extra work. The vineyards were quiet, and it would get him out of the house, where the kids were bouncing with excitement about Santa coming. I asked him to clean the pantry first because we planned to donate one of its two freezers to the Fiddletown Community Center. We were also anxious to move some clutter out of our garage (such as cases of new wine and olive oil bottles) to the spacious pantry shelves once they were clean. I worked in the kitchen because I couldn't stand to look at the grimy handprints on the refrigerator, stove, and work surfaces another minute.

Carlos was listening to music as he worked. "This is great work for me—so relaxing," he said. I could see how indoor cleaning would be much easier than the labor he typically does outdoors, like picking fruit for long hours in the sun or building rock walls on cold, wet days.

Carlos asked if Deborah and I planned to stay in Fiddletown for Christmas. I said yes, we were planning a quiet Christmas for a change—cooking, reading by the fire, and taking America for long walks. Most years in the past, we'd traveled east to be with relatives, but this year we wanted to stay home and enjoy a quiet holiday.

"You two will be alone on Christmas Day?" he asked. Yes, I said. He looked stricken with concern. Being without extended family at Christmas was incomprehensible.

"Don't worry! We'll be fine. We like it this way. We look forward to it," I insisted.

I'm sure it was hard for him to imagine how we could enjoy the holiday alone. Carlos had his wife, kids, and numerous siblings living nearby—each married, with spouses and children, nephews and nieces, and in-laws. Large parts of the extended family would get together all day on Christmas Eve and Christmas Day. I asked if they would roast a turkey. No, he said. Their feast would involve taquitos, tamales, menudo, and pozole. He said he would drop off a plate of prepared food for us on Christmas morning. I thanked him but said there was no need for that. He'd be busy with his family, and we had many holiday treats in store for ourselves. When I told him friends were coming from the Bay Area to spend New Year's Eve and New Year's Day with us, his look of concern diminished somewhat.

I offered to invite his kids to our house to decorate cookies if he and Lola needed time to wrap presents or cook without children underfoot. "That's okay," he said. "We're going to be busy all the time. So many things are planned." He looked a bit overwhelmed by all those things—shopping, cooking, parties, and kids' activities.

I was pleased to take a break from the typical "Merry Excess" this year. But it was also touching to see how the Mexican families living around us joined together for holiday celebrations and wouldn't have it any other way.

PAEAN TO A DUMPSTER

How many love songs, country and western tunes, and poems essentially say: "I didn't know what you meant to me until you were gone"? Scads.

Deborah and I had worked at the Moose Lodge through the weekend, clearing out more trash—expired packs of tartar sauce, empty cans and bottles, and many more boxes of obsolete paperwork. We took a break when the dumpster was half-filled. We wanted to leave room for more trash we planned to bring from our house and barn.

The big trash truck came to empty the dumpster every Wednesday morning, so we returned on Tuesday afternoon to fill it to the top. We'd loaded our pickup with broken lawn chairs, bent fenceposts, cracked plastic buckets, and kitchen trash. I pulled up in front of the lodge and backed up to facilitate unloading. But...but...the dumpster...was no longer there! It was GONE!

"Oh no," I wailed, looking at the naked concrete pad.

"Holy cow," Deborah said. We sat for several moments in stunned silence, staring at the blank spot, hoping the dumpster might miraculously reappear. I called Joe to see if he knew anything about it.

"You mean you weren't paying for the service?" he asked. "I thought you were!" Nope. We felt like idiots. *Of course*, Moose International would eventually realize they were paying for services no longer needed at a property they'd sold. I'd taken the trouble to switch the electric bill to my name but hoped the trash service was billed quarterly. That way, we'd have more time to spend with that lovely dumpster, filling it weekly with crap from the lodge, before our satisfying and productive relationship would come to an end.

"If only we'd had it another month, or even a couple more weeks, we might have had the junk cleared out of the attic and storage rooms," I said. I was nostalgic about that green dumpster sitting loyally near the back door, ever ready to have its black plastic covers thrown back to accept anything we threw into it without judgment. It would swallow whatever unsightly, rusted, busted, dusty, or rotten crap we found to throw into it. Having a personal, private dumpster was a surprising source of inexplicable joy. It had put an unexpected spring in my step.

Weeks earlier, we'd had a locksmith come to the lodge to rekey all the doors (again) to prevent unauthorized entry. I asked if he could remove the padlock that someone had put on the dumpster. He said sure—and he'd do it for no charge if he could keep the lock. That way, he could rekey it and sell it to someone else.

"Go for it," I said without a moment's hesitation. When Deborah and I returned a few days later, we'd found the unlocked dumpster loaded with someone else's trash, including old pants and moldy bread. We immediately slapped our own padlock on it. After all, it was on our property. But now it was gone altogether, padlock and all.

With heavy hearts, we unloaded our trash next to the concrete pad where the dumpster once stood. We'd have to figure out another way to have it hauled away. The mouse-infested sofa in the smoking annex would also have to go. I had no idea how we'd manage that.

We decorated a real Christmas tree at home, though there were not many gifts to put under it. We didn't care. After all, we'd just acquired five acres of land with a big clubhouse. We'd installed fencing, hung a new gate, fixed the well, and bought insurance. Who needed anything more?

On Christmas morning, Deborah slept in as America and I took a walk around the property. I made a note to install a gate in the deer fence we'd built between our original acreage and the lodge, so we could add five more acres to our daily dog walk circuit.

We made biscuits with ham and scrambled eggs for breakfast and then opened the few gifts under the tree—mostly novels and cookbooks and some sweets from family members. We spent a leisurely time sipping coffee and reading new books by the fire.

Finally, we dipped into our Christmas stockings, where Santa usually puts practical stuff like lip balm, notepads, and warm socks. Mine had a folded piece of paper deep down in the toe. I opened it and saw a printed email confirmation from Aces, our local trash company. It indicated a two-yard dumpster would be delivered to the former Moose Lodge on December 27, when weekly service would resume until canceled.

"Hallelujah!" I shouted, startling America into barking as I did an exuberant happy dance around the living room. "That Santa sure knows the way to a girl's heart!"

We didn't keep the dumpster forever, just long enough to empty the lodge of useless stuff and to clean out our barn, as well. One week we replaced it with an even bigger dumpster, about the size of a shipping container. Our neighbor Javier came over with his forklift to help us load big items like the mouse-infested sofa and a broken Xerox machine into it. I enjoyed that dumpster while we had it, but at the end, I finally felt ready to let it go. Spring was upon us and there was plenty to do in the vineyard and gardens.

RITES OF PASSAGE

Carlos and Lola's youngest child was about to turn three years old. In Mexican culture, a Tres Años party is a big deal. It is held to celebrate a child's survival of the perilous early years (due to historically high infant mortality rates) and to welcome the young boy or girl into the community. The parents asked if they could hold a Tres Años party at the lodge. We said yes.

They invited relatives and friends. Lola hand-cut a gazillion colorful paper decorations. She taped them to string and hung them to flutter above the gathered guests. The cooking went on for days to prepare an elaborate buffet. And of course, there was a special cake with lots of white icing.

It was a sweet party. Children ran around the cavernous hall playing tag while teens clustered around the dartboard next to the bar. Adults sat at tables sharing conversation, sodas, and beer while enjoying tacos the men prepared on an outdoor grill. The young guest of honor, dressed in a traditional charro outfit complete with an oversized sombrero, had a meltdown from all the attention and had to be taken home for a nap.

That party was so successful that our neighbor Javier asked if he could hold a similar event at the lodge to honor his three daughters. He and his wife had worked so hard that they never found time to throw parties for their kids. No birthday parties, no confirmation parties, no Quinceañeras. Their oldest daughter had just married and moved to Modesto. Javier wanted one celebration to acknowledge all the rites of passage for all three of his girls at once. We said "Sí" to another excellent community party.

One subsequent event got a bit out of hand, resulting in a noise complaint from a neighbor. We made new rules: drinking and conversation should be confined indoors; events must end by 9 p.m.; Carlos would be present at any parties involving his friends or relatives; one more noise complaint from neighbors, and there would be no more parties at all. When a group of teens from Plymouth asked if they could use the lodge for an unchaperoned graduation party, we said no.

When the mid-term elections rolled around in 2018, I got involved in the local supervisors' race. I hosted some meetings at the lodge aimed at identifying a viable candidate who might beat the incumbent. When a woman named Andrea stepped forward, we rallied to support her. She was a mom and a businesswoman who'd raised her kids in the county, and she was an active volunteer for local emergency service providers. I offered to help with her campaign.

We had to gather enough signatures to get Andrea's name on the ballot. I first knocked on the doors of friends, then neighbors whose political instincts I thought were aligned with mine. Needing more signatures, I drove to Bev and Leon's place. When I explained my cause, Leon replied, "But you Democrats always want to give everything away!" I glanced at his hat rack: MAGA, Support NRA. Oops. After some friendly banter, Leon agreed to sign the petition, making it clear this was to support the democratic process. He would help me get this name on the ballot as long as I didn't expect him to vote for the woman. Fair enough.

Deborah and I made the lodge available for campaign meetings and agreed to host a fundraising dinner there. An event committee took care of much of the planning. Most people attending would be folks we knew and liked—fellow blues in a predominately red county. There would be good food, fine wine, live music, and a silent auction.

We decided to spruce up the building for the big event. We'd already steam-cleaned the kitchen and painted the interior, but the main hall had as much ambience as a school cafeteria. We hired a company from Sacramento to install a new epoxy floor, which made the place sparkle. Now it looked more inviting, like a respectable community center. Volunteers set the rented tables and festooned the place with red, white, and blue flags and streamers.

The day before the event, our neighbor Pam, who'd bought a ticket, informed me she'd be unable to come. "It's a good cause. I don't want a refund. But you should let someone else take my place," she said. "Perhaps someone who might not be able to afford to buy a ticket." I called our neighbor Anna.

"I'd like to come," she said, "but it depends on how things go here." She was providing elder care to Zack and his wife, preparing meals and driving them to appointments. Doris needed to be driven to Sacramento three times a week for dialysis, and Zack recently had been in the hospital. He was home now but not doing well. She'd attend if she could but couldn't promise.

I walked America around the vineyard the morning of the event before heading to the lodge for a final check. My phone vibrated with a message from Anna: "I can't attend the dinner tonight. Zack died this morning. My priority is being with Doris now."

I stopped in my tracks and took a slow breath, feeling my chest expand and my heart thump. A surge of emotions washed through me. I felt the universe tilt. Things would be different now. But how? And what could it mean that the man who'd presided over the lodge for years died on the day of this particular event? A fundraiser for a liberal candidate who, unlike Zack and his pals, believed in representing everyone, regardless of race, religion, or beliefs.

I looked heavenward and saw dark clouds roiling across the sky. I instinctively leaned toward a cypress tree for protection, as if a lightning bolt might shoot from those clouds straight at me. As if Zack could carry on his campaign of intimidation from another world. His death seemed momentous. It would alter my neighborhood, my life. But there was no time to ponder all that. There was too much to do to prepare for the dinner, which would cater to a diverse crowd very different from the old guard who'd occupied the barstools in the lodge for decades. Zack's death seemed to mark a changing of the guard, a farewell to the old boys' clubhouse and firm movement in a new direction.

The fundraiser was a great success. Still, Andrea lost the election. Dark forces had funneled money into the incumbent's campaign to ensure he'd remain in office. There were so many election irregularities that elected officials called for a special investigation. Changes in how poll workers were selected and trained would be made in the future to improve voting accuracy and fairness. But the election results held. It was a 60-40 loss. The voters had spoken decisively.

Nine months later, I ran into our reelected supervisor at the farmers' market in Plymouth. A stormy look crossed his face when he spotted me. I congratulated Brian on his election win, but his mouth remained twisted. I suggested it was time to bury the hatchet. He raised his eyebrows.

"My first question to you," he said, "is where'd you want to bury it?" I guffawed.

"That's hilarious, Brian," I said. I was going to extend my hand for a shake but could see he was not going to let go of a good grudge so easily.

PART FIVE

BARREL AGING

VERAISON

We returned from an excursion to San Francisco on a Friday afternoon in summer. After unloading the car, I took America for a lap around the vineyard. I returned to the house to report that veraison was underway.

"Are you sure?" Deborah asked. I showed her the cluster of zinfandel I'd plucked for evidence. Many of the grapes were still green, but more than half had plumped up to full size and begun to soften. About a third of the berries were various shades of purple.

Veraison is a French word for this stage in the grape ripening process. It is a critical marker along the road to fruit maturity. A general rule of thumb is that once 75 percent of the grapes have gone through veraison, harvest is approximately six weeks away. Yikes. We had no buyer for our crop nor, with Mark out of the business, a winemaker to produce wine for our own label this vintage. It was panic time.

I wondered if *veraison* might be related to another French word: *verité*—or truth. Because this felt like a moment of truth. We could no longer ignore the fact that we were in a serious pickle. Shortly after the previous harvest, we'd received a notice from our buyer, one of the big wineries in the Shenandoah Valley, informing us they would not be renewing our annual contract. We were not alone; the winery had canceled many of its grape contracts. Their new vineyards were beginning to yield a crop, and they had a surplus of wine to sell from previous vintages. *No hard feelings, that's business,* I thought.

We were grateful they'd given us ample notice—but then we'd done little about it. I'd made a few inquiries over the winter and into the spring, and we'd put the word out to friends and acquaintances in the industry. We visited some of our favorite wineries and winemakers, but they all said they were set for the coming year. We spoke with the head of the local Vintners Association. He knew of no one looking for zinfandel. We asked the local home winemaking group. Nope, they were buying French varietals this year.

Deborah and I are not prone to excessive worrying. We're comfortable letting things slide for a while, hoping for the best, assuming "something will turn up." But veraison is a wake-up call. Suddenly, we could see the grapes ripening before our eyes. In a matter of weeks, we'd have six to eight tons of fruit demanding to be picked. Again.

Deborah suggested sending an inquiry to our new vineyard consultant in Napa. After the recent fires, she thought perhaps someone in that part of the state might be looking to buy grapes from the foothills. It was a good idea, but Napa is cabernet, chardonnay, and pinot noir country. I was skeptical but contacted Derek anyway. He didn't know anyone looking for zinfandel but suggested placing an ad on a wine industry website with advertising services.

I didn't expect much, but within twenty-four hours, we had a nibble, an inquiry from a home winemaker in Sacramento who wanted to buy zinfandel. A half-ton. One thousand pounds. We needed to find a buyer for tons of grapes, not mere pounds. Within forty-eight hours, there was another inquiry, this time from someone interested in buying our entire crop. That sounded great until we learned that his winery was in Ohio. The logistical issues seemed mind-boggling.

Next, a winery in nearby El Dorado County contacted me. The winemaker, Eric, was interested in buying three tons of the "pampered zinfandel" grapes we'd advertised. Delivering them to Eric would be much easier than orchestrating cross-country transport. And if one three-ton buyer popped up, perhaps there might be others.

We were so excited to hear from Eric that we decided to take a road trip to meet him. His tasting room was just off Highway 50 near Placerville, about a forty-minute drive from our vineyard. We were impressed with the tasting room amenities: ample parking, well-kept grounds, an attractive arbor for wedding ceremonies, and an outdoor patio for live music and wood-fired pizzas on summer evenings. The tasting room was small yet cozy and charming—filled with Eric's personal artwork—portraits of family members painted on wooden barrel heads. He served us samples of his wines, each paired with a perfect bite of artisanal cheese. We enjoyed each of the wines Eric poured and liked the man, too. He was friendly, relaxed, and jovial, as well as competent. Cool.

We asked Eric how he sourced his grapes and learned that he sometimes did custom crushing for others in exchange for fruit. Deborah and I exchanged glances, realizing we might have found a solution to our need for a new winemaker, too. Soon, we sealed a deal to deliver six tons of zinfandel to Eric in September. He would purchase three tons to make wine for his own label. And he'd take three more tons at no cost in exchange for a specified number of cases of finished wine that we would bottle and sell under our own label. We were all pleased with this arrangement. Harvest suddenly became something to look forward to rather than dread.

We were delighted to have both a buyer and a winemaker again. However, we still faced the problem of how to deliver six tons of grapes to El Dorado County. We could only haul one ton at a time with our truck and trailer. Our previous buyers were located in the Shenandoah Valley, a mere five miles away. We would drive there, unload, and return to the vineyard in about twenty minutes—just as our picking crew would need more empty bins. Making six round trips with our own equipment was not going to work this time. We'd need a flatbed truck and a forklift, and we owned neither.

We made a test drive to Eric's winemaking facility in Shingle Springs. Mark, our former winemaker, was in town and asked if he could come along for the ride. We meandered along twisting roads through a part of El Dorado County we'd never seen before. We passed open meadows, densely forested areas, clusters of ranch homes, and a scattering of industrial parks. Finally, we reached Eric's home, where his grandfather had built a straw bale winemaking facility. As we pulled up the steep driveway, I spotted Eric operating a forklift. Two young helpers were loading grapes into a stemmer-crusher. Eric took a break to show us the winery, which was filled to the ceiling with racks of wine barrels. He and his crew were getting ready to bottle to make room for the new vintage.

Mark and Eric hit it off immediately. They talked about winemaking techniques in their private language as Deborah and I sipped the barrel samples Eric had poured. On the way home, Mark summarized his impression of Eric: "He's super talented, yet unpretentious. Creative, smart, and a solid winemaker. I like him *a lot.*" Mark was relieved that, since he wouldn't be making our wine anymore, at least we'd be in capable hands.

We still had to figure out how to transport six tons of fruit. After numerous calls, we were referred to a woman named Milly, who lived in the Shenandoah Valley. Her family was in the trucking business, and she had her own rig that could transport five or six tons of grapes at a time. We arranged to have her meet us at 10 a.m. on harvest morning at a nearby winery, where our neighbor had agreed to let us use his forklift in exchange for a few cases of beer.

As harvest approached, we walked the vineyard frequently, tasting grapes and scaring off birds. "I think we have more than six tons here," Deborah said. "We should start dropping fruit."

"But why?" I asked. "The crop is ripening well, and there's no sign of rot or mildew."

"True, but what will we do with the extra fruit?" I wasn't sure, but I had a few ideas.

When harvest day dawned, the grapes looked and tasted fabulous. The Brix and pH seemed perfect. Our small picking crew filled twelve half-ton bins within a few hours. There were still quite a few vineyard rows we hadn't touched. We'd deal with those later. First, we had to deliver fruit to Eric. Deborah departed with our friend Marco and our Dutch friend, Tecla (whom we'd met through the WWOOF program), to deliver one ton of grapes with our own truck and trailer. I stayed behind to watch Joe load Milly's rig.

There are always some glitches during harvest, involving lost tie-downs, missing ball hitches, or a blown tire. This time, it was Eric's forklift that broke down. He needed a new hydraulic hose, but the local hardware store didn't have one, so he and Marco got busy trying to adapt a barbeque hose for the purpose while Tecla began manually shoveling grapes from the half-ton bins into the crusher in case of prolonged equipment trouble. Fortunately, by the time Milly arrived with the other five tons, the forklift was working again. Unloading went smoothly. Milly departed, saying she'd mail us an invoice.

After that harvest weekend, Deborah had meetings to attend in San Francisco. I stayed in Fiddletown to deal with our remaining fruit. I thought it was the best crop our vineyard had ever produced. The clusters were dense, beautiful, and scrumptious. They deserved to fulfill their destiny and be made into wine—or something, even if juice or jam.

I called that Sacramento home winemaker who'd wanted to buy a half-ton of Zin but by then, he'd made other arrangements. I received a late call from another home winemaker looking for only one hundred pounds of grapes for his winemaking experiment in the East Bay.

"Why bother?" Deborah asked. I thought it better to let someone come pick a hundred pounds of grapes in exchange for a bit of cash than to let them rot on the vine.

"Let's charge him a buck a pound for such a small amount. A crisp Ben Franklin is better than a poke in the eye with a sharp stick," I said.

I called Eric to ask if, by any chance, he could use more zinfandel. He said he had all the grapes needed for his wine. "But I could take another half-ton to blend into a zinfandel port I'm making." He offered to barter some of the future port in exchange for the grapes. *Perfect holiday gifts,* I thought.

I called our friend Vicki to ask if she'd sold all of her grapes. "The barbera and syrah are all sold, but I still have sixteen tons of zinfandel left," she said. "Everyone seems to have too much zin this year; nobody wants it."

The following weekend, we picked another half-ton of grapes to deliver to Eric for his port. Tecla and her husband, Bruno, helped, along with a few other friends. We harvested the half-ton in just over an hour (it would have taken a professional crew about ten minutes).

A home winemaker friend arrived with his wife, and we picked another half-ton for them. We wouldn't be paid in cash for those grapes, but our friend is a renowned woodworker and bowl maker whose work we cherish. He promised to give us a case of finished wine and two hand-carved wooden wine sippers he'd carve from local walnut.

There were still beautiful grapes hanging. Tom, our former winemaker, was now working at a custom crush facility and event center in San Francisco. I called and asked if he could use more fruit. The answer was no, but he said he could take a ton to do a custom crush for us if that would help. *Why not?* It would be fun to compare the wines Eric and Tom would produce from the same vineyard and vintage. We picked another ton of zinfandel, and I delivered the load to San Francisco the same day.

Tecla was restless. "Mara, there's still more fruit hanging out there. We have to do something..." I called the local food bank to see if they wanted some fresh fruit for their clients. They'd never heard of using wine grapes as fresh produce. I explained that zinfandel grapes are sweet and delicious but have seeds like the old-fashioned table grapes consumers used to buy. They agreed to try some, so we picked ten lugs to deliver to Jackson the following day.

Our hundred-pound customer showed up soon afterward. Tecla and I helped him harvest, just for the fun of it. Even after that, we still seemed to have over a ton of gorgeous grapes hanging.

I contacted a man I knew in the food business and asked if he knew anyone who made frozen desserts like sorbets or popsicles. I thought perhaps we could make Zin-sickles out of our sweet, dark juice. But the guy was a cheese specialist; he didn't know anyone like that.

I called our friend Karen, who has a winery and vineyard about a twenty-minute drive away. She was not particularly interested in buying more grapes, but I offered her the rest of our crop for free.

"Well, why not?" she replied. "I've been thinking of making a dry rosé again like I did a few years ago. This sounds like the perfect opportunity." She showed up the next day with her own picking crew. To my relief, they took all of the remaining fruit, which filled three half-ton bins.

"My crew is just gushing," Karen said. "They say these are the best grapes they've ever harvested." She was excited about the wine she would make from them and promised to give us some rosé in exchange for the free fruit. It was something else to look forward to, but mainly I knew I would sleep better knowing our grapes had all gone to good homes.

I was satisfied with the harvest, but Tecla was still agitated. That woman could not stand to let *anything* go to waste. She made one more pass through the vineyard, picking lovely, fat clusters that others had missed. She brought two full picking lugs to the house on a wagon, and we put them in the wine cellar for safekeeping. I was too tired to deal with them; I'd think about making them into juice, jam, or sorbet later. Right then I needed to collapse on a sofa.

A week later, I went into the wine cellar to fetch a bottle and saw the two bins of grapes that Tecla had scoured from the vineyard. I'd forgotten about them. They'd shriveled a bit, making me think it might be fun to try an amarone-style wine experiment. Italians encourage this grape withering on purpose to concentrate the juice. The fruit was still in decent shape.

I could hear Deborah asking me if I'd lost my mind. We had enough projects going already. Right. I carried the lugs to the new compost heap that Tecla and I had started a few weeks earlier. I tossed those beautiful grapes onto the pile and shoveled falling leaves on them for a proper burial.

"Tecla might be disappointed, but I think you'll be proud of me," I told Deborah when I returned to the house. "I put those last grapes she gleaned on the compost heap!"

"What was the alternative—letting them rot in the cellar?" she asked.

"That or going out to buy pectin and spending all day making grape jelly that no one wants," I said.

"Well, then, you did the right thing," she said. She gave me a pat on the back, knowing how wasting things is hard for me, too. But the older I get, the better I am at choosing to occasionally waste some "stuff" over wasting my time, which grows more precious with each passing year. Besides, by next fall, those grapes would be transformed into lovely compost to use in our raised garden beds, so they would not truly be wasted.

MORE FLAMES

The 2019 Super Bowl game had just ended—Patriots winning yet again, ho hum—when we heard an explosion. It sounded a bit muffled, not super close, yet distinct. Deborah and I looked at each other with "what the heck?" expressions. Then we heard a second explosion. Deborah leaped to the window and yelled, "There's a huge fire down the hill. Call 911!"

I grabbed my phone and dialed. As it rang, I moved onto the front patio. Yes, an impressive fire was blazing in downtown Fiddletown, with its historic wooden buildings that can burn like tinder. It looked as if an entire structure was engulfed in flames. I heard a third explosion just as the operator answered.

"Where are you calling from?" she asked.

"Fiddletown," I replied.

"We're on it," she said. "Firefighters are on the way now." I could already hear sirens wailing. The fire continued to intensify, even though it had been raining heavily for several days. We were experiencing one of those "Pineapple Express" storm systems that hit California in winter, bringing waves of water off the Pacific to fill ponds and turn dirt roads to muck.

"Thank God it's not fire season," Deborah said. The wildfires in California had become frightening, violent, and lethal annual events. If something in our neighborhood had to burn, this was probably the least dangerous week of the year to have it happen. Still, any fire could set us on edge now. After many years of drought, we learned that even wet wood could readily ignite and burn super-hot.

We had no urge to jump in the car and drive down the hill to witness what was happening. For one thing, it was dark, cold, and drizzly. For another, we didn't want to get in the way of emergency responders. Instead, we watched the fire from our safe vantage point up the hill. We remained on alert in case it should spread in our direction.

I called Joe, who usually knows everything, but he had no idea what was happening. He and Michelle were heading home from a Super Bowl party, so he hadn't heard the explosions. He said he'd go investigate.

I tried calling Katherine and Herb, who live close to the post office. No answer. I called Alan and Marsha, whose home is right across from the post office. I was slightly annoyed with Alan because of the piles of scrap metal growing in his yard. However, I was mainly miffed because of the signs he'd hung on his fence supporting our incumbent supervisor during the 2018 election (when I was working hard to elect his opponent). However, we'd previously invited Alan to graze some of his sheep on our land. That was before we'd deer fenced the entire property. A predator slaughtered the two baby lambs, leaving only scraps of wool pelt near our seasonal creek, so the ewes returned home.

"This is Alan. How can I help you?"

"Hey, Alan. It's your neighbor Mara calling. We can see a big fire burning in downtown Fiddletown. Do you know what's up?"

"Yes, I do. The building behind the old house on the corner is on fire. The barn and workshop are fully involved, but not the home. The firefighters should be able to save that." The house on the corner, right next to the post office, was an eyesore, with shingles missing, paint peeling, and numerous inoperable vehicles parked in the yard.

I thanked Alan for the information. "It looks like a big deal from up here on the hill. Glad to know you and Marsha are safe."

"It's good to hear from you," he said. "Feel free to call me anytime to talk about anything." *I should take him up on that offer,* I thought, *instead of letting my annoyances smolder or letting political differences interfere with being neighborly.* We have some disagreements, but we also share common ground. We use the same post office, participate in many of the same community meetings and events, and share information about threats like fire. We'd help each other out in any emergency. We're polite and respectful to each other. That's worth something.

I called Pam, whose home is across the road from ours, further up the hill. She has a similar view over the town, with picture windows along her south side for a clear view of our small valley with its rolling hills and waving vineyards. When she answered the phone, I asked if she was watching the fire. "Of course

I am," she replied. "You know me. I see everything that goes on from up here. I actually called it in."

"So did I," I said, "but they were already on it." I shared what I'd learned about where the fire was burning.

"See—that's just what happens when the county lets properties get run down and filled with junk," she said. "Fires and explosions. It's no wonder!"

Soon the firefighters had gained the upper hand. We stopped monitoring the situation and made dinner.

The following day, our local newspaper carried a story about the dramatic Sunday night fire in Fiddletown, with photos of men, trucks, and hoses battling the flames. There was a reference to the many "antiques" stored inside the building that had burned. Apparently, these included a collection of historic wooden-wheeled wagons that were brought out annually for a reenactment of the Kit Carson wagon train ride. Every April, dedicated locals dress up like pioneers or mountain men. They parade their horses, mules, and historic wooden wagons through our foothill communities, stopping to camp in the late afternoon. The event would last several days, culminating with a parade through downtown Jackson. It's a spectacular sight, a step back in time, and it looks like a lot of fun. Perhaps our neighbors on the corner were regular participants in that event. Of course, it would be sad for them not to participate because their wagons had burned.

Entries about the fire were popping up on the Fiddletown Facebook page, among notices for found or missing pets and complaints about tourists speeding through town. Initial inquiries like "What were those BOOMS?" quickly turned into condolences to the family for their loss and expressions of gratitude that no one was injured. They were considerate, neighborly posts. That's what the community where we live is like. Well, most of the time...

WINTER TREATS

It rarely snows in Fiddletown, but in early February, we had two snowstorms in a single week. It turned our dormant trees and vines into a delightful winter wonderland. Whenever this happens, it seems magical and wonderful—until we remember that olive trees are not accustomed to snow. The weight of it can break their branches. We quickly don warm, waterproof clothing, grab rakes and brooms, and head outdoors to knock the snow off our hundred olive trees.

As we were liberating the Kalamata tree beside our house, Al and Billy came up the driveway in their black pickup, their Aussie shepherd yapping from the rear window. It seemed a long while since we'd seen them.

"We've been confined to the house by a series of damn head colds," Billy said.

"It feels like it's been a long winter already," Al added, "and I know it's not over yet, but look at this!" He reached into the truck and pulled out an egg carton. He opened it to display a dozen freshly laid eggs. "The girls seem to think it's spring already."

"You've got to be kidding," I exclaimed. "Your hens decided to start laying eggs *now*, just as we're getting freezing rain and snow? This should be their 'off' season."

"Well, yes. It's all a bit of a mystery. Our hens just do their own thing. Like us, I suppose," Al said.

We look forward to regular egg deliveries from our neighbors in spring and early summer, when we trade asparagus, boysenberries, apricots, tomatoes, and zucchini for them. But fresh eggs laid by free-range chickens in February are a rare treat. Perhaps those pampered hens produce out of sheer joy, living as they do in a chicken palace Al built for them. It's decorated like a Bavarian alpine cottage with a spacious fenced yard—a poultry playground with chicken swings, benches, feeding trays, and plants for shade and nibbling.

I asked the men if they'd observed the dramatic recent fire. They had missed it entirely. They'd been watching a movie in their upstairs loft when it happened. But they'd heard about it somehow and seemed particularly saddened by the loss of the historic wagons.

"One of the vehicles lost in the fire was a horse-drawn hearse from the 1800s," Al said. "*That's* a real shame." Perhaps Al could picture himself being transported to the Fiddletown Cemetery, where he owns a plot, in such a grand, antique vehicle.

"Anyway, we thought since the hens have decided to come out of their winter hibernation, we should do the same thing," Al said. "Why don't we get together for dinner one day soon?"

Deborah and I had a growing list of new places we wanted to try. We'd heard about a new bistro and a new Indian restaurant in Jackson, both getting good reviews. One of the B&Bs in Sutter Creek was hosting community dinners one Friday a month that sounded like fun. And a new restaurant had opened in the Plymouth Hotel. It was only open three nights a week, but it was rumored to have an Asian-fusion menu not typically seen in the area. Since the Plymouth option was closest, we made a date to go there the following weekend.

On Friday evening, Al and Billy drove over to hitch a ride with us, claiming their own truck smelled too "doggy" for driving ladies to dinner. We took the scenic route to Plymouth, through the Shenandoah Valley vineyards. We drove around the new traffic circle, down Main Street, passing Taste Restaurant and Vintage Market. Both were excellent eating spots that had sprung up since we'd built our Fiddletown homes.

"Remember the old days?" I asked. "A quarter-century ago, there was *nowhere* you could get a cappuccino or a croissant in the entire county, but baby, look at us now!"

"Has it really been that long?" Al asked. "Where does the time go?"

"Who'd have thought we'd have such good restaurants one day, let alone ethnic options, a bakery, a cheese shop, and a brewpub?" Deborah said. "We're getting spoiled!"

"And the wineries!" I added. "When we first moved here, there were only about a dozen. Now there are more than forty, and they seem to get better all the time. And lots more are springing up just over the river in El Dorado County."

"Please don't tell me we're going to become like Napa," Billy said. "I prefer things the way they are."

"So do I," I said, "but I've liked things the way they are for almost three decades now. There's more to do here all the time—concerts, art classes, wine tasting events, films and lectures, and new restaurants to try. We haven't been ruined with tourist traffic jams yet."

"I do like to stay home on those weekends when the huge wine festivals happen," Deborah said. "When the roads are choked with stretch limos and traffic checkpoints, and 'our' tasting rooms are packed with strangers." We all agreed there were a few inconveniences, but generally, life was very good in the foothills.

We parked and entered the hotel, where several couples sat intimately at the bar. They studied the four of us: two men and two women, yet we didn't look like typical couples. Deborah and I had changed out of our work duds into our going-out clothes, while Al had on his flannel shirt, paint-splattered jeans, and work boots. Billy wore clean jeans and a sweater, but that man looks gorgeous in anything, and he's quite a bit younger than the rest of us. The spectators didn't seem malicious, just curious. They soon turned back to their cocktails and conversations.

We claimed a free table and reviewed the eclectic menu. Al ordered a prosciutto salad. Billy ordered the *Lomo Saltado*, a Peruvian stir fry. I ordered beef sliders with a side of roasted Brussels sprouts, and Deborah ordered lettuce cups and lumpia. We shared bites of everything and a bottle of excellent local red wine, as we mused on the past, present, and future.

Toward the end of our meal, Al said: "I know you are a licensed minister, Mara. Is there any chance you might be available to perform a spring wedding this year?" Smiles erupted around the table.

I'd become a card-carrying Universal Life Church minister more than a decade earlier. Since then, I'd had the privilege of legally marrying gay couples and even a few straight ones. I do it for free because I don't think basic rites of passage should come with a price tag.

"Of course I'm available," I said. "I don't plan on going anywhere for a while."

PRESERVATION

Linda Sue and Terryl had bought tickets to the Fiddletown Preservation Society dinner and invited me to go with them. Deborah was out of town, so they offered to pick me up. Terryl pulled up in a car I'd never seen before—a vintage, pearl white convertible with the top down.

"What's this?" I asked.

"Meet Pearl," Terryl said. "She's a 1962 Plymouth Valiant I've had since my thirtieth birthday. A friend of a friend in Marin was selling her, and I bought her on a whim."

"Pearl never fails to put a smile on our faces," Linda Sue said.

I was smiling, too. "Pearl looks like a real Good Time Gal," I said.

"She is! And I never have to work on her," Terryl said. "Her motor is indestructible. I can park her for months at a time, and she fires right up whenever I return, ready to hit the road and be seen lookin' good." Pearl did look good with her almost-perfect paint job, red leather upholstery, and gleaming chrome trim. I was delighted to hop in and ride in style to the dinner venue.

The Fiddletown Preservation Society had rented a historic building on Lodge Hill in Plymouth for their fundraiser. None of us had seen or known about this gem before. It was an Odd Fellows Hall, built in 1879. The Odd Fellows must have been something like the Moose Lodge of their day. They were clearly well organized and had raised enough money to construct a solid, two-story building on top of a hill that now overlooks the county fairgrounds. A peach of a location.

We entered the building and saw many of our favorite Fiddletown neighbors, the ones who care about preserving our town's history and maintaining the character of historic buildings like our one-room schoolhouse and the rammed-earth buildings that had been important gathering places for Chinese residents during the Gold Rush. (The Chew Kee store, located in downtown Fiddletown, is a remarkably well-preserved specimen of an authentic Chinese apothecary.)

Dinner guests were encouraged to do a self-guided tour of the Odd Fellows social hall upstairs and then return to the ground floor dining room for drinks and dinner. Terryl wandered off to chat with some neighbors while Linda Sue and I perused the silent auction items—the usual array of books, gourmet food baskets, wine packages, restaurant coupons, and gift certificates for services ranging from massage and haircuts to oil changes. But one item stood out from the rest.

"Hey, Mara, look at this," Linda Sue said. "Rick donated one of his Highland cattle. Have you ever seen anything so cute?" She held up a flyer showing a beautiful specimen with blond locks hanging over its eyes. Highland cattle, originally from Scotland, are a hearty breed with shaggy coats and long horns. Rick was dedicated to breeding his stock back to their historic small size. In his quest for classic cows that conformed with his ideals, he'd culled his herd of the ones he thought too tall or lanky. He didn't want those in the gene pool, so he would sell them for pets or grazing animals. (Our neighbor Al had bought two of them, named Moo and Moe, to eat grass and keep his Sicilian donkeys company.)

We saw Rick in the crowd and asked him more about his offer. It was not any particular cow or bull, he said. The auction winner could choose from several animals he was planning to cull. He encouraged us to bid, saying he'd be happy to escort us into the hills above Fiddletown to see his family property and meet the herd. "We could take some margaritas, corn chips, and salsa for a sundown Happy Hour," he added. That sounded like fun.

There was a call to be seated for dinner. Guests took their seats at the round tables decorated with dark green linen and potted lavender plants. Linda Sue took one more cruise past the auction table. She reported that most of the auction items had bids on them by now, but no one had bid on the Highland cow.

"Maybe people are waiting until the last minute to bid on things," I said.

"Maybe the bidding will heat up after people have had more wine," Terryl said.

"C'mon, Mara, why don't you bid on it?" Linda Sue asked.

"Because Deborah would kill me if I came home with a cow," I said.

"I mean, just write down the minimum bid. That usually sparks interest and gets other people bidding."

"Why don't you bid on it?" I asked.

"Because we're going to Mexico soon. It would be too complicated to care for it," Linda Sue replied. "How about I put both of our names down and offer a hundred bucks. That'd be just fifty bucks each to get the bidding started for a good cause." I acquiesced.

The meal was good, the atmosphere festive, and the company excellent. A local artist played mellow guitar tunes in a corner as folks sipped local wines. Before dessert was served, someone announced that the silent auction would close in ten minutes. Interested parties got up to look the items over one last time or hover by a prize they were particularly interested in to protect their final bid.

As volunteers cleared plates and served coffee, the auction winners were announced. When it came to the Highland cow, four words hung in the air: "Linda Sue and Mara!"

Really? We're the winners? This wasn't supposed to happen. How will I explain it to Deborah? What the heck will we do with a cow? Terryl was asking Linda Sue similar questions.

"It could be an excellent, adorable lawn mower," Linda Sue said. "We could split the services between Deb and Mara's place and ours. Or they could just keep it since we already have two horses on our property. We could occasionally visit to comb its bangs and say hi."

"There's no way Deborah will want a cow," I said. "Our fencing is not up to snuff, and we're gone too much. We don't need another responsibility. But maybe we could split a freezer full of local, free-range Highland beef burger."

Terryl looked horrified. She held up the flyer with the color photo. "I could never eat anything with bangs!" she declared. We were at an impasse. We decided to sleep on it. Maybe a path forward would occur to us.

We took Rick up on his offer to visit his hilltop wonderland. Deborah rode with Linda Sue and Terryl, and I rode shotgun in Rick's pickup. As we approached the property, Rick noticed a bull had broken out of its enclosure. "I have to get him back inside," Rick said. "How about I go open the gate, and you ladies usher him back into his pen. Just walk behind him in a semicircle waving your arms like this and making noise so he'll want to move."

I got out and explained to the ladies in the next car what Rick wanted us to do. "He wants us to do what?" Deborah asked. She was wearing shorts and flip-flops. We stumbled along the ditch, hoping to avoid snakes and herding the bull as Rick suggested. Only later did we wonder what the chances of a goring might have been.

Once the bull was safely contained, we proceeded to the hilltop and parked. The vistas in every direction were amazing. It felt like the top of the world. Rick gave us a tour as he explained his family's history with this beautiful piece of land. He then showed us the herd and pointed out which cows were available for selection.

We still weren't ready. We asked Rick to give us some time to decide what we would do with our prize. He said there was no rush. We sat on logs as we sipped margaritas, relishing the views and sharing stories. Eventually, we headed back to our homes.

Our impasse was never resolved. Linda Sue and Terryl wanted a lawnmowing pet; Deborah and I preferred meat in the freezer we wouldn't have to care for or worry about. We could have had one party buy out the interest of the other, but this wasn't about the money. No one regretted donating fifty bucks to a good cause, but none of us had her heart set on owning the animal.

I called Rick to explain our dilemma. I asked if it would be okay if we took a pass on his Highland cow and donated it to the Farms of Amador fundraiser instead. They were planning a similar dinner soon, with another silent auction. Rick was agreeable. He liked the idea that one of his cows could end up helping several local non-profits.

Later, Deborah and I worked out a barter arrangement with Rick and his wife. Once in a while, we'd trade a case of our estate-grown wine for a box of their free-range Highland beef burger wrapped in frozen one-pound packages. We all won.

OUR TWENTIETH HARVEST

We were setting up the pressure washer, getting ready to wash our half-ton bins in preparation for the upcoming harvest, when Deborah said: "Hey—I just realized something. I think this is our twentieth harvest from the DAMAS vineyard."

"You're right!" I said, after pausing to do the math. Our first harvest was in 2000, so 2019 would be the twentieth. We reached for our water bottles and clunked them together in parody of a toast. "Perhaps this deserves some sort of celebration…"

We weren't in a particularly celebratory mood, though. We felt tired. The vineyard had demanded a lot of attention lately. More than any other year we could recall.

Every grower worries about mildew, which can infest grape clusters under and ruin the fruit. Growers with head-trained vines have to worry even more, because once the canes grow long enough to slump down into the aisles, you can no longer drive a tractor into the vineyard to spray mildew control products.

In 2019, we had five inches of rain in May, followed by relatively cool weather in June and July—perfect conditions for mildew proliferation. Every summer, we remove canes and pull leaves from the center of our vines to improve natural air circulation and discourage mildew formation. But this year, we'd done a lot more of that. Our neighbors with trellised vines continued applying sulfur to suppress mildew (or mineral oil to kill it), while we had only limited, labor-intensive options available to us.

Despite our best efforts, the fruit developed strangely. As the season advanced, we observed speckled grapes, split grapes, blackened grapes, uneven ripening, and lots of "shot" clusters whose berries filled out unevenly. The previous year we'd had a fabulous harvest, excellent in both quantity and quality, with grapes I thought were the prettiest we'd ever grown. And now this. Many clusters were just plain ugly. *How could juice from these monstrosities possibly make good wine?* I wondered. And then mildew showed up.

Carlos came to the house looking flustered. "We did so much cane thinning and leaf pulling" he said, "but I think we still have a problem. I think you should talk to Pat. See if he can bring his cane-cutting machine here to cut canes back, so we can spray once more with his skinny tractor."

Deborah and I were skeptical. We had never done such a thing. We'd never cut our canes to spray so late in the summer. But now the fruit was sprouting dusty white spores, on top of its other blemishes. We had to do something fast, or risk losing the entire crop. I called Pat.

Pat is a super busy vineyard manager. Normally, he would not consider taking another customer, let alone one as tiny as us, with our two-acre vineyard. But he is always willing to help us in a pinch because we're friends of Vicki's, and she and Pat were an item in the past.

"Any grower who says they don't have mildew this year has not spent time in their vineyard," Pat said. "It's everywhere. Some places are worse than others, and some varietals are worse than others. But it's everywhere, believe me." His words were little comfort.

Pat dispatched one of his workers, who arrived with a narrow-gauge cane-cutting tractor to work its magic. Then, the same tractor was used to spray Stylet oil, an organic mildewcide, on our vines. (I made a note to add a "skinny tractor" to my Santa wish list.)

Our efforts paid off. The mildew subsided. Nonetheless, Deborah and Carlos and I spent many more hours in the vineyard dropping clusters we thought looked too ugly to make good wine. Between the three of us, we probably dropped three tons of fruit.

"Think of it as adding organic matter to the soil," Deborah said when she saw the disgusted look on my face.

"Okay, but I'm not sure we can save any of this crop," I said. "It's discouraging."

"The vineyard has been a real pain in the ass this year," Deborah said. "This morning, I woke up thinking maybe we should just pull the whole damn thing out. That would save us a lot of trouble and make our lives easier. We could turn the two acres over to local organic farmers, like the cute young couple who started Upcountry Farms. They could grow flowers and vegetables here, and maybe we could retire."

"Well, that's a radical thought," I said, wondering if she meant it seriously. Ripping out vines that we'd babied along for almost a quarter-century seemed harsh. Yet I'd heard of some other vineyard owners doing just that recently, finding grape farming no longer worth their money and time. The intense labor shortage didn't help matters.

"Or maybe we could strike a deal with Carlos'," she said. "We could have him take over managing the vineyard without us. He could get his friends and family to help him do the work, and then he could keep all revenue from grape sales at the end of the season."

"You are full of creative ideas today," I said, "but it's complicated. Carlos would be using our equipment, fuel, and water. How would those expenses work? And what if he can't find a buyer for the crop? And what about the fact that you actually like getting out and riding your tractor through the vineyard in the spring?"

"I'd be willing to do some mowing and mulching just for fun," she said. "But it's true that marketing is not easy these days. It deserves more thought."

Our friend Marco arrived to help us wash bins, even though his back had been bad lately. He enjoyed helping us harvest but he had a schedule conflict this year. At least he could help us get ready.

Once the bin washing was done, we sat down to have sandwiches and iced tea and catch up on news of our various summer travels. We all felt a bit subdued. For Marco, it was his bad back and some family issues. For us, it was a touch of jet lag from our recent short trip to Italy, as well as fatigue from the extra vineyard work lately. We were also bummed because almost none of the friends who'd been our regular harvest helpers in previous years were available this year. Some were traveling, some were sick, some had weddings or funerals to attend. At least we had a picking crew arranged. We felt grateful for Carlos and his brothers and friends. They are all hard workers who can be counted on to make themselves available, as long as we're able to harvest on their day off. But we still had to supply drivers and leafers. This year, Joe and Deborah and I would do all the driving ourselves, each of us handling a truck and trailer combination. Most years, we had enough hands to have two people for each delivery team. I didn't see how the three of us could also do all the leafing, a sticky job involving leaning into the half-ton bins to pull out any leaves, twigs, insects, etc., that might get mixed in with the grapes.

"I think we're going to be short-handed," I told Deborah after Marco departed. "I should try to round up a few more people to help with leafing." She thought it couldn't hurt.

I texted some friends and neighbors to see if anyone might be available to help for a few hours on Sunday morning. When Michelle and Kate replied that they could come for at least part of the time, I felt better. We'd manage somehow.

Joe showed up in the afternoon to see if we had all the hitches and tie-downs we'd need. "Where are Kay and Linda?" he asked.

"They're in Iowa tending to Linda's brother, who recently moved into a care home and is not the least bit happy about it," I said.

"Well, what about Marco? I thought I saw him earlier. Did he take off already?"

"He had to attend an important family gathering in Elk Grove," Deborah said. "At least he came by to help us wash bins. He shouldn't have done that with his back a mess."

Joe asked about Mike and Molly. "At a wedding in Santa Cruz," I said.

"What about Linda Sue and Terryl's? I told him Terryl's parents had died recently, so they were up to their ears sorting out the estate.

"Let's face it, Joe. All of our friends are getting old—and so are we," I said.

"Yeah, well, what can you do? You've got to just keep putting one foot in front of the other. That's what I do, anyway." *Me, too,* I thought. *But sometimes lately, it feels like a trudge.*

After Joe left, I went over our harvest punch list:

- Identify picking crew and leafers
- Mark the center of each vine row with bright tape
- Wash picking lugs
- Wash half-ton bins

- Round up 3 trucks and 3 trailers
- Find trailers, hitch pins, balls, safety chains
- Sort out tie-downs for each trailer
- Clean and sharpen all the clippers
- Arrange for a forklift to be available when needed
- Buy lunch supplies and drinks for the crew
- Find and clean the water jug and coolers
- Don't forget to buy ice
- Put out trash receptacles
- Place a few chairs in the shade
- Check paper towels and toilet paper supplies
- Chill beverages overnight
- Make muffins and chop fruit for breakfast

Once I'd checked every item twice, I felt as prepared as possible. Deborah and I had a soak in the hot tub, ate a light supper, and went to bed early. When the alarm went off at 5:30 on Sunday morning, it was still dark out. Deborah and America ignored me as I got up and dressed. They both sighed, turned over, and went back to sleep.

I put on the coffee and then went out with a flashlight to feed the barn cats, open the front gate, and turn on the light in the guest cottage so workers could access the bathroom. Back in the kitchen, I laid out muffins and fruit out of habit, even though this year we had no house guests who'd be getting up soon to help. I filled the big water jug, adding a block of ice to keep it cool, and set it on one of the trailers so it would be available in the vineyard once the sun came up and pickers grew thirsty.

Joe showed up at six o'clock like I'd asked him to and started loading empty half-ton bins onto each trailer. I went out to help, taking two fresh cups of coffee with me. He seemed grumpy.

"I don't know why you had me come so early," he said. "It's too dark to start picking anytime soon. I know Carlos said they'd start by six twenty, but there's no way that'll happen, unless they wear headlamps. I guarantee you, they won't be picking until six forty-five or later."

"Well, I wanted time to get everything ready, go over the harvest plan again, and get the trucks and trailers positioned," I said. "Besides, isn't it nice to take a minute to drink coffee and admire the sunrise before all hell breaks loose?" I handed him a cup and asked if he'd like a muffin.

"Nah, I've been up for a while. I made oatmeal and made extra for Michelle. I told her she better eat something before coming over here, because you used to always make muffins for harvest, but you haven't done that for a few years now."

"That's because Kay usually shows up with that cinnamon-nut loaf from Acme Bakery in Berkeley. Since that's not happening this year, I actually did make muffins," I said. "Go help yourself if you want one."

At 6:15, I heard car doors slamming and saw men wandering out into the dusky vineyard with a knife in one hand and a yellow picking lug in the other. Carlos was not around, so I told the men where to start picking. By 6:20, five men were harvesting fruit quickly. Joe didn't say anything. He handed me his empty coffee cup, got into his truck, and drove it to the top of the vineyard, where half-ton bins would be needed any minute. I went to the house to tell Deborah the harvest had begun. We'd need to start leafing right away.

I drove a second truck into position behind Joe's. The pickers were already emptying their lugs, each holding forty or fifty pounds of grapes. I leaned into the half-ton bin and began picking out MOG.

"Incoming!" Joe would yell each time another worker ran up to dump his lug of grapes. I'd duck out of the way so each man could jettison fruit and race back into the vineyard for more. I pulled out leaves and inspected the fruit, rejecting any clusters that were underripe, overripe, or odd looking. Carlos and friends picked the first ton in thirty-five minutes and immediately started on the second ton. They were singing, shouting, and yelling jokes as they ran along the vine rows.

Joe drove the first ton to the winery a quarter mile up the road. The forklift was waiting outside, so he was able to unload and return to the top of the vineyard with fresh bins quickly. By then, Deborah was leafing beside me, and America was sniffing around, excited by the commotion.

Michelle arrived around 8 a.m. This allowed me to take a break, check for calls, make more coffee, and fetch a bucket of water for handwashing so we wouldn't have to put sticky hands on steering wheels. I texted Milly, the woman we'd hired again to haul our grapes to Shingle Springs, to update her on our progress. Kate showed up around 9 a.m., after her morning walk with a friend. She'd never done leafing before, but quickly got the hang of it and thought it was fun. Joe stepped back, claiming that five leafers was way too many and that we'd only get in the way of the pickers. Deborah wandered off to pour herself a second cup of coffee. I paused to take some photos, as Michelle and Kate continued leafing.

The crew finally finished picking the zinfandel—all but the fifteen shortest rows, which were reserved for another buyer. They quickly harvested our small block of Petite Sirah, which had only fifty vines. Soon, it was all over, at just a few minutes past 10 a.m. The pickers gathered under the oak tree to wash their bins and knives and hands and crack open cold beers. Each man had picked and carried a ton of grapes. I marveled to think these guys usually pick many hours longer. At the peak of harvest, they are in high demand. Winemakers prefer to keep the grapes cool, so picking at night has become popular. A crew can start at midnight and pick straight through the night, working under portable stadium lights until the sun comes up. They often keep working through the morning, harvesting four or five tons each before finally stopping for rest. I couldn't imagine how exhausted they must feel at the end of such a work shift.

I rode with Joe and Michelle as they hauled the last two bins up the hill to be weighed. Milly was there, waiting with her yellow truck and big flatbed trailer. We shook hands and chatted as Joe carefully weighed the last bins, documenting the weights on his spiral pad. Then he used the forklift to load containers onto the big flatbed trailer under Milly's watchful eye. I'd promised her the load would not exceed five tons, but with the weight of the bins themselves plus a few extra grapes, the total weight came to 11,102 pounds. She expressed concern, saying her engine had been overheating on hills lately.

I called Deborah and asked her to come over with our truck and trailer. We'd have to drive a ton to Shingle Springs ourselves. It was already 11 o'clock, and Eric had asked us to arrive no later than noon. He and his wife were hosting an event at their winery that afternoon. I urged Milly to finish tying down her load and hit the road as soon as possible.

Deborah arrived with America riding shotgun. Joe loaded the last two bins onto our trailer. We secured them and departed, arriving at the winery ten minutes ahead of Milly. Eric was ready with his forklift.

When Milly arrived, she said she was happy we'd taken two of the bins, as her engine had begun to overheat on the twisting inclines along Highway 49. She explained why her truck had been overworked lately. Her family's trucking company had won the contract to haul debris out of Paradise, the town destroyed the previous fall by the Camp Fire, the deadliest and most destructive wildfire in California history. Dispatching all the trucks required for that job was the most challenging work they'd ever done. "We actually hauled more ash and molten metal and concrete out of Paradise than had been hauled away after the Twin Towers fell in New York on 9/11, if you can imagine that. And all that debris had to be sorted to send to different landfills or recyclers." They'd called on extended family to help, even hiring her nephew Bud who, until recently, was living in the guest cottage at our neighbor Al's place. I asked her how Bud was doing.

"Bud's settled down a lot," Milly said. "He actually has a boyfriend now—a tall, handsome fellow from Placerville, a really nice young man."

When I'd first met Milly a year earlier, she and her husband struck me as conservative old-timers. I presumed our values and voting patterns were miles apart. Yet here she was, embracing and employing the black sheep of the family and even supporting his choice of a same-sex partner. I was in awe. *Open-mindedness can take root in unexpected fissures,* I thought. I reminded myself not to make snap judgments about the people living around me.

Deborah and I drove through the community of El Dorado on our way home. I offered to buy lunch at Poor Red's Barbeque, but she didn't want to spend time on a sit-down meal. Instead, we went straight home, noticing for the first time the "Original Pony Express Route" markers along the highway.

"I feel whipped," I said when we finally sat down to eat a sandwich at home.

"Well, no wonder," Deborah said. "You just finished working about eight hours straight!"

"I guess that could explain it," I said. "But just think—in the old days, we'd be gearing up to host a Harvest Party for thirty or forty people tonight."

"Good grief," she said. "I don't know how we ever pulled that off. I don't think I could do it now." She asked what I wanted to do with the rest of the day.

"I want to sit somewhere quiet and not move. Maybe do some reading or a bit of writing, maybe take a nap." That was fine with her. We did wander out eventually to empty the water jug and coolers, put away chairs, and collect the cups, cans, and bottles scattered around the vineyard.

The next day we returned to the winery to pick up our empty bins. We could fit only half of them on our truck and trailer combo. Eric agreed to return the rest of them to us later that day. I asked him to bring a sample of the juice from our crushed grapes.

Eric arrived in the afternoon with the rest of our bins, as promised. We helped him unload, and then he handed me a small bottle of liquid. It was a lovely, deep pink color, a bit cloudy with particles of pulp. I carried it carefully to the kitchen. When I removed the lid from the bottle, the liquid bubbled over the top, like champagne. Deborah grabbed a glass to capture the flow.

"Wow, this is a frisky puppy!" I said.

"Yeah, fermentation is going gangbusters," Eric said. "That sample kept leaking into my shirt pocket on the drive over here." I poured three tastes, and we each took a sip.

"That's absolutely delicious," Deborah said.

"It's amazing," I said.

"Yeah, I'm delighted with it, too," Eric said. "I think this is going to make some mighty fine wine. I have to compliment you ladies on the job you did growing these grapes in a particularly challenging year. Congratulations! In fact, even though your production is relatively small, I'm thinking I should make your grapes into a single vineyard-designated wine, rather than blend it with zin from my other sources. Mostly because this juice tastes so damn good, but also because my other growers don't use the sustainable farming methods you two do."

Deborah and I exchanged a glance to communicate our pride and delight.

"I've been thinking about how to make the transport easier in future," I said. "Maybe next year we should rent a truck with a lift gate. That might work better than having Milly drive that huge truck and long trailer up the mountain, and it would be a lot easier to turn around in your tight loading area."

"Actually—I have news," Eric said. "We're going to construct a brand new winery building. I hope to start before the end of the year. It'll be up in Camino, where our tasting room is. There's a lot more space up there. Plus, it will be a lot more convenient to do my winemaking there, instead of off-site. I'll be able to work on the wines when the tasting room is slow.

"The building will have a circular driveway that goes right through it," he continued. "You'll be able to pull up, unload, and be on your way. Way easier than it is now!"

We congratulated Eric on his plan. Deborah mentioned we'd run short on space for storing our case goods and asked Eric if he happened to know anything about the new wine storage facility in Mount Aukum.

"I don't," he said, "but I'm overbuilding the new winery building, because I don't want to find myself in constrained space again anytime soon. I should have extra room to spare for years to come, so it would be an option to keep any wines I make for you stored right there until you need them. You could come pick up your wines ten or twenty cases at a time if you want."

Ah—so there might be a future, after all. For here we were—Deborah, Eric, and I—standing around our kitchen island discussing it with enthusiasm, contemplating it with pleasure.

THE EXCHANGE

When the pandemic arrived in March 2020, Deborah and I began to stay virtually full-time in Fiddletown. The city became eerie and depressing. Its boarded up storefronts and empty streets seemed surreal. In the foothills, we felt better prepared than many to weather the storm. We were more grateful than ever that we'd bought land and nurtured it over the decades. We had a safe, beautiful spot to shelter in place. We had a bountiful garden and a well-stocked pantry and wine cellar. Parties and meetings at the lodge would cease for a while, but we could use the space as a private gym and art studio. There were always endless outdoor tasks to take our minds off the state of the world.

We tried to use the strange time well. Deborah threw herself into improving her Spanish language skills. I had a book of stories to work on.

One day, I had a dump run and a few wine deliveries to make in Jackson and realized it was Wednesday. That meant the new community market I'd been reading about would be open, so I could swing by and check it out. Some of our friends and neighbors had run an organization called Motherlode Harvest for a decade before it disbanded. Their goal was to connect local farmers with consumers to improve access to fresh, organic, and sustainably grown local foods. They worked hard but had a series of financial challenges—website crashes, not enough subscribers, few offerings in wintertime, and long distances to travel for deliveries.

One of the members decided to try a different approach, opening a year-round market called The Exchange. There, growers and vendors could sell their goods to the public under one roof. She rented the historic Chichizola Store on Jackson Gate Road. The landmark building still had the original shelves and sales counters, giving it an authentic, old-time feel. The Motherlode Land Trust, which owns the building, moved its offices to the second floor, making the downstairs space available for the new market. The Exchange was open only a few days a week. Still, because it's indoors, it can remain open year-round, unlike seasonal farmers' markets.

As I approached the market, I was pleased to see patrons coming and going, the adjacent parking lot almost full. I entered the room and bumped into Michelle, our friend and masseuse, on her way out with an armload of goodies. We greeted each other, chatted briefly, and confirmed an upcoming massage appointment. I strolled to the nearest table to find it occupied by our neighbor Alice, who runs a B&B and organic farm on family property in Fiddletown. I bought some of the homemade English muffins and strawberry jam she offered.

I surveyed the room to see if anyone was selling eggs. I recognized Ron, who grows lavender and makes wreaths out of dried wildflowers. I walked over to say hello and told him he was welcome to harvest eucalyptus leaves from the trees on the former Moose Lodge property. He said he'd come check it out.

I passed Robert, co-owner of Rosebud's Restaurant. He was trying to sell some ladies one of his specially forged augers that could be attached to a power drill. I told them I how much loved mine, saying it had made planting my tomatoes a breeze this year.

Our local caterer, Lucy, had a table offering organic salads, soups, and desserts she'd made from scratch. Lucy had relocated from Napa to Volcano and created a new commercial kitchen inside a shipping container. I picked out some lunch items and asked her to hold them for me until I finished shopping. She refused my cash, reminding me I still had credit from a previous olive oil exchange.

I spotted fresh eggs on the next table. I picked up a dozen and chatted with Caroline—a retired schoolteacher-turned-farmer whom I'd met through Motherlode Harvest. It had been a while since I'd seen her, so I asked about her new lambs. I paid for the eggs and bought a few red-speckled butter lettuces that looked so fresh I couldn't resist them.

When Luisa and her husband, Kevin, came in, I walked over for hugs. Luisa had sent me an email that morning inviting Deborah and me to share their table at the annual College Connect fundraiser in a few weeks. (Since our county has no community college, this non-profit group helps local students complete degrees via online courses.). I told them we'd love to come.

I circled back to pick up my lunch from Lucy. She commented that I seemed to know everyone in the room, and I realized she was right. "This doesn't happen when I walk into any store in San Francisco," I said. I marveled over how this happens, how you can move somewhere new, begin finding kindred spirits, form relationships with neighbors, and make new friends. Add some tincture of time— and voila! You discover that a strong sense of community materialized while you weren't paying attention.

I glanced at the tables and chairs at the back of the room, where patrons could sit and enjoy their lunch. I realized I'd rather chat with Lucy than anyone else. I asked her if I could pull up a chair and sit with her while I enjoyed her cooking. She scooted over on the large cooler serving as her bench to make room for me. Deborah and I had recently had brunch with Lucy and her husband, Bill, but we still had things to discuss and some future social plans to finalize.

Lucy took advantage of my presence to use the restroom. While she was gone, I sold a few slices of her carrot cake and lemon cheesecake. She rewarded me with an extra pint of soup to take home. As I walked away with my goodies, I felt warmed by the sense of belonging and fellowship I'd experienced at The Exchange.

I drove home through the bright green hills dotted with orange poppies under a sky full of puffy spring clouds. Farm chores awaited me—weeding, weed-whacking, mulching, turning garden beds, fixing irrigation lines. The usual. I couldn't wait to dig in.

HERD INSTINCT

I've always wanted farm animals on our land in the Sierra foothills, but Deborah thought taking care of them would be troublesome and time-consuming. (In the early years, when we were busy professionals spending most weekdays in San Francisco, this was certainly the case.) We've always kept a few barn cats, but they don't count. They're just our four-legged rodent patrol.

For years, I thought the mural of farm animals I'd painted on the wood shed had taken care of my "animal fever," but one day, I discovered it had not. I was walking around the vineyard when I saw a flock of sheep on our neighbors' land, just across the fence that separates our vineyard from their open pasture. A dozen pregnant and lactating females with some young, adorable lambs scattered as I approached.

When I returned to the house, Deborah looked up from her computer and asked: "What are you smiling about?" I hadn't realized how delighted I felt until she asked.

"There are sheep in the old Thorpe pasture," I said. "I don't know why, but they make me feel happy. Just looking at them gives me a sense of contentment. Weird, huh?"

I sent the neighbors a text message, thanking them for getting sheep. Our properties instantly seemed much more pastoral, with lambs romping on the grass. The neighbor replied that they enjoyed watching the lambs, too, but the flock did not belong to them. They didn't know where the sheep had come from but figured they'd go home for dinner. I wasn't so sure. They seemed to enjoy grazing right where they were.

Then our neighbor Anna called. "Hola, Mara. Have you, by any chance, seen some sheep? Mine are missing. I think they found a way through the fence and headed in your direction." I told her where I'd seen the flock and gave her the names and phone numbers for our new neighbors.

Soon, the sheep were back where they belonged, but I missed them with a physical pang. I pondered why the sight of sheep should make me feel so happy. I couldn't come up with any rational explanation, but I concluded that if such a simple thing could give me such pleasure, it was darn cheap post-pandemic therapy.

"Wouldn't it be nice to have a flock of our own?" I asked Deborah, fully expecting her to pooh-pooh the idea as she had done in the past. To my surprise and delight, she did not.

"Why don't you talk to our neighbors who have sheep to learn more about it? They should all be having lambs about now. Maybe you could get a few 'starter lambs' from Art and Bonnie, or from Anna, or the couple who live at Steve's place on Tyler Road." The idea of having a "training flock" made me grin.

However, the more I thought about getting a flock of my own, the more daunting it seemed. Inoculations, live births, hoof care, shearing. I didn't know anything about all that. Did I really need a new project of this scope when I already felt busy enough? Hosting someone else's flock seemed easier than owning and managing one of our own. We'd achieve the thrilling, pastoral look of a flock romping or grazing contentedly on our land without the ownership responsibilities.

I called Anna. "Hey, Anna. I'm glad your sheep got home safely. I've been wondering if you might be interested in letting them graze on our land sometimes."

"That might be a good idea," Anna said. "My ewes will need a lot of grass while they're feeding their new babies. I'm swamped this week, but I'll try to come over soon to talk about it."

The more Deborah and I discussed it, the more problems we identified. "Providing water for them would be easy, but how would we transport the sheep from one place to the other?" I asked. "And we'd have to repair our fencing." Several oak trees had fallen in the last winter's storms. A few of those landed on our ranch fencing, crushing almost a hundred-foot stretch. We'd managed to cut, split, and stack the firewood and burn the brush and stumps, but we still had to fix or replace the fencing that had been damaged. We had some extra metal fence posts and even a roll of wire fencing left over from a previous project, but it was tough to find experienced labor to help.

"I've never been crazy about wire fencing," Deborah said. "Maybe it would be better to remove that section rather than replace it." *Oh no, here we go again*, I thought.

"And by the way, didn't I read in *Hobby Farm* magazine that sheep need a safe place to shelter at night?"

"Really? I don't recall reading that," I said. We'd subscribed to *Hobby Farm* for years. It was full of practical ideas and tips about raising crops and animals. They even had special issues devoted to chickens, pigs, goats, and sheep. Apparently, I don't retain everything I read.

"Do you suppose Anna brings hers in at night?" I asked.

"Maybe her sons do it. But I wouldn't want to. Would you?" she asked.

"No," I said. I do enjoy feeding cats and dogs first thing in the morning, but at dusk, I'd prefer to be reading by the fire or enjoying a glass of wine, not stumbling around in the dark trying to lure animals into a shed.

I called our handyman, Joe, who'd once been very involved in the local 4H sheep project. He confirmed what Deborah had said. "You have to protect sheep from predators like coyotes or mountain lions at night. They have to have secure shelter and someone to get them into it every night. Either that or a guard dog," he said. We had neither a predator-proof shelter nor a guard dog. I couldn't stand the idea of finding lambs slaughtered by a mountain lion on our land. I felt my flock dream slipping away again. *Why complicate our lives? Let things be. Enjoy your mural.*

With the arrival of warmer weather, grass sprang up everywhere. Joe usually did a lot of weed-whacking for us, but this year, he was booked with other projects and was behind schedule due to the late spring rains. Other laborers we knew were busy pruning fruit trees or grapevines. We were beginning to feel desperate when Joe told us about a guy doing some grading work at Pam's place. Joe said Gilberto worked hard and did a good job (a rare compliment from Joe, with his impossible-to-meet standards). "He works for a local contractor five days a week and likes to spend Sundays with his family. But he said he's looking for extra work, like weed-whacking, he can do on Saturdays." We jumped at the chance to talk with him, so Joe said he'd give Gilberto my contact information.

Gilberto had his teenage son Gilbert call me. The boy said his dad didn't speak English well, so he would act as an interpreter. We arranged for his dad to work for us the following Saturday. Father and son both came by on Friday afternoon to see where we wanted him to work, so everything would be clear, and he'd be able to start at 7 a.m. without needing further direction from us.

Gilberto was indeed a hard worker, and his work was tidy and thorough. His command of English seemed much better than expected. Or so I thought—until I explained his next task: trimming the grass between the main road and our fence. When I checked, I found him weed-whacking the olive trees along the driveway.

I asked Deborah if she would explain task priorities to him. Her pandemic project (improving her Spanish language skills) was going well. She'd been studying hard, had a weekly online class, and even a one-on-one tutor she met with weekly on Zoom. Her facility with the Spanish language was now well beyond mine. She agreed to speak with Gilberto.

She was gone for some time, no doubt taking advantage of the opportunity to practice her Spanish conversation skills. When she returned, she reported having a successful talk with Gilberto, who was now weed-whacking along the front road. "He's smart and delightful," she said. And then she asked, "Do we want a herd of goats here?"

Huh? Wasn't she the one who thought a flock of sheep was infeasible or just plain crazy? What in the world was she talking about? She had my full attention.

She explained that Gilberto happened to own a few dozen goats—a mix of adults and babies and even a few sheep. They'd been grazing at a ranch on Hale Road but had to be moved to new pasture. He realized our land would be perfect for them. Instead of paying him to trim our grass, his herd could do it for free. He seemed eager to move them and even asked about the possibility of bringing them the following day.

"Well, that's not possible," I said. "We haven't made the fence repairs. And what about the shelter issue?" She said Gilberto had offered to finish the fence repairs himself, and his herd, which included a few sheep, would come with their own guard dog. He'd even bring his own troughs for feeding and watering.

"Well, then, why not?" I said with a rush of excitement. Sheep and baby goats and a dog? What could be better? I texted Anna to let her know we'd identified a tribe of goats that would come with a guard dog, so we were thinking about hosting them. "That sounds best, since I don't have a guard dog," she replied.

Gilberto returned the following day with his son and several friends. They removed bent fence posts and installed straight ones. They stretched and attached wire fencing where it was needed. A few more men arrived to help check the entire perimeter in case foxes or coyotes had made tunnels beneath our fence. The men used more wire to secure the five gates whose bars were far enough apart for a baby goat or lamb to slip through. Gilberto declared the fencing to be secure and departed.

A few hours later, we were surprised to see a large flatbed truck outfitted with wooden slats arrive and park at the gate beside our upper garden. We suspended dinner preparations to see what was happening. Gilberto had brought the herd! Four other men whom we recognized from vineyard work and labor contracting emerged from a car to help unload the animals.

I asked Gilbert how they got the animals into the truck. Had they lured them with alfalfa or some such? No, he said. The men lifted each one into the back of the panel truck. I imagined a chaotic scene with men whooping and running after goats, feeling like genuine gauchos.

The son disappeared briefly and returned with a big, shaggy white dog on a leash. It was a classic guard dog, a Great Pyrenees. I walked over to greet him, asking if the dog was friendly. Yes, Gilbert said. He told me the dog's name was Beethoven.

I extended my hand to Beethoven. He sniffed it and let me scratch his muzzle and ears, wagging his bushy tail lazily. He seemed like a sweetheart who'd immediately move indoors onto the sofa if invited. But he had an important job to do outside.

I counted twenty-eight animals in the field, including the dog. There were three large sheep and three young lambs in the mix. Gilbert grinned as he told me this enterprise had started with a single goat someone had given his family. After that, people kept giving them more animals, including the sheep and even the guard dog.

Gilberto was prepared to come by daily to feed the dog and give the herd whatever supplements they might need. I volunteered to feed Beethoven in the mornings since I had to feed the barn cats early, anyway. I enjoyed doing it and was sure I could get Carlos to cover for me on the rare occasion when I might be away. Gilberto accepted gratefully.

Before the men departed, someone remembered that they'd put the billy goat in the cab of the truck when they'd run out of space in the back. One of the men dashed off and returned carrying a large goat with a brass bell on a leather collar around his neck. Now there were twenty-nine four-legged mammals to amuse us. The rustic look I sought was complete, accompanied by delightful audio effects—tinkling bells, bleats, and baaaahs.

It was even more thrilling than I'd imagined. I loved this motley crew of mixed animals. Goats and sheep. Large, medium, and small. Mellow and feisty. They were all beautiful to me.

The next morning when I went to check on the animals, I saw one tiny goat crawling inside a hollow tree stump and wondered what was happening. I went to investigate. The goat was shivering and looked very weak. I pulled it out of the tree, but it immediately crawled back inside. I looked up and realized one of the ewes had a thin string of bloody tissue hanging from her rear. She had just given birth to the baby goat, which had a chocolate head like a German Shorthaired Pointer and four perfect, round brown spots on each knee that resembled knee pads. I felt a surge of fondness for this kid born on our property but resisted the urge to name him. Now the menagerie had thirty members. I made it a habit to count them daily, to make sure Beethoven was doing his job and we hadn't lost anyone overnight.

Of course, I paid particular attention to the new baby. He seemed very weak the first few days, but he finally got the hang of feeding. He grew stronger quickly and soon was romping with the slightly older kids. As he grew, the white streak on his brown head stretched and began to look like a lightning bolt on his forehead. I began to think of him as Harry Potter, though I never said his name aloud.

When I posted photos and videos of our new visitors on Facebook, friends responded with comments about how cute they were or requests to come by to admire them. Our friend Anne called to ask a few hard questions: Were there any things growing inside the fenced area that we might want to protect, "because goats will eat *everything!* And do you have electric fencing installed?"

"No electric fencing, but the men did a great job securing our wire ranch fencing and all the gates, too," I told her. Some young oak trees were growing in the back acres scarred from Zack's fire years earlier. I'd rather have those survive, but it seemed like too much trouble to install protective fencing around each tree. I didn't mind sacrificing them, given how frightening wildfire season has become in California. I knew goats eat the grass and brush, and they'd trim every mature oak tree as high as they could reach. That all seemed good for fire protection. Anne wished us luck. I detected a note of skepticism.

People kept asking how long we'd be hosting the herd. I had no idea. Deborah told someone she thought it would be for a few weeks. I thought it would take much longer for the animals to eat all the grass and brush inside the five or six acres now securely fenced. I didn't know how long we would get to enjoy them, but it wasn't a question that troubled me. Like everything in my life, this was a work in progress. I'm comfortable with uncertainty. I enjoy experimenting, allowing for the possibility of success or failure. Either way, I'd likely learn something valuable to apply in the future.

I went out to admire the animals again after dinner. One ewe had stuck her head through the fence and was busy trimming a box of chrysanthemums now within her reach. Oh well. Almost everything else we valued was set back further from the fence and should be safe. Undoubtedly, there'd be a few unanticipated casualties. Hopefully, no significant damage would occur to our gardens and vineyard—or the animals would have to go. I understood that. But I felt relieved I wouldn't be blamed when or if something went awry. After all, this was Deborah's idea.

WINTERIZING

Each year around Thanksgiving, the annual feeling of a "wrap" settles over me. The grapes have been crushed, pressed, and fermented. Their juice is resting in barrels to become what we hope will be fine wine. The walnuts are in their drying racks in the top of the barn. The olives have been milled into oil that will make the many chefs and gourmands in our lives deliriously happy for another year. We've finished delivering fresh pears and figs to local restaurants or preserving them one way or another (pear sauce, pear chips, dried figs, chutneys). We still have the pomegranates to process. We'll seed some to use fresh on salads and juice others. We'll drink some of the pungent-sweet juice but boil most of it down to an intense molasses that freezes well for future use in marinades or homemade pomegranate soda.

There are specific tasks we have to do to prepare for the possibility of freezing temperatures. Most of these involve managing our water system. We shut off and drain the vineyard and orchard irrigation lines, remembering to open faucets so any water in them will push out instead of expanding to burst pipes. We've tried to make this job easier over the years by installing underground utility boxes with master valves that can shut off the water to numerous faucets with a single turn. However, there are still some old faucets around the barn and old trailer that remain active. These we wrap with insulated hats (created from strips of fiberglass insulation stuffed into an upside-down plastic flowerpot or small bucket) to warm them. We remove any battery-operated timers from garden patches and remove the batteries for storage. We roll up hoses and stack them in the top of the barn, so they'll be out of the way when spring mowing and weed-whacking begin. We have a few tons of organic compost delivered, so we can spread it in the vineyard before the winter rain starts in earnest.

This particular point in our annual farm cycle makes us sigh with relief.

With the major chores done, crops harvested, and equipment put away—it's time to relax and kick back. We can hunker down for winter, looking forward to rainy days, perhaps even a few dustings of snow, and long evenings spent reading by the fire.

I used to feel more carefree this time of year. Now it seems harder to achieve a sense of peace and contentment moving toward the new year when there are so many things to feel frantic about: environmental collapse, social injustice, economic disparity, and a political situation in America that feels like a civil war much of the time. Once, the planet felt stable beneath my feet, but now it feels more like a lurching boat, bashed by waves, buffeted by storms, and riddled with leaks requiring constant bailing. We have not cared for our planet (or each other) well enough. The world can seem angry and volatile. Unprecedented superstorms, fires, hurricanes, and flooding occur with regularity. There seems to be no safe harbor anymore.

In 2019, I sent out my annual holiday greeting, with its summary of the year's events and activities, in a somber mood. I concluded my bulletin with these words: "Life seems rich and mostly good. I worry about politics. I worry even more about the planet. I carry on; I keep moving forward. I try to help in the ways that I can — I contribute to causes, I volunteer for non-profits. I write. I love. I work. What more can one do?"

A Canadian friend replied: "I read your news, and I'm so glad you two are still thriving at your farm and enjoying life. That farm was the best idea you ever had. You have surely made the most of your time there and love it all."

Yes. In hindsight, buying rural property in the Sierra foothills was the best idea we ever had. Though it's not clear it ever was an idea. It's not something we planned. It came to us more like a happy accident, the way love can blossom suddenly, or a child can be conceived unexpectedly. Thankfully, we had the good sense to be open to it, commit ourselves to it, and make the most of it, even when it seemed most challenging. Especially then.

TEN REASONS, THIRTY YEARS LATER

Ⅰ asked Deborah to list ten reasons she likes to be in Fiddletown, three decades after we launched our adventure in country living. I said I'd do the same.

Deborah's List:

1. Things are tidier and better organized than they used to be.
2. I know exactly where my food (and even my wine) comes from.
3. The internet is fast enough that I can work efficiently from home.
4. I sleep well now that I can use my noise-canceling headphones to eliminate the sounds of barking dogs and crowing roosters in the early mornings.
5. There's a barn full of sharp tools, ready to use.
6. I can study Spanish while I mow and disc.
7. My family and friends like to visit (except during pandemics).
8. There are always more improvement projects to plan and do.
9. I've mastered keeping the chain saws tuned and sharpened.
10. The new pool is a dream, with jets that allow me to swim laps in place.

Mara's List:

1. I get to look at that majestic, centuries-old oak tree while I work in the kitchen.
2. The land is teeming with life: squirrels, skunks, foxes, voles, moles,

mountain lions, bobcats, snakes, tarantulas, lizards, frogs, and so many birds.

3. There is never nothing to do.
4. I can hear Al's donkeys braying and Bev & Leon's cows mooing daily.
5. The air is fresh and clean (except when wildfires are raging).
6. Even repetitive tasks (pulling weeds, stacking wood) seem satisfying somehow because you can do whatever you feel like doing and leave the rest for later.
7. There is always something fresh to snack on in the garden or orchard.
8. We can afford to hire more helpers when we need to now (if we can find them).
9. The barn cats are ecstatic to see me coming every morning.
10. I never tire of the views from the barn, patios, garden and vineyard.

SMOKE TAINT

On August 18, 2021, the Caldor Fire erupted just ten miles northeast of our home and vineyard. The fire doubled in size daily and eventually consumed around a quarter million acres. It callously demolished the community of Grizzly Flats, only fifteen miles from us.

The winds worked in our favor, blowing the flames away from us and toward Lake Tahoe. We thought we were relatively safe—until we received an automated call from the sheriff's department. Meteorologists predicted a 180-degree shift in wind direction with gusty winds over the next few days. They'd expanded the Caldor Evacuation Warning Zone to include our property. They advised us to prepare to leave immediately.

We decided to go, even though our vineyard was ripening quickly. Our personal safety was more important than the crop, although we worried about being away from the vineyard at such a critical time. We needed to check the Brix for our buyer, so we could finalize a picking date and organize a crew. We had to prepare equipment, pressure wash bins, pump up truck and trailer tires, round up ball hitches and tie-downs, and buy ice and beverages for the crew. The usual pre-harvest ballet.

Wildfire season was becoming a bit much. We'd evacuated several times beginning in 2019—mainly due to dense smoke from fires burning elsewhere in Northern California and throughout the west. In 2020, when fires were incinerating Napa and Sonoma, the air quality could be as bad, or worse, in San Francisco or Sacramento than in the foothills.

"I used to take breathing clean air for granted," I said to Deborah. "But no longer."

"Damn climate change," she said, poring over the latest California fire maps online. We'd become obsessed with monitoring fire, smoke, and air quality data during fire season, which seemed to start earlier and last longer each year. We were constantly plotting where to escape flames and smoke, should we have to leave on a moment's notice. Could we breathe better if we drove to the coast, southern California, or the mountains? We installed a Purple Air monitor on-site, so we could get real-time smoke air quality readings at our vineyard, no matter where we might be.

With the terrifying Caldor Fire, we escaped disaster once again. The sky above us was hazy, but the smoke stayed high and didn't settle into the vineyard. This was good because the fires that decimated vineyards in Napa and Sonoma taught us that, even if your vineyard doesn't burn, the grapes can be ruined by smoke exposure. This can lend an ashtray taste to the wine—not a flavor most consumers appreciate. Amador grape growers worried about this possibility, but our risk seemed low compared to our El Dorado neighbors, who were more impacted by the fire.

Eric was reeling from the effects of the pandemic and the wildfires. He'd been forced to evacuate both his home and his wine tasting room. He was helping home-school his kids. He'd sold his house (including his winemaking facility) just as the pandemic began and wouldn't obtain a building permit to build a new winery facility for over two years. He was making wine in rented space at a wine storage facility.

Eric told us he wouldn't be able to do any custom crush work until he had his own winery again. Fortunately, we were able to find a new buyer for our grapes. Most of our crop would go to a premium winery in the Napa Valley this year. The owners had come to meet us, inspect the vines, and collect samples. They were pleased with what they saw and tasted. They contracted to buy six tons of our fruit, asking us to pick it in two stages because the upper vineyard was ripening faster than the lower vineyard.

Labor was becoming ever harder to find. We were fortunate to have Carlos living in the caretaker house on our property. Typically, he can round up his siblings and friends to pick for us on a Sunday—their day off from other jobs. I was concerned they might not be happy about picking twice instead of once.

"It's no problem," he assured me. "In fact, it's easier. The guys are getting older. They prefer not to work on their day off now. They like to relax and spend time with the family on Sundays. A small job—three or four tons—is easy. My brothers and I can each pick a ton before we go to work. Any weekday is okay. Just give me a couple days' notice to arrange it."

Harvest day dawned clear and smoke-free. The crew began picking at first light. Soon, they were dumping lugs of grapes into the half-ton bins Joe pulled around the vineyard on a trailer as Deborah and I did the leafing.

We thought we had a good crop. There were lots of clusters hanging on the vines, but they turned out to be smaller and lighter than usual. It took us longer than expected to fill eight half-ton bins. By the time we finished, we'd harvested about three-quarters of the vineyard rather than half. We realized we wouldn't have another two tons of fruit to deliver to our new client after all. The grapes just didn't seem to contain much juice this year. We were not alone. Most vineyards in our region were seeing low yields. We were better off than some growers, who found their crop 50–60 percent lighter than average. The vines were struggling from years of drought.

Once the grapes were delivered, we received a message from our buyers asking us to call ASAP. "Bad news," they began. They'd received more lab results, and these ones concerned them. They didn't want to pay for our fruit until they knew more. That got our attention.

The initial testing found no "free" guaiacol (a chemical marker for smoke taint) in the juice pressed from our grapes, but a more complex analysis indicated there was guaiacol bound to sugar molecules. It seemed possible that the guaiacol might release as the sugars converted to alcohol during fermentation. This could result in a smoky taste—then or sometime later. No wine purveyor looks forward to a customer asking for a refund on a bottle of wine they bought years earlier because now it tastes of ash.

The art of smoke taint is a new one, born of several years of extreme drought and severe wildfires in wine-growing regions of Australia and California. The science is inexact and changing all the time, but experts suspect volatile phenols to be chemical markers for potential smoke taint, with guaiacol being a primary suspect.

I attended a webinar on smoke taint sponsored by UC Agricultural Extension and starring Anita Oberholster, a respected enologist with expertise in this topic. My main takeaway was that little is known, and more research is needed. Most of the research to date had been done on cabernet sauvignon. No one is sure how findings might translate to other varietals, some of which (like syrah) have naturally occurring high levels of volatile phenols, including guaiacol. No meaningful research had been done on zinfandel.

Oberholster said the most significant factor in smoke taint is the "age" of the smoke, rather than smoke visibility or smell, or even the presence of ash in the vineyard. Smoke from an area that burned within the previous thirty-six to forty-eight hours is cause for worry. Older smoke drifting in days later does not appear to cause smoke taint. That's something, I thought, but when smoke appears over the vineyard, we have no way of knowing how old it is. When the Caldor Fire was closest to us, the prevailing SSW winds were in our favor. Smoke seen or smelled later could have been drifting from areas burning far away—or could be from Cal Fire doing control burns nearby.

We understood our buyer's concern. They'd just weathered two vintages in which Napa fires created havoc for winemakers. That experience was too fresh. Perhaps they'd sought grapes from outside the region because of it—only to discover wildfires can occur anywhere.

To limit their risk, they decided not to accept any more fruit from our vineyard this vintage. This was fine with us as we didn't have the additional two tons they'd contracted for, anyway, and preferred to keep whatever crop remained for our own use.

Despite the lab results, we felt reasonably confident that our grapes were okay. Our vineyard had not been exposed to as much smoke as in some recent years. The juice tasted as intense and delicious as ever. We decided to go ahead and pick the remaining fruit to make wine for our own label. Time would tell who was right and how this wine would turn out.

The lower quarter of the vineyard yielded just 1.25 tons of fruit. We sorted it carefully and sent it to San Francisco, where our first winemaker, Tom, now working at a new custom crush facility, would make wine for us once again. Tom was familiar with smoke taint. He'd seen and tasted it in grapes from fire-affected areas during the last couple of vintages.

"I'm not concerned about your zin," Tom said. "Last year, we could taste the taint on Napa grapes at crush. Your fruit looks beautiful, and the juice tastes great."

Tom's excitement was contagious. Soon one of his small custom crush clients asked if they could purchase a barrel of our zin for their private label, even knowing about our Napa buyer's angst. We made him happy by agreeing, thus pocketing at least a small amount of cash for this vintage's efforts.

"Thank god that's over," I said to Deborah as we put away the last of the lugs, bins, and hitches.

"Yeah, done for another year," she said. "I'm not sure how many more years I can deal with this kind of excitement."

Over the next few weeks, temperatures dropped substantially. We even had three showers deliver just over an inch of rain. People were jubilant about the moisture and the arrival of cooler days. We knew fire season was not over yet, but it didn't feel quite as terrifying anymore.

We had heavy rains through November and December, beating the previous winter's rain record before the calendar year ended. The parched landscape absorbed every drop greedily, and the snowpack in the Sierras reached normal levels. That was a promising start, but it would take many more storms and wet winters before drought conditions could be declared over.

Just before Christmas, we made a quick trip to San Francisco to do a few errands and barrel taste the wine Tom was making from our grapes. We were pleased with it and could not detect any hint of smoke.

On New Year's Eve, we received a note from our buyer. They'd tried some innovative winemaking techniques, including letting the juice pressed from our grapes sit on lees from other grapes with no detectable guaiacol. Once the wine completed fermentation and tasted fine, their concerns subsided. They said they were mailing a check for full payment on our four tons of estate-grown zinfandel. And they confirmed they'd like to continue our buyer-grower relationship with hopes the new year would be less anxiety-provoking for all of us.

Cheers to that. Deborah opened the last bottle of zin Tom had made from our very first vintage in 2000. We toasted the good news.

I no longer sip wine carefree. Once you are involved in producing wine, as a grower or vintner, you're constantly analyzing a wine's characteristics and unique flavors. Is it true to the grape varietal? Is there a hint of pepper, leather, or herbs? Does the fruit taste more like plums or dark berries?

Now, I can't help tasting for hints of climate change.

Photo by Mike Rafferty

VINIFICATION VINDICATION

Afⁱⁱᵉʳ the driest first quarter on record, we had unusually ample April rains in 2022, followed by a warm spell that lasted a couple of weeks. Everyone donned T-shirts and planted tomatoes, only to have them hailed on in early May. But the brief hot spell inspired wine store and restaurant owners to restock their white and rosé wines for summer sipping.

We received an order from a unique small business in Plymouth called Amador 360. The place acts as a central tasting room for local wineries that are too small or too remote to have their own public tasting rooms. The owner wanted to stock up on our 2020 Shenandoah blanc, a white Rhone blend of viognier and roussanne that is a customer favorite. He encouraged us to enter it in the 2022 Amador County Fair Wine Competition. I was pretty sure we'd entered it the previous year. But when I checked my records, I realized I'd confused it with our Sauvignon blanc, which won a silver medal at the 2021 fair. The 2020 Shenandoah blanc had been bottled after competition entries had closed last year. I thanked Brian for the prompt and told Deborah I was going to enter it in this year's fair.

"I agree. We definitely should enter it," she said. "We might also want to enter the 2019 zinfandel Eric bottled recently." I filled out forms, paid fees, and delivered samples to be judged in the upcoming competition.

We'd run out of labels while bottling the 2019 estate-grown zin, so we had several cases of "shiners," unlabeled bottles we could not sell legally. We'd been enjoying those with dinner and guests. I thought it was excellent. Perhaps the best zinfandel we'd ever produced. And it was the result of our twentieth harvest, the most challenging year of vineyard management we'd ever experienced. Eric had done a great job making it, blending it with our small lot of estate-grown petite sirah before bottling.

I didn't think much more about the fair wine competition until I received an email from Steve, a Fiddletown neighbor who'd coordinated entries for the wine competition:

> *Hi Mara!*
>
> *The judging went well, and I am happy to tell you your zinfandel not only won Class 9 with a Double Gold but also Best Amador Zinfandel!*
>
> *Your Shenandoah blanc also won Gold. The full results will be emailed to you shortly. Congrats and thanks for entering. :)*
>
> *Steve*

I read the note three times, my smile growing wider with each reading. I wanted to shout and tell Deborah the amazing news. But it was a Sunday afternoon and Michelle had come over with her massage table. Deborah had gone in for her massage a half hour earlier. Mellow harp music was tinkling through the house. It would not do to start yelling and dancing around in the next room. I wondered if telling her the news when she emerged would ruin the effects of her massage, but as soon as she appeared in her bathrobe looking blissful, I said, "I have big news."

"What?"

"I just got the results of the county fair wine competition."

"And?"

"Our Shenandoah blanc won a gold medal. But our 2019 zinfandel won—are you ready for this?" She nodded. "It won not only Double Gold and Best of Class, but also Best Amador Zinfandel, period," I said.

"I know that zin is good, but are you sure?" I showed her Steve's note, and we did a high five. We decided not to spread the word until we saw the official results in print. We wanted to be sure there'd been no mistake.

The final results of the judging were distributed the following day. There it was in black and white, confirming Steve's report. More than fifty Sierra foothill zinfandels had been entered in the competition, and ours was judged to be the best of them all. Our tiny operation beat family-owned wineries that have been making wine in the area for generations. Not to mention the bigger new corporate wineries that had moved in more recently. *How did that happen?* I wondered. It seemed such a random, unexpected fluke. Welcome, yet surprising.

We'd never set our aims on being the best producers of zinfandel in the Sierra foothills. With our history of rotating wineries and winemakers, we did not have a stable situation for ensuring this would be duplicated year after year. Sure, we were serious about our viticultural practices. And we had worked extra-hard wrestling that 2019 vintage into submission. That had worked out well, it seemed. It was sweet to have our hard work acknowledged, but we are tiny self-taught producers, flying by the seat of our pants most of the time. We've been creative. We've worked in the interstices of the industry to find places to have our grapes crushed and tended. We've been fortunate to find talented, flexible people who can turn the juice from our grapes into very good—even excellent—wine. We stay involved in tasting and blending decisions.

Is this what success tastes like? I wondered. It was delicious to savor the moment, even though it did feel a bit random, surreal.

In case you are wondering, no, we did not beat Easton's zinfandel—because it was not entered in the fair competition. Bill views these competitions as unscientific, with non-reproducible results. The same panel of judges might taste a group of wines one day, then taste the same wines a few days later, and arrive at completely different results. He prefers to submit wines to wine writers and journalists who blind-taste wines multiple times with a variety of people, scoring them over and over until a consensus is reached with time. That is how his Terre Rouge Ascent syrah was awarded 100 points by *Wine Enthusiast* magazine in 2016, becoming the first Sierra foothills wine to achieve the perfect score. And the same Syrah scored 100 points again in 2018, an unprecedented feat. So no, Bill didn't enter random one-day tasting events that he viewed as a crapshoot.

We had a healthy skepticism about wine competitions, too. We'd stopped entering most contests but continued to enter the Amador Fair Commercial Wine Competition mostly for fun, to support the fair and to stay involved in our community. And now this had happened. Perhaps on another day, the results might have been different, but we were confident our 2019 zinfandel was excellent. And so was everyone we'd been sharing those shiners with.

We blasted the news to family and friends, and I wrote a news release to send to our wine club members and post on our website. As orders for our wines poured in as never before, I reflected on the years Deborah and I had spent in this Fiddletown experiment. We were never sure where or how it would end but continued taking one step at a time, feeling our way toward an uncertain goal. We worked hard, aimed for excellence, and tried to keep it fun. Now that our efforts were acknowledged and our hard work rewarded, the attention seemed surprising. We were collecting the love, the ribbons, the medals, and a brief bit of media attention. But we never could have reached this point without the help of many others—our grape growing mentors (Dick Cooper, Mr. Ferrero, Scott Harvey, Bill Easton, Charles Spinetta), our winemakers (Tom, Mark, and Eric), the wineries that took us under their wing (Drytown Cellars, Bray, Andis, Chateau Davell), and the countless vineyard workers who helped us plant, prune, nurture, and harvest over the years.

I realized I should let Eric, the man who'd made this award-winning wine, aware of the honors. I texted him the good news.

His reply was simple: "Cool."

How cool, indeed. Deborah and I stepped innocently into the Flying Saucer in San Francisco in 1991, and the flight since then has been out of this world.

EPILOGUE

I've kept a journal on and off through most of my adult life, including during the years spent discovering Fiddletown. I write not so much to remember what happened as to ponder events in hope of achieving a deeper understanding of them, the role I played in them, and how things might have gone differently. Finalizing these stories has provided an opportunity to take a protracted glance in the rear view mirror, savoring accomplishments, reliving defeats, and marveling at all the living and learning that can be packed into the middle years of adulthood.

I feel fortunate to have stumbled upon Fiddletown and to have had the gumption to embrace it fearlessly. The Middle Age Spread still inspires me every day—the natural beauty, the spectacular skies, the weather (both mild and wild), and all the things this land and its varied inhabitants have to teach me. I never seem to tire of it or take it for granted. My favorite oak tree on earth, the one I see from my kitchen window, still takes my breath away every day, whether it is naked and dusted with snow or leafy green and filled with birdsong. I can only hope to age that gracefully!

Yet some things are also constantly changing, mostly in subtle but sometimes in dramatic ways. This season, the wild turkeys have not come around. I miss them, but a huge flock of collared pigeons has taken up residence, gracing the sky with their frequent aerial ballet displays.

After Zack died, his property was bought by an established winery that wants to grow grapes there, not open another tasting room or event center. I introduced myself to the new manager, only to discover he is from a small town in Australia very close to where my father grew up. I sense a good neighbor there now. As for the old lodge, it continues to be both quiet and active. It is the buffer we wanted, but it's also a place for building community. We host fundraisers for local non-profit groups there, as well as birthday parties, Quinceañeras, and holiday celebrations. Its uses continue to evolve in positive ways.

New challenges constantly arise, too. With climate change and the advent of mega storms and lethal wildfires, our need for woodland management has intensified in ways we would never have predicted. And we are searching for a new winemaker again. Mark is gone forever, having lost his battle with addiction and died at all too young an age. We miss his talent, engaging presence, and loyal friendship. Tom, much as he loves winemaking, has realized he should get a "real" job before it's too late, so his availability has declined sharply. Eric's winery building is finally complete and has excess capacity. We could work with him again and enjoy doing so, but we'd prefer to find a viable option closer to Fiddletown, if possible. Deborah has suggested we take a year off from making wine and simply sell all of our grapes to our Napa buyer this year. At first I resisted, but I've come around to seeing the advantages of this plan. Why not make things a bit simpler for a change?

Making things easier wherever possible (or at least once in a while) seems to have become a guiding principle. Last year, we let our neighbor Ron, who has a lavender farm nearby on the Cosumnes River, plant a field of sunflowers on our land to sell at local farmers markets. We provide the space and water, and Mother Nature provides the sunlight. We get to enjoy the cheerful sight of colorful sunflowers (and a steady stream of cut flowers in season) while someone else provides most of the labor. That is smart, cooperative farming, so we hope to continue it.

Our annual winterizing rituals feel more poignant to me now, knowing that another precious year has ticked by—so quickly! I can't help but wonder how I should prepare for the final season of my own life. I sense the sand trickling through the hourglass more acutely as the future shrinks and the past expands. There's no ignoring the fact that most of our years are behind us now and precious few remain ahead. It's obvious we won't be farming for another three decades. But it's tough to think about the inevitable transition to living somewhere else, especially as we have no certainty about when or how that time will come, or with what urgency. It's hard to imagine living anywhere else when we love Fiddletown the way we do. The idea of trading the Middle Age Spread for a room in a senior care home seems preposterous. Instead, we try to relish every minute of country living afforded to us. For now, we take life one day, one season, another year at a time.

Photo by Kay Ellyard

FIDDLETOWN   CALIFORNIA

SCHOOLHOUSE   150 YEARS

Art by Terryl Tagg

ACKNOWLEDGMENTS

These stories improved from the close readings and comments from a variety of friends and neighbors, including Kathleen Jones, Nancy Nieland, Don Miller, Pam York, Jane O'Riordan, Bob Kleinbrahm, Terri Houseman, Jeff Muscatine, Marc Ellen Hamel, Deirdre Mueller, Margaret Grover, Laurie Pollack, Joan Ramo, Barbara Campbell, Liz Kantor, Jacqueline Bogard, and Vicki Delpart.

Many thanks are due to two amazing proofreaders: Ericka Lutz and Christine LePorte. Same goes for Julie Price for her endurance in laying out proof after proof. And thank you, Deborah, for not complaining too much about the remarkable amount of time and attention I devoted to finishing this book to my satisfaction.

I appreciate the extensive research and writing on Fiddletown's history done by my neighbor, Elaine Zorbas. Kudos to the hardworking members at the Fiddletown Preservation Society who work to maintain both that history and key local monuments. And hooray for the Fiddletown Community Center volunteers who keep this community's heart beating.

ABOUT THE AUTHOR

Mara Feeney was born in Canada but has lived in Northern California since 1980. She went to college intending to become a novelist but fell in love with Anthropology instead. This led her to live and work in the Canadian Arctic, especially in Inuit communities around Hudson Bay. Her first book, *Rankin Inlet: A Novel*, is based on those experiences, as is a short story that won First Prize in the Great Northern Canadian Writing Contest in 2009.

After her stint in the far North, she attended the University of British Columbia and obtained a Masters degree in Community and Regional Planning. She traveled around the world for a year before settling into a career as an environmental consultant, authoring numerous technical studies on the social and economic impacts of large development projects (dams, pipelines, mines, toxic cleanups) on existing communities.

When she and her partner bought a hobby farm in the Sierra foothills, Mara began to write short stories about that place, the landscape, the people, and lessons in farming. Those stories are the basis of this book. Now retired, Mara spends her time gardening, writing articles, and trying to stay fit. She is passionate about life and animals and has written hundreds of adoption success stories for rescue dogs.